the
KAMADO GRILL
cookbook

FRED THOMPSON

STACKPOLE
BOOKS

Published by
STACKPOLE BOOKS
5067 Ritter Road
Mechanicsburg, PA 17055
www.stackpolebooks.com

Printed in the United States of America

10 9 8 7 6 5 4 3 2 1

First edition

Cover design by Wendy A. Reynolds
Cover images by the author

Library of Congress Cataloging-in-Publication Data

Thompson, Fred, 1953-
 The kamado grill cookbook / Fred Thompson. — First edition.
    pages cm
 Includes index.
 ISBN 978-0-8117-1468-6
 1. Outdoor cooking. 2. Barbecuing. 3. Stoves, Earthenware. I. Title.
 TX823.T494 2014
 641.5'78—dc23
                          2014026689

To the next grillmaster:
Carter Bailey Wilkerson

*Smoked Chicken Wings
(page 69)*

Contents

······ **Acknowledgments** ······

Acookbook is never just the work of the person whose name is on the cover. While I get to play the role of author and fire-lighting expert, this work is a collaboration by many good folk.

Pam Hoenig, my editor, is the best. She brought this project to me and, through some difficult times with my mother's illness and eventual passing, guided me with love and patience to mold this book into what you are reading today. We've worked on many projects together and Pam has always made me look better than I probably am. Thank you, Pam, for being, as you like to say, "the silent partner."

The staff at Stackpole Books wrapped their arms around this book with excitement and vigor. Thanks to publisher, Judith Schnell, for her support of the project, and to the Creative Services department, and editorial assistant Tim Gahr for everything they did to bring this book out in record time. Stackpole has been a first-rate publisher to work with.

To make this cookbook a work that an owner of any kamado grill could use with confidence, I wanted to test the recipes and methods across several different brands of kamados. Primo, Grill Dome, Kamado Joe, and Bayou Classic made that possible by furnishing grills. Check out their websites. My neighbors loved the smells when all of these grills were fired up at the same time. I also

received great counsel from Derald Schulz of Primo on all styles of kamados and especially the Primo Oval. Ashish Kohli, with Grill Dome, also added his expertise on the ways of kamado grilling. Thank you both for always taking my calls and keeping me on prudent paths.

I hope the photography for the book makes you hungry and want to light a fire. Kyle Wilkerson did much of the food styling, and I even let him take a turn or two with the camera. Much of the composition of the photos came from his creative mind and we made a great team and had lots of fun and good food. Kyle, being a chef, was also a grand sounding board for flavors and culinary ideas. My buddy and partner in Dinner Plate Productions, Drew Herche, also did some of the styling. He is the best at making a pizza and was amazed by the results that a kamado grill could achieve, so we made lots of them. His technical support and extra eyes were a huge help as I took the photos.

Belinda Ellis, prop stylist supreme, encouraged us to take chances with the photos. She also was invaluable with her professional knowledge of all things involving flour and baking, even while she was working on her own cookbooks.

As you read the introductions to the individual recipes, please take note of the many folks who shared recipes or inspired them. Kamado grilling is about regular people cooking great food at home, and without the input of my friends and colleagues, this book would be much less than what you see before you. Thank you all for sharing and keeping the fires burning.

Thanks to all the great writers, editors, and design folks who kept *Edible Piedmont Magazine* running while I worked on this project. I couldn't have finished this book without you. A special shout-out goes to executive editor Belinda Ellis and designer Melissa Peterson.

Thank you, Nikki Parrish, for suffering through another cookbook with me. I'm a writer who doesn't type very well and Nikki has handled my word processing issues with grace and patience.

Thanks to my daughter, Laura, for giving me, and the world, my grandson, Carter. I'm certain he will keep the grill hot for his generation. Also to Kathleen, for encouraging me early on in my career change into the food world that I love.

My mom was always confused about me not having a "real job," but boy, would she swell with pride when a new book came out. Mom was a super cook and an even better eater, and I learned much from her. During the last year of her life she was always worried that I was spending too much time with her and not enough on this book and my other work. Mom, I wouldn't have had it any other way, and I'm thankful for every minute we had. With much love, you will be missed.

Spicy and Sweet Smoked Chicken Thighs (page 70)

Introduction

If you were to mix the Chinese Qin Dynasty (221 to 207 B.C.), Japan in 400 A.D., American servicemen returning from the Pacific theater after World War II, and NASA, what do you think you would wind up with? A very utilitarian, multi-functional, some say funny-looking, elliptical cooking machine: the kamado. Notice I didn't say grilling apparatus, or smoking contraption, but "cooking" machine. Certainly you can grill and smoke on a kamado, but you can also roast, sauté, steam, braise, and bake, all within the confines of the kamado's dome.

The kamado finds its very early beginnings in the simple domed clay cookers of the ancient Chinese. It was then adopted by the Japanese, who gave the cooker the name *kamado* and probably first put a slotted grate into the dome. American GIs discovered the grill while stationed in Japan during the Second World War and, finally, it was the development by NASA of super ceramics for the space program that allowed the kamado grill to evolve into the superior cooking machine it is today, earning a well-deserved cultlike status among serious backyard culinary folk.

And I count myself as a convert. Over the past three decades, I've cooked on every conceivable type of grill, written multiple books on all manner of outdoor grills and smokers, sat and jawed all night about flame-based cooking with great pit-masters, interviewed folks all over the country on their methods and recipes, and even dug pits for pig-pickings. I can say, without a doubt, that the kamado is my favorite way to cook outdoors. No, it isn't as easy as turning the valve on a gas grill, but what it lacks in immediate convenience, it more than makes up for in versatility and—most importantly—delicious, succulent food.

Moisture—what most of us think of as juiciness—is the carrier of the natural flavor of whatever it is we are cooking; its presence helps to spread that flavor across our taste buds. Ceramic cookers retain a food's moisture better than any other device I've ever cooked on. Why? The design. The thick ceramic walls have better heat retention than any metal grill and the heft of the dome lid, coupled with the gasket, ensures a tight seal, creating a moist cooking environment inside. The draft system is centuries old and has changed very little over that time because it works, creating a swirling flow of air that bathes food in the trapped moisture instead of blasting it with dry heat. The dampers control temperature with unwavering precision. I've had several models of kamado cookers maintain a steady 200° F, without any additional fuel, for eighteen hours. In all my years of smoking and grilling, I've never seen another grill duplicate that feat.

The kamado can go as low as 150° F, perfect for "cold smoked" salmon, to more than 600° F, hot enough to sear a steak to caramelized perfection.

Are you a fan of brick-oven pizza or crusty Old World–style bread? The kamado is at your command. Roast your next holiday turkey in the kamado and you'll be guaranteed moist breast meat without the constant basting necessary with indoor roasting. The kamado will also steam shellfish for a crowd, impart a delicious char to burgers, give long-cooking stews a righteous flavor, and even bake your favorite pie, all of this while imparting an additional nuance of flavor that only cooking over coals can achieve.

And then, of course, there is what the kamado does best—cooking low and slow. For me, the versatility of the kamado harkens back to my grandmother's wood stove, days of campfire cooking with my daughter, afternoons of beer and friends spent around the barbecue, and the sear of a steak at Peter Lugar's.

The ancient Chinese and Japanese did all their cooking on a kamado, which in Japanese has three meanings—"oven," "stove," and "kitchen." The grill is perfectly named, because it can do it all, and this book will lead you through the different cooking processes as executed in the kamado and the awesome taste that lies on the other side of the "dome." The kamado really offers cooking—not just grilling or smoking—perfection. It truly sits at the crossroads of the "art" and "science" of outdoor cookery. Come join me on this delicious journey of discovery!

Kansas City Prime Rib (page 27)

Kamado Basics

For most of us, the kamado will not be our first grill purchase. Many will come to the kamado after experience with a covered kettle-style charcoal grill or a gas grill. Some techniques for the kamado will seem radically different from those cookers but there are a lot of similarities. Some folks believe that it takes several years to become well versed in kamado cooking and to that I say, "hogwash!" Those who speak of the challenge of cooking in the kamado just don't want you to outcook them. There certainly will be a learning curve, but that's to be expected. I guarantee you, within a couple of months, you'll be at the top of your kamado game. That said, you never really stop learning on the kamado, but that's because the possibilities of what the grill can accomplish are so vast.

Why the Egg (or Oval) Shape?

This configuration allows for very efficient airflow, the capture of heat, and the formation of steam. The airflow is almost circular in nature and the steam, which collects inside the high dome, acts like a basting brush, keeping your food moist. Primo offers an oval-shaped kamado, which preserves the benefits of the egg design but also offers added features, like a divided firebox, which allows for indirect cooking without the use of heat defusers.

The divided firebox of the Primo Grill (note the divider on the right).

What is a Kamado Grill?

Simply stated, a kamado grill is an egg- or oval-shaped grill built from materials with superior heat retention, with a heavy dome-shaped lid and gasket that create an airtight seal when the lid is closed. The kamado's heat retention and airtight seal, combined with its unique damper system, allow the cook to hit target temperatures with remarkable precision and to maintain them, with no added charcoal, for hours on end. When it comes to cooking slow and low, you will not find a better grill—call it the "set it and forget it" grill for smokers!

But the kamado is not just about smoking. In fact, though it's a considerable investment, I would recommend the kamado for use as a primary outdoor grill to anyone who is more than just a dabbler in grilling. Here are my reasons:

- *Versatility.* A kamado grill can maintain temperatures from as low as 150° F to over 700° F with amazing precision. This unparalleled range means you can use your kamado to cold and hot smoke, roast, bake, braise, steam, and grill.
- *Quick warm-up time.* Most charcoal grills can take from 30 to 40 minutes to be ready to cook on. A kamado can generally be ready to cook in 15 minutes.
- *Ease of use.* Once you hit your target temperature, a kamado require less fuss than a gas grill or any other type of charcoal grill. I cooked on multiple brands of kamado grills and can tell you from firsthand experience that a kamado can maintain a temperature of 200° F for 6 to 12 hours, depending on the brand, with no additional charcoal needed. Kamado grills also produce about one-third the ash of regular charcoal grills and smokers.
- *Durability.* Weighing in at 250 pounds and built from ceramics developed from NASA technology, kamado grills are built to last a long time; in fact, many models come with a 20-year warranty. The ceramics don't rust and a kamado can be used in almost any type of weather.

The Components of a Kamado Grill

Though there are some differences across brands of kamado grills, almost all share these features:

- A ceramic-insulated firebox or fire ring.
- A heavy dome-shaped lid (I refer to it simply as the "dome" throughout the book), also constructed of ceramic.

- A felt gasket that sits on the grill body and makes contact with the dome lid when it is closed. The gasket is key to the airtight seal of the kamado.
- A banded hinge attached to the dome, which makes the dome easier to lift and position on the gasket.
- A fire grate to hold the charcoal (this can be made of ceramic or cast iron)
- A grill grate for cooking; for most brands of kamado, this will be porcelain-coated cast iron.
- The damper system, which consists of a bottom damper located underneath the fire grate and a damper at the top of the dome. The dome damper can be one solid piece or include what is known as a "daisy wheel."

What to Look for When Buying a Kamado

First, understand that when you buy a kamado, you are making an investment. Expect to spend from $800 to $1,500 and up. And if you buy any accessories, like a cart or ceramic plates for smoking, you can easily drop another $500. But you are also buying a grill that will likely last for 20 years and, depending on the brand, may come with a 20-year warranty.

As with any significant purchase, shop around and look at all the different brands available. Also, check the web for reviews and visit the online chat rooms of the different kamado manufacturers to see what people who already own the different models you are considering have to say about them.

SIZE

Kamado grills come in different sizes, so your first consideration will be the diameter of the grill. A 12-inch-diameter grill should be large enough to serve the needs of a family of four. But if you want to be able to cook a turkey or larger cuts of meat like a pork shoulder or full-size brisket, an 18-inch-diameter grill is a necessity. Think about how you'll be using your grill—will it strictly be for preparing family dinners or will this be a party grill? If the latter, you might want to opt for the larger grill size.

STURDINESS OF CONSTRUCTION

The thicker the ceramic walls are, the more durable the grill, and the greater its ability to retain heat and moisture. Lift the dome and look under the "hood." Do the walls of the firebox look sturdy and well made? Look at the hinge for the dome. Is it sturdy and well made? Look at the gasket and then close the dome. Get down and look at the seal at eye level. Do you see any gaps where the dome makes contact with the gasket? Remember, it's the seal between the dome and the gasket that is key to the success of the kamado.

Porcelain-coated cast iron grill grate

FIRE GRATE

The grate that holds the charcoal can be either ceramic or metal. Every brand has designed one to work efficiently with that brand of kamado. Some have more holes than others, which makes a difference with airflow. There are kamado grill masters who prefer more holes for increased air flow, and if you are going to do a lot of grilling (vs. smoking), it's something to consider. A charcoal grate with fewer holes just takes slightly longer to get to searing temperature. Both are good for indirect cooking.

TEMPERATURE GAUGE

You want a model that has a sturdy, easy-to-read built-in temperature gauge, one with more heft than you would normally see on a regular charcoal grill. The temperature gauge is going to be your best friend when cooking kamado style.

An easy-to-read temperature gauge on the grill dome is key to kamado success.

COLOR

Kamado grills are available in a wide range of colors. My only advice—make sure you love whatever color you pick, because that grill is going to last you a *long* time.

KAMADO GRILL ACCESSORIES WORTH INVESTING IN

Each kamado manufacturer offers lots of add-ons for purchase. These are the ones I have found particularly useful:

- *Ash tool*: This is great for cleaning out the ashes from the bottom of the firebox.
- *Grill lifter*: This makes moving the racks around much easier.
- *Heat diffusion plate*: Made out of ceramic, this item looks like a pizza stone and goes by different names, depending on the manufacturer—plate setter, D plate, etc. If you're going to smoke, you'll want one; it's inserted between the fire and the food for indirect cooking. You may need to purchase an additional rack to set the plate in.
- *Upper or "extender" racks*: These sit atop the base grill grates and can double your cooking surface. My favorite way to use them is to place a brisket on an upper rack and a pan of beans or potatoes on the base grill, which allows the meat juices to drip down into the beans or potatoes. So good!
- *A mobile cart*: While the feet that come with every grill will allow it to sit safely, even on a wood deck, the extra elevation provided by the cart makes cooking and cleaning the ash from the grill much easier. A cart will also allow you to move the grill without breaking your back or calling in reinforcements for help.

Getting Started with Your Kamado

There are quite a number of different brands of kamado grills on the market. Each has its own particular learning curve, but none are radically different from the others. Your first step after buying a kamado is to very carefully follow the manufacturer's instructions for putting the grill together, unless you are having it set up and delivered by a dealer. If you didn't opt for a cart, think long and hard about where you're going to locate your kamado. These grills weigh 250 pounds and up, so once you get it on a deck or elevated patio, I think

An extender rack can almost double your cooking area. You can also use one for a set-up like this: As the lamb cooks, its juices drip off and baste the potatoes set underneath it. (For this recipe, see page 61.)

that's where you're going to want to leave it. Also consider where you will be keeping charcoal and any accessories and how convenient they will be to the grill. I would also recommend the purchase of a side table. I have a rolling stainless-steel table purchased from a warehouse club next to my grill. It's my holding station for food going onto or coming off the grill, as well as any sauces or bastes I may need to apply during cooking.

Fire and the Kamado

Once you've got your kamado in place, it's time to build a fire. But before you build that fire, be sure to read this section in its entirety. Your first fire will cure the kamado, and it must be done correctly. Also, there a number of fire-making dos and don'ts that are particular to the kamado. Learn them, and you'll have kamado success; ignore them, and you could possibly ruin your grill and void your warranty.

THE CHARCOAL

Let me be unequivocal: Briquettes have absolutely no place in kamado grilling. The only fuel you should use is all-natural hardwood lump charcoal. Lump charcoal is made by partially burning wood or heating it without oxygen; this process removes or vaporizes all water, hydrogen, methane, and tars from the wood, reducing it to carbon. Using lump charcoal is also better for your health, as it's those tars that contain most of the carcinogenic compounds associated with charcoal grilling. Lump charcoal contains no additives or petroleum byproducts; it also lights faster, burns hotter

and much, much longer than briquettes, and produces less ash. From this point forward, know that the word "charcoal" refers only to natural lump charcoal.

Every kamado manufacturer sells its own proprietary blend of charcoal, but any brand of lump charcoal will work fine and you'll find it for sale in large supermarkets, hardware stores, and many big-box retailers. Most all lump charcoal sold for cooking is a mixture of hickory, maple, and oak; this happens to be a blend that many of the great barbecue houses in this country prefer.

Size Matters

Open a bag of lump charcoal, and you will see that the chunks are not uniform in size; this is a

Charcoal from a bag sorted into large, medium, and small pieces.

good thing. When you build your fire, start with a base of larger chunks; this will provide for better air flow, allowing the fire to get going more quickly. If you need to add more charcoal once the fire is going, use the smaller pieces.

When I buy a bag of charcoal, I pour it out, then sort out the pieces, which I then store in two big airtight, waterproof containers (like pet food containers) that I keep near my kamado, one for the larger pieces and another for the medium to small chunks. Yes, it's kind of a mess to do this but it's a mess once and then I can get my fires going quickly without rooting around in the bag looking for pieces of the size I want. You can use gloves when you do this, but if you do it barehanded, which I do, the charcoal residue washes off easily with soap and water.

BUILDING THE FIRE

Make a generous pile of large chunks of charcoal in the kamado. Arrange your fire starter of choice in the charcoal; this can be a paraffin-based lighter

block, a compressed wood fire starter, an electric starter, or rolled newspaper. (I haven't found chimney-style starters to be as effective as any of these methods, and some kamado manufacturers out-and-out recommend not using them.) Open the bottom and top dampers as far as they will go.

Whatever you're using, light the charcoal pile with a match or, my favorite, a propane torch. DO NOT EVER USE LIGHTER FLUID IN A KAMADO.

When starting the fire, both top and bottom vents should be wide open. **Left:** *Fire starter options, clockwise from left to right: paraffin starters, compressed wood strips, Green Egg Starters, Primo Quick Lights.*

Once the fire starter is in place, light the charcoal (here, with a propane torch).

When the charcoal just begins to ash over, close the dome and let the temperature build in the kamado.

The chemical residue will be absorbed by the firebox and any food you cook in the kamado from that point on will taste like lighter fluid.

Once lit, leave the fire alone for 10 to 15 minutes. If your experience with grills is using briquettes, you'll be used to waiting until they burn to ash gray. Forget you ever did that. If you do that with lump charcoal, you're wasting fuel. Look for just a little gray to form, but not much.

BRINGING THE KAMADO UP TO TEMPERATURE

At this point, close the dome and wait for the temperature to build inside the kamado. Whatever the target temperature is for your recipe, let it build beyond that. For example, if the target is 200° F, let it build to 300° F, then open the lid and add any needed equipment, such as the grill grate, or a heat diffuser if you're smoking (more on that later). Doing this will likely drop the temperature down below your target. Close the dome, wait for the temperature to build up to your target, then add your food, close the dome again, and adjust the dampers to maintain the temperature you want. Keep a close eye on the temperature for a while to make sure you are in the range you want.

From this point on, you should not have to add any additional charcoal.

DAMPERS, AIR FLOW, AND GRILL TEMPERATURE

The kamado has two dampers, one at the bottom, located directly under the fire grate, thst controls air flow to the fire, and the other at the top of the dome (in some models, this vent takes the form of a daisy wheel), used to draw the heat, smoke, and steam up through the grill.

The top and bottom dampers work in concert. When you start the fire, they should both be wide open, as you want maximum air flow to get the fire going. During cooking, you'll need to manipulate the dampers to arrive at your target temperature. Every model is different, so these instructions are guide, not gospel—you're going to have to experiment, but this gives you a place to start. The bottom damper will be your primary focus in getting to the target temperature, and I have found that every ½-inch movement in either direction will increase or decrease the grill temperature by about 25° F. The top damper is meant for fine-tuning the temperature in the grill, and should be moved in ½-inch increments. Every time you make a

THE WORD ON TEMPERATURE

Method	Temperature
Grilling	450°–700° F
Most roasting and baking	350°–450° F
Steaming and braising	300°–400° F
Hot smoking ("low and slow")	200°–250° F
Cold smoking	150° F

Left: To get the high temperature you want for grilling, you want maximum air flow, with the bottom vent wide open. *Center:* For roasting, baking, steaming and braising, you'll want to cut back somewhat on the air flow. *Right:* To maintain a smoking temperature of 200° to 250° F (or lower, if you're cold smoking), your bottom damper will be open just a crack.

Left: Daisy wheel–style top vent wide open for grilling. *Center:* Top vent open for roasting, baking, steaming, and braising. *Right:* Top vent open for smoking.

change in the damper, check back after about 10 minutes to see what's happening with the temperature gauge.

If you want to drop the temperature in the grill quickly, close both dampers and open the dome slightly to let some heat escape, then readjust the dampers to get to your target temperature.

ADDING SMOKE

When cooking with lump charcoal, you're already adding wood smoke flavor to your food. That said, you might want to layer in additional nuances. Check the chart below for the most commonly used woods and their suggested uses. I like to mix woods as well, hickory and apple being my favorite combination. Cherry and apple is another good mix. Hickory and mesquite are both very strong; most all the great pit masters temper these woods with the addition of a fruitwood or oak. Start slow when adding wood flavor, especially if you are new to lump charcoal.

SMOKING WOODS

I've listed these woods from most commonly used on down.

Wood Type	Characteristics	Good With
Hickory	Bacon-like, smoky	Most anything but fish
Mesquite	Pungent but sweet; burns hot, so take that into consideration	Made for beef and lamb, but also good with veggies
Oak	Mellow; is the traditional mix with hickory for barbecue of all types	Brisket, pork shoulders, pork of all types
Apple	The darling of the barbecue circuit; mild, sweet, dense smoke—my favorite	Pork, all poultry, especially duck and turkey
Cherry	Mild and sweet	Duck and other poultry, pork
Alder	Light and delicate	Great with salmon and most all seafood—veggies too
Pecan	Strong and nutty; burns cool, which makes it great for low and slow cooking	Wild game, pork, and chicken
Pear/peach	Woodsy and sweet, but rich	Poultry, pork, and fish
Grapevines	Mild and easy; great for quick-cooking foods	Poultry parts, pork
Wine and whiskey barrel pieces	Fun and different; oak and wine nuances	Beef and poultry

Chips or Chunks?

When I want to add smoke to an item that's going to cook quickly, I use chips, soaked in water for about 30 minutes, since they only last about 20 minutes. You can layer the chips in from bottom to top as you build your charcoal base; doing this will extend the smoke.

However, when I want smoke for an item that will take an hour or more to cook, I use chunks of wood and I don't bother soaking them. In fact, I use chunks 90% of the time when I'm cooking in the kamado. Because they're slow-burning, I can get the grill to temperature, put my food in, close the dome, and not have to fiddle with the grill to add another handful of chips somewhere along the line. But be careful: Too much smoke will make your food bitter.

Direct vs. Indirect Cooking

The difference between these two methods of cooking is simple: With direct cooking, the food is

Add smoke by setting wood chunks on the charcoal fire; no need to soak them!

set directly over the fire, meaning there is nothing between the food and the fire but the grill rack. With indirect cooking, the food is not exposed to the flames.

When using a regular charcoal grill or a gas grill, indirect cooking is accomplished by establishing a cooler area in the grill by either turning off gas burners or by pushing the coals to one side of the grill. In the kamado, for indirect cooking, the food is separated from the flames by inserting a ceramic plate (a heat diffuser) over the fire. You can get the same effect by putting your food on a pizza stone or in a cast-iron pan, Dutch oven, or other pan set on the grill grate.

Direct cooking is fast and hot, and it's the method of choice for thin, tender cuts of protein and sliced vegetables. The kamado is well known as a superior smoker, but it can also achieve the high temperature you want for a good sear. And with the dome down, you eliminate flare-ups. Instead, any juice drippings evaporate into steam and recirculate in the closed atmosphere of the kamado, eventually being redeposited on the food they came from, creating even more layers of delicious flavor.

The ceramic plate inserted for indirect cooking.

You'll find in the roasting chapter that for that method I like to use a combination of direct and indirect cooking, first searing the protein on the grill grate over the flames for some tasty caramelization (see below for more on searing), then transferring it to a roasting pan.

To a great degree, whether you use indirect or direct cooking will be determined by what you're cooking. The charts on pages 14–15 will help you sort it all out.

SEARING IN THE KAMADO

Searing, with all its tasty caramelization, is part and parcel of grilling, but it is also used in roasting and braising—the protein is first seared directly over the flames to develop flavor, then transferred to a cooking vessel to finish cooking indirectly.

Two factors contribute mightily to a good sear. First, cast iron is best—invest in a cast-iron grill

grate if your kamado did not come with one. Second, preheating is key—let that grate heat up while the kamado builds to temperature. Follow those rules and I'll guarantee you a mouthwatering sizzle the second your food hits that grate, and grill marks that will be the envy of any steakhouse.

Many models of kamado have grill grates that can be flipped to allow the grate to be closer to the fire, accenting the searing process. I've flipped the grate to its lower position to sear, then pulled the food off and quickly flipped the grate to the higher position to finish the cooking, but it seems to me to be a lot of work for a small result. But if you have a model that allows you to do this, try it and see if you like the results. Searing in this lower position is fine for steaks and such, but don't do it with more delicate items like fish.

Caring for Your Kamado

The good news is that very little is needed to care for your kamado. It is basically self-cleaning. There is no need to try to clean the firebox or charcoal rack. Just heat the grill to 500°F and that will pretty well incinerate any food buildup or other debris stuck to the inside of the grill. You may have to run a grill bush over the grill grates, but if you do that while the grill is hot, any residue will come right off. The only cleaning the outer surface of the kamado requires is wiping with a damp cloth to remove dust and pollen.

You do need to clean the ash trap, as any buildup there will interfere with the air flow of the grill, which is central to the functioning of the grill. Do this using the tool designed for it for your particular kamado, though I have heard of folks using a shop-vac. The ashes should always be cold when you do this chore. I recommend doing it before each use of the kamado.

Follow your manufacturer's recommendations for keeping the hinge bands for the dome tight. If they get too loose, the balance of the grill will be off and the grill could topple. Also, the gasket will need to be replaced periodically to ensure that tight kamado seal when the dome is closed. A sure

Recommended Cooking Methods

These are guidelines only; specific recipes may vary.

BEEF

Tender Cuts (direct heat)

Filet mignon, rib eye steak, Porterhouse steak, New York strip steak, T-bone steak

Less Tender Still But Tasty Cuts (direct heat)

Hanger steak, skirt steak, flank steak, top sirloin, flat iron steak, London broil

Big Cuts to Roast or Smoke (indirect heat)

Whole beef tenderloin, strip loin, standing rib roast, tri-tip roast

Tougher Cuts for Smoking or Braising (indirect heat)

Chuck roast, eye of round, brisket, short beef ribs, dinosaur beef ribs

PORK

Tender Cuts (direct heat)

Pork tenderloin, bone-in pork chop, boneless pork chop, country-style ribs, ham steak, shoulder blade steak, sirloin chop

Large Tender Cuts (combination of direct and indirect heat)

Boneless pork loin roast, rack of pork, sirloin roast, cured ham

Ribs (combination of direct and indirect heat)

Baby back ribs, spareribs

Large Tough Cuts (indirect heat)

Boston butt, picnic shoulder, ham, pork belly

LAMB AND GAME

Tender Cuts (direct heat)

Lamb tenderloin, lamb rib chops, lamb loin chops, venison loin chops, venison tenderloin steak, bison rib eye steak, bison filet mignon, bison sirloin steak

Less Tender But Still Tasty Cuts (direct heat)

Lamb shoulder chops, lamb leg steaks, deer leg steak

LAMB AND GAME *continued*

Big Cuts to Roast (indirect heat)

Bone-in leg of lamb, boneless leg of lamb, deer ham, venison sirloin roast, whole venison tenderloin, lamb crown roast

Tough Cuts to Smoke or Braise (indirect heat)

Lamb ribs, bison ribs, lamb shanks

POULTRY

Boneless Parts (direct heat)

Chicken breasts and thighs, turkey cutlets, butterflied quail, duck breasts

Bone-In Parts and Larger Boneless Pieces (direct and indirect heat)

Cut-up fryers, chicken quarters and other pieces, butterflied chicken, turkeys, or ducks, turkey drumsticks, boneless turkey roasts, Cornish game hens cut in half, whole squab

The Whole Bird (indirect heat)

Chicken, turkey, duck, game hen, capon, goose

SEAFOOD TYPES

Meaty, Firm, and Thick Fillets (direct heat)

Grouper, salmon, tuna, swordfish, monkfish, mackerel, catfish

More Delicate But Still Fairly Meaty Fillets and Steaks (direct heat)

Mahi-mahi, Chilean sea bass, halibut, red snapper, trout, striped bass

Whole Fish (indirect heat)

Mackerel, bluefish, grouper, snapper, striped bass, trout, sardines

Shellfish (direct heat)

Shrimp, scallops, lobster, oysters, clams

sign that it's time to replace it is smoke escaping between the grill bottom and dome. Refer to your owner's manual for how to replace it. You'll also want to lubricate all the moving parts of your kamado once or twice a year; again, refer to your owner's manual for instructions.

If a crusty buildup develops on the ceramic plates, scrub them with warm water and a mild abrasive cleaner like Bon Ami. Once you use these plates, they will never again look like the day you bought them, so don't kill yourself doing this. Truthfully, I only do it when I have caked-on buildup.

Cleaning the ash out the kamado.

Some Barbecue Basics

What follows are tips, techniques, and more that I've found useful in my forty years of barbecuing, no matter the grill.

GENERAL BARBECUE EQUIPAGE

Beyond the kamado and its accessories, here are the tools and supplies I like to have on hand when cooking out of doors.

Must-Haves

- A good pair of barbecue mitts.
- Multiple pairs of tongs. You'll need one to handle raw food and one to switch over to for cooked food to prevent cross-contamination. Restaurant supply houses are a great source for good, sturdy, inexpensive tongs. Spring-loaded tongs are best; the kind that breaks apart into a spatula and fork is hard to work with sometimes.
- Spatulas. Have several sizes with sturdy blades. Long handles are nice but not necessary. I particularly like fish spatulas for turning fish on the grill.
- A sturdy, brass-bristle grill brush. If your kamado has cast-iron grates, you will need to get a brush with stainless-steel bristles. Don't skimp here; buy quality.
- A probe-type thermometer for checking the internal temperatures of meat and poultry. The probe eliminates the need to open the dome to check on the temperature. You can even buy them with alarms on them to tell you when you've hit your target temperature. I also like OXO's probe thermometer, which includes

My basic griller's toolkit: From left to right, tool to remove ash, long-handle spatula, tongs, fish spatula, probe thermometer, instant-read thermometer, grill lifter, and saucepan and brushes.

both the USDA-recommended and "Chef-preferred" temperature settings. You will also need an instant-read thermometer to use on quicker cooking items.

- A couple of timers. They'll keep you on your toes through cocktails and beer.
- A few basting brushes. Have a small one for brushing oil on the food before grilling and a longer-handled one for basting food on the grill. Heat-resistant silicone brushes are great. They are easy to clean and carry a good amount of product with one dip. There's one available now that looks and acts like a "mop" brush.
- Disposable aluminum-foil pans are a godsend for many chores around the grill. Use them to transport food or as drip pans. Keep a good supply on hand.
- Skewers. Given a choice, I will always use metal rather than bamboo for the better heat transfer. Buy flat-blade skewers; otherwise your food will spin when you go to turn it on

the grill. You might want some double-prong skewers, but that's not a must-have.
- Loads of heavy-duty aluminum foil and ziptop plastic bags for marinating.
- A good-quality injection syringe if you plan to do long-cooking meats
- A restaurant-quality half-sheet pan. This will carry all your stuff to the grill without buckling under the weight, and it can also double as a roasting or drip pan.
- A pepper mill. Please grind your pepper fresh; it makes a huge difference.

Nice to Have

- Racks. I have both a standard-size rib rack and one big enough to hold a whole rack, as well as a "V"-style roasting rack (turn it upside down and you can use it as a quick rib rack). You can also purchase a beer-can chicken rack if you want, but the kamado keeps poultry so moist that I don't even cook chickens this way anymore.

Food Safety

- Wash your hands often in hot, soapy water during food preparation.
- "Room temperature" means 65° to 72° F, no higher.
- Defrost foods in the refrigerator.
- Cross-contamination is real and can ruin your day. Keep tongs, cutting boards, platters, and anything else that touches raw food away from cooked food. Wash everything that has been in contact with raw stuff in hot, soapy water.
- If reusing a marinade as a sauce or basting medium, place it in a pot over high heat, bring to a boil, and boil for at least a full minute. Start timing when a full boil is reached.
- If a sauce is to be used as a basting sauce and also passed as the table sauce, divide it before use. This is preferable to boiling a basting sauce after use; heat can sometimes radically change the flavor.

- An outdoor grill light
- A pizza peel. Buy a large one, wood or stainless steel.
- Assorted cedar planks for smoking. They should be 1 inch thick, at least 4 inches wide, and 10 to 12 inches long, and untreated.
- A pan, pot, and baking pan or two that are very heavy duty, for use on the grill. My top choice for this is Lodge preseasoned and porcelain-coated cast-iron cookware. I also really like their carbon-steel pan for searing and grill roasting
- A spice grinder
- Microplane zester
- A vacuum sealer. I use it to pack up leftover barbecued or grilled items. To reheat, just drop the bag in simmering water for a few minutes. Before you know it, you'll be enjoying right-off-the-grill flavor.

THE BARBECUE PANTRY

These are the ingredients I like to have handy in my culinary tool chest. Pick and choose as you like.

- Kosher salt, especially Morton's, and gray sea salt. I like the feel and the melt of Morton's kosher salt, and have found that gray sea salt doesn't seem to affect my blood pressure too much.
- Black pepper. It adds volumes of flavor. Please use only fresh ground!
- Good oils. Have olive oil (no need for extra-virgin) and canola or another neutral oil. A little truffle oil is nice for finishing simply grilled food.
- Unsalted butter—that way you control the seasoning.
- Hot pepper sauces. For the recipes in this book, I used Texas Pete, Frank's, and Tabasco. Also have an Asian hot sauce like Sky Valley's Sriracha on hand.
- A good-quality mayonnaise. Being from the South, for me that's Duke's. Pick a mayonnaise that has little or no sugar. But if a recipe calls for a particular mayonnaise (like Hellmann's), then use it; it's part of the flavor profile.
- Brown sugar, local honey, high-quality molasses like Muddy Pond, grade B pure maple syrup, and plain old white sugar.
- Bourbon, for the food and the cook.
- Ketchup. I really like the flavor of organic ketchups, Hunt's regular ketchup, and Dickinson, a specialty ketchup from J.M. Smucker. But when you're using it in a barbecue sauce that's going to get cooked, a store brand is fine.
- Tamari. I prefer this over soy sauce. It's better tasting, lower in sodium, and slightly thicker than regular soy sauce; it's also sold in most large supermarkets these days.
- Worcestershire sauce. Try the recipe for homemade on page 252 but store-bought is fine.
- Distilled white, balsamic, and cider vinegars.
- Mustards: Yellow American-style, Gulden's Brown, and Maile Dijon-style mustard are my choices. I use only Colman's dry mustard.

Bourbon-Glazed Bone-in Rib-Eye (page 102)

- When you don't have time to make your own barbecue sauce, look for Bone-Suckin' Sauce in the supermarket—it's exceptional.
- Fresh spices and herbs. If they are older than six months, they have lost their oomph and need to be thrown out. I make sure I always have on hand a few pure chile powders (especially chipotle and smoked paprika), crushed red peppers, granulated garlic and onion, and a barbecue rub.
- Fruit preserves such as peach, jellies like red currant, guava, plum, and hot pepper, and orange marmalade. They can be used for quick glazes and sauce ingredients.
- Prepared horseradish and wasabi in a tube—forget the powder.
- Lots of onions, yellow and sweet, fresh garlic, and shallots, lemons, limes, and oranges—all these ingredients add immediate flavor.
- Italian salad dressing for an emergency marinade; my favorite is Good Season's.
- Red and white wine, and sherry. Since box wines have gotten so much better, I keep a box of red and white wine just for cooking; I find the wine stays fresher in the box than a bottle. Remember, it must be drinkable. Vermouth is also nice to have on hand.
- Herb pastes. These can be found in the produce sections of most large supermarkets. I particularly like garlic, Italian herb blend, and lemongrass pastes.

"COOK IT TILL IT'S DONE"

Ask a chef how long to cook something and invariably the smart retort will be, "cook it till it's done." The only absolute in the timing for any recipe in this book or any other grilling book is that there are no absolutes! Grilling is more art than science, which is a big part of why most of us are drawn to it. Way too many variables have an effect on outdoor cooking, and you should never accept any timing guideline as gospel: Wind, the outside temperature, and rain can all affect timing.

In cold weather, you will need to adjust your temperatures upward, especially if you want to maintain a consistent temperature for indirect cooking. Wind can be your toughest adversary. If possible, position the grill so that the wind is blowing perpendicular to the dampers.

So how do you know when something is done? Each recipe in the book will provide you with clues to doneness, whether it be internal temperature or a visual cue. For tender cuts, there are also the touch tests, outlined on page 21.

I routinely tell my cooking classes and neighbors, "It's easier to put cook on than to take cook off." When checking for doneness, always err on the side of checking it too soon. Remove the food from the grill and check it after letting it rest the suggested amount of time (put the dome down on the grill while you're doing this), then and return it to the grill if it's not cooked enough.

Face Touch Method for Doneness

For this, you will touch the food, then compare its firmness to different parts of your face.

If it feels like your cheek, it's rare.

If it feels like the tip of your nose, it's medium.

If it's as firm as your forehead, it's well done.

Hand Touch Method for Doneness

For this, you will touch the food, then compare its firmness as you use different fingers to touch your thumb.

Rare

Medium rare

Medium well

Way past done

Smoky Slab of Beef Ribs
(page 34)

2
Smoking in the Kamado

I know why you bought a kamado grill. You went to a friend's house and they cooked the most amazing barbecue you've ever eaten on a kamado, and you just had to have one. Congratulations, you are now the owner of a lean, mean backyard smoking machine!

Whether you are smoking a tender cut like beef tenderloin, which will be ready to enjoy in just an hour, or tougher cuts like brisket or pork shoulder, which will stay in the kamado for many, many hours before falling into delicious strands at the prod of a fork, you're embarking on a culinary adventure with a reliable guide at your side, the kamado.

I've smoked on just about every imaginable grill available to the home pitmaster—side-box smokers, bullet smokers, kettles, even oil drum rigs. Nothing has outperformed the kamado.

Smoking temperatures usually range from 150° F ("cold smoking" and perfect for fish) to 225° F, with the outside range being 275° F. Times for smoking can run as short as an hour, or 8 hours or more. It takes precision with temperature to smoke properly. If smoking isn't your day job, the kamado is your precision tool.

The insulating properties of the ceramic-clad kamado, coupled with its damper system and elliptical or oval design, are a match made in smoking heaven. With the kamado, temperature control is almost as easy as flipping a switch once you become familiar with your particular grill. Of the five different grills from five different manufacturers that I have cooked with while writing this book, I have been able to maintain 200° F in all but one for 16 hours without adding any more charcoal. Imagine loading your kamado with charcoal and knowing that chances are you will not have to mess with your fire again!

Also, most foods will cook or smoke faster in the kamado because of its tight seal and superior insulation, and when there is no need to lift the lid to restoke the fire, the heat retention is even greater.

Smoking can often cause foods to dry out. That's why, when smoking, you're often instructed to put a water pan in the grill. But not in the kamado. The tight seal keeps water from evaporating and instead it condenses at the top of the dome. A few years ago at the Big Apple Barbecue Block Party in New York City, I asked pitmaster Mike Mills, a past Memphis in May Champion and Bill Clinton's go-to guy for ribs (Mike had clearance on Air Force One to deliver ribs), why there was so little smoke coming from his rig. His response made perfect sense: "If you see smoke, then the smoke's not going on the ribs." With the kamado's tight seal, you can replicate Mike's setup.

The setup for smoking in the kamado differs slightly for each brand (be sure to read your manual), but basically it's the same. A fire is built, then a ceramic plate (think of it as flame tamer) is set over the fire on the lower rack, under the grate where the food will sit. This blocks the food from the direct heat of the fire. An alternative is setting a cast-iron skillet or grill pan on that lower rack. I've had good success doing this.

When getting ready to smoke, I have found that running the temperature past the target smoking temperature, say 300° F when I want to smoke at 225° F, is helpful. By the time I've opened the dome, inserted the ceramic plate, and put my food on the grill, my temperature has usually dropped to my target temperature and I'm ready to cook. I then adjust the dampers to maintain that temperature. With almost every model of kamado that I tested, I try to have the top damper open only slightly, and the bottom open about an inch or two.

Your food will end up with a pleasing smoke flavor if you just use lump charcoal and nothing else, but you can add wood chunks to amp up the smokiness or add another flavor profile. For every recipe in this chapter (except for of a handful of recipes where I think additional smoke doesn't work with the flavors involved), I give you my recommendation of what wood will work best; you can also leave out the wood entirely. You can soak the chunks or not, it's up to you. I find it unnecessary—chunks smoke from the get-go and as they burn they become their own charcoal. Also, don't stress too much about having the chunks smoking through the entire cooking time. Most proteins take on the lion's share of their smoke flavor in the first two hours of smoking.

Smoked Garlic Beef Tenderloin

Serves 8 to 12

10 cloves garlic

1 teaspoon kosher salt

1 tablespoon chopped fresh thyme

1 tablespoon chopped fresh flat-leaf parsley

1 (4-pound) beef tenderloin roast, trimmed of silverskin

Freshly ground black pepper

Prepared horseradish sauce

. . . .

Recommended wood: Hickory

Beef tenderloin is always a treat. Add smoke and low and slow cooking and the result is a butter knife–tender piece of beef infused with the essence of wood. This method adds so much flavor to the tenderloin, actually enhancing its beefiness. It's a perfect choice for large gatherings and delicious warm, at room temperature, or even cold (it makes a killer roast beef sandwich). For a flavor change-up, swap out the regular garlic for smoke-roasted garlic (page 90).

1. Using the butt of knife, smash each garlic clove on a cutting board and peel it. Sprinkle all the cloves with the salt and, again, using the butt of the knife, mash the garlic into a paste with the salt, working the knife back and forth. Place the garlic paste in a small bowl and work in the herbs. Smear the paste all over the beef, making sure you get the ends as well. Liberally season with black pepper. Place the tenderloin on a wire rack and then place the rack in a disposable aluminum-foil pan to catch the drippings.

2. Light a fire in the kamado grill using your favorite method. After about 10 minutes, close the dome and open the upper and lower dampers all the way. When the temperature reaches 300° F, place the wood chunks around the fire and add any accessories necessary for smoking on your particular grill, along with the grill rack. Close the dome, let the temperature build back to between 200° and 250° F, and wait for a little smoke to accumulate. Adjust the dampers to maintain the temperature in this range.

3. Place the pan on the grill, close the dome, and smoke the roast for about 2 hours, until the internal temperature in the center reaches 125° F for rare or to your desired degree of doneness.

4. Transfer the roast to a cutting board and let rest for about 30 minutes, tented with foil, if desired. Slice the roast thinly and serve with horse-radish sauce on the side and any accumulated pan drippings.

Kansas City Prime Rib

Serves 8 to 10

1 bone-in standing rib roast (about 6 pounds), trimmed of excess fat

6 large cloves garlic, peeled

2 tablespoons fresh rosemary leaves

2 tablespoons fresh thyme leaves

Kosher salt and freshly ground black pepper

3 tablespoons coarse-grain Dijon mustard

3 tablespoons olive oil

Prepared horseradish sauce

. . . .

Recommended wood: Hickory

D o you remember back in the '80s when every restaurant had the ubiquitous prime rib night? It may have fallen out of favor with restaurant diners, but savvy cooks know better. Taking the time to smoke a prime rib adds that final nuance of delicious flavor to this exquisite cut of meat, elevating it to a truly regal status.

1. At least 1 hour before you're ready to begin cooking, remove the roast from the refrigerator. In a food processor or mortar, combine the garlic, rosemary, thyme, and 2 teaspoons each salt and pepper. Pulse to finely mince or crush with a pestle. Add the mustard and pulse or mix to combine. Slowly add the oil with the food processor running or slowly mix in with the pestle until a paste forms. Smear the paste evenly over the entire surface of the roast. For a more intense herb flavor, let the roast sit at room temperature for 2 hours or wrap and refrigerate overnight.

2. Light a fire in the kamado grill using your favorite method. After about 10 minutes, close the dome and open the upper and lower dampers all the way. When the temperature reaches 300° F, place the wood chunks around the fire and add any accessories necessary for smoking on your particular grill, along with the grill rack. Close the dome, let the temperature build back to between 200° and 250° F, and wait for a little smoke to accumulate. Adjust the dampers to maintain the temperature in this range.

3. Place the roast, bone side down, on a rack in a disposable aluminum-foil pan (this pan is going to catch all the delicious meat juices so you can make gravy). Place the pan on the grill, close the dome, and smoke until an instant-read thermometer registers 130° to 135° F. Make sure to insert the thermometer away from the bone. Usually this takes about 4 hours, but begin to check after $2\frac{1}{2}$ hours.

4. Transfer the roast to a cutting board, tent with foil, and let rest for at least 30 minutes to let the juices settle. If you wish, make a quick pan gravy (see left) out of the drippings. Carve the meat into thin slices and arrange on a warm platter. Serve at once with horseradish sauce and the gravy.

Making Gravy

Pour all the accumulated fat and meat juice into a fat separator. Return 2 tablespoons of fat to the pan and discard the rest of it, leaving behind the meat juices. Add enough beef broth to the meat juices to equal 2 cups. Place the pan over medium heat over two burners of your stove. Throw in some chopped shallots and sauté quickly until softened. Add 2 tablespoons superfine flour or cake flour, stir into the fat, and cook for 2 to 3 minutes, stirring. Whisk in the broth. Add a thyme sprig and cook for about 5 minutes. If the gravy begins to get too thick, add more broth. When the gravy has thickened to your liking, gild the lily. Swirl in 2 to 4 tablespoons unsalted butter, 1 tablespoon at a time. Want to really crank this up? Use a combination of unsalted butter and truffle butter. Keep warm over low heat until you serve the roast.

Gilroy Smoked Tri-tip

Serves 6 to 8

1 tri-tip roast (3 to 4 pounds)

1 tablespoon chili powder

1 teaspoon garlic salt

Copious amounts of freshly ground black pepper

Your favorite fresh salsa and pinto beans cooked with bacon for serving

. . . .

Recommended wood: Hickory; I usually say soaking doesn't matter, but soaking the wood in beer for an hour brings a nice flavor to the tri-tip

S moked tri-tip is to central California what pulled pork is to North Carolina, ribs are to Memphis, and brisket is to Texas. On a trip along California's Coast Highway, I stopped at a convenience store/farmers' market near Gilroy, south of San Francisco. The store had a small grill serving local favorites and tri-tip sandwiches were on the menu. I had heard a lot about this style of barbecue, sometimes referred to as Santa Maria barbecue, and was eager to try it. After about two bites I was back in the kitchen talking the cook out of his recipe. I think you will enjoy this change of pace on smoked beef. Tri-tip sometimes needs to be special ordered, but I've found that most of the price clubs have it on a regular basis.

1. At least 1 hour before cooking, remove the roast from the refrigerator. Season all sides with the chili powder, garlic salt, and lots and lots of black pepper.

2. Light a fire in the kamado grill using your favorite method. After about 10 minutes, close the dome and open the upper and lower dampers all the way. When the temperature reaches 300° F, place the wood chunks around the fire and add any accessories necessary for smoking on your particular grill, along with the grill rack. Close the dome, let the temperature build back to between 200° and 250° F, and wait for a little smoke to accumulate. Adjust the dampers to maintain the temperature in this range.

3. Place the roast on the grill and smoke until an instant-read thermometer registers between 130° and 140° F, about 2 hours. Transfer the roast to a cutting board, tent with aluminum foil, and let rest for 15 minutes. Slice very thinly against the grain. Arrange on a platter and pour any accumulated juice over the top. Serve with salsa and pinto beans.

Hugh Lynn's Texas Brisket with an Onion Twist

Serves 12, twice

2 (5- to 6-pound) beef briskets

12 cloves garlic, thinly sliced

2 tablespoons Texas Brisket Rub (page 233)

4 large onions, quartered

Texas Barbecue Joint–Style Sauce (page 249) for serving

. . . .

Recommended wood: Mesquite

The Texas Crutch

On the championship barbecue circuit, wrapping a piece of meat in aluminum foil is called a "Texas crutch." It's a fairly foolproof way of insuring juicy results. I've found the construction and design of the kamado really prevent the beef from drying out the way many grills tend to do, thus there is no real need for the "crutch." But if it makes you feel better, you can wrap the brisket after about 3 hours.

Sugarland, Texas, is a hot spot of Texas-style beef brisket perfection, and fortunately for me, my friend Hugh Lynn is a native of the region. Hugh has somehow managed to have all his work assignments in cities with great barbecue culture: Austin, Kansas City, Raleigh, and now Memphis. Hugh and his wife, Jean, taught me how good a beef brisket could be—quite a feat considering I'm a pork shoulder–loving North Carolinian. Hugh believes you should be gentle with your seasoning and keep the fire low. With a kamado, draft control is so precise you should never, ever end up with a tough, dried-out brisket. One of the secrets to Hugh's brisket success is that he adds onion quarters to the fire. Not only will it drive you insane with the delicious smell, it imparts another layer of flavor to the finished brisket.

Even with the kamado, smoking brisket is a real commitment of time, so I always cook two at a time and throw one in the freezer.

1. Using a knife, cut small slits into both briskets and slide a slice of garlic into each slit. Sprinkle each brisket with 1 tablespoon of the brisket rub and work it into the meat. Let sit at room temperature until you're ready to cook.

2. Light a fire in the kamado grill using your favorite method. After about 10 minutes, close the dome and open the upper and lower dampers all the way. When the temperature reaches 300° F, place the wood chunks and the onions around the fire and add any accessories necessary for smoking on your particular grill, along with the grill rack. Close the dome, let the temperature to come back to between 200° and 250° F, and wait for a little smoke to accumulate. Adjust the dampers to maintain the temperature in this range.

3. Place the briskets on a rack in a drip pan, then place the pan on the grill grate; the pan will catch the drippings, which are good for making sauce or seasoning baked beans (see the recipe on page 91). Smoke the briskets for 6 to 8 hours. After 6 hours, check the meat at its thickest point with an instant-read thermometer; 180° F is where you want to be.

4. Remove the briskets from the grill and wrap each in aluminum foil. Let one brisket cool completely, then wrap it again in foil and freeze it; it will keep up to 3 months. (To reheat, let it thaw overnight in the refrigerator, then put it in a preheated 350° F oven until warmed through, about 30 minutes.) Let the other brisket rest for 15 to 20 minutes, then slice thinly across the grain and serve. Pour any accumulated juices over the meat. Serve the sauce on the side.

Sweet Jewish-Style Brisket

Serves 8 to 10

½ cup olive oil

½ cup cola

½ cup dry red wine

¼ cup honey

5 tablespoons ketchup

2 cups finely chopped onions

½ teaspoon dry mustard, like Colman's

½ teaspoon smoked paprika

1 (5- to 7-pound) beef brisket

3 tablespoons unsalted butter or pauvre margarine

3 tablespoons gravy flour or all-purpose flour

Kosher salt and freshly ground black pepper

....

Recommended wood: Cherry or wine barrel chunks

Against the Grain

Cutting against the grain is your key to tenderness, when it comes to tougher and more muscled cuts, like brisket and skirt steak.

This recipe is based on my high school buddy Steve Grossman's mother's recipe. I always jumped at the chance to eat with the Grossmans; their food was so different from my mother's Southern fare. His mom would braise this dish, but I found a way to smoke it and still have a moist brisket and gravy.

1. In a medium bowl, whisk the oil, cola, wine, honey, ketchup, onions, mustard, and paprika together.

2. Place the brisket in a 2½-gallon zip-top plastic bag or other container large enough to hold it. Pour in the marinade and squish everything around. Seal the bag or cover the container and marinate overnight in the refrigerator, turning the bag or brisket over occasionally. About an hour before smoking, remove the brisket from the marinade; reserve the marinade.

3. Light a fire in the kamado grill using your favorite method. After about 10 minutes, close the dome and open the upper and lower dampers all the way. When the temperature reaches 300° F, place the wood chunks around the fire and add any accessories necessary for smoking on your particular grill, along with the grill rack. Close the dome, let the temperature build back to between 200° and 250° F, and wait for a little smoke to accumulate.

4. Place the brisket on a rack in a drip pan, then place the pan on the grill grate; the pan will catch the drippings, which are good for making sauce or seasoning baked beans (see page 91). Close the dome and smoke for 5 to 6 hours, until an instant-read thermometer inserted at its thickest point reads 180° F. Remove the brisket from the grill and let cool. When cool, trim off the heavy fat layer, if desired. Wrap the brisket in aluminum foil and refrigerate overnight (trust me, you want to do this; the brisket flavor gets even better). Also refrigerate the brisket drippings and marinade.

5. Preheat the oven to 350° F. Reheat the brisket (still wrapped in foil) for about 20 minutes (until heated all the way through). While the brisket reheats, make the gravy, if you like (and I highly recommend that you do). Melt the butter in a small saucepan over medium heat. Add the flour and whisk for 3 to 4 minutes. Very slowly and whisking constantly, add the reserved marinade and drippings from the meat. Cook, stirring, until the gravy thickens to your liking, then taste and season with salt and pepper. Keep warm.

6. Slice the reheated brisket against the grain into thin slices and serve with the gravy poured over.

Freezing and Reheating Pastrami

When grocery stores put their corned beef on sale, I will buy several and cook at least three at one time because any that I don't eat right away will freeze perfectly for at least 3 months. I wrap each pastrami tightly in plastic wrap, put it in a freezer bag, force as much air as possible out, and freeze for later use. To use a frozen pastrami, let it thaw in the refrigerator for a couple of days. Then set up a large pot for steaming and steam the thawed unwrapped pastrami for 20 to 30 minutes. You'll have perfect hot pastrami.

If you have a vacuum sealer, use that to store and freeze the pastrami. To reheat, just drop the pastrami package in a large pot of simmering water and let simmer for 20 minutes.

Shortcut Pastrami

Serves 4 to 6

1 corned beef brisket (4 pounds), low salt preferred, with its spice packet (if there isn't one, use 2 bay leaves and ½ teaspoon yellow mustard seeds)

1 tablespoon coriander seeds

1 tablespoon black peppercorns

....

What's a Southern boy to do when he can't get to Katz's Delicatessen for a nice pastrami sandwich? Make the pastrami himself! No, this isn't the exact recipe from Katz's but the end result is pretty darned close. Pastrami is a three-step process which involves corning (which is brining) a piece of meat, typically brisket, for several days; coating the meat with spices and smoking it; and, finally, slowly roasting it with a bit of liquid. After years of going through all three steps, I had a eureka moment. Buy already-corned beef. This works well for a couple of different reasons: First, it saves time, and second, when you buy corned beef, you're dealing with smaller pieces, which are easier to store and freeze.

The best way to reheat pastrami is do it the way they do it at good delis. Place it on a steamer rack and steam it until warm; this will keep your pastrami moist, juicy, and oh so good.

1. Open up the corned beef brisket and cut away any excessive fat. You do want to leave a small fat cap. Pat very dry with paper towels. Grind the contents of the spice packet, the coriander seeds, and peppercorns in a spice grinder or mortar into a coarse mixture. Rub this mixture over all surfaces of the corned beef.

2. Light a fire in the kamado grill using your favorite method. After about 10 minutes, close the dome and open the upper and lower dampers all the way. When the temperature reaches 300° F, add any accessories necessary for smoking on your particular grill, along with the grill rack. Close the dome, let the temperature build back to between 200° and 250° F, and wait for a little smoke to accumulate. Adjust the dampers to maintain the temperature in this range.

3. Place the corned beef on the grill, close the dome, and smoke until the brisket registers an internal temperature of 150° F. I try to keep my grill temperature closer to 200° F because I want the brisket to absorb as much smoke as possible. This process usually takes about 2 hours.

4. Transfer the brisket to a disposable aluminum-foil pan and fill with enough water to come up about ½ inch. Cover the pan with foil and crimp it tightly. Place the pan back on the grill, close the dome, adjust the dampers so the temperature is between 200° and 250° F, and steam-roast the brisket until it is extremely tender, which will take another 2 to 3 hours. Remove from the grill, uncover, and let rest for about 10 minutes. Slice the pastrami against the grain and serve as you prefer (I would suggest rye bread, spicy mustard, and sauerkraut).

Smoky Slab of Beef Ribs

Serves 4

2 racks beef ribs, 8 bones each

1 tablespoon granulated garlic

1 teaspoon granulated onion

1 teaspoon dried thyme

Kosher salt and freshly ground black pepper

Your favorite barbecue sauce for serving (Texas Barbecue Joint–Style Sauce on page 249 is a good choice)

. . . .

Recommended wood: Pecan or cherry

It used to be difficult to find a slab of long-bone beef ribs, but not anymore. Most major grocery stores carry them and they make a nice change of pace from pork ribs. When cooked low and slow, they come out exceedingly tender, with a wonderful beefiness that you only get from the lesser cuts of a steer. The caveat here is if you cook them too fast or at too high a temperature, they will be tough and pretty much inedible, so treat them right. Cooking them on a kamado, you're going to end up enjoying a wonderful eating experience. (See photo on page 22.)

1. At least 1 hour before you're ready to grill, remove the ribs from the refrigerator. With a sharp knife, remove the thin membrane from the back of each rack and trim off any excess fat. Season the ribs on all sides with the garlic, onion, thyme, and a fairly generous amount of salt and pepper.

2. Light a fire in the kamado grill using your favorite method. After about 10 minutes, close the dome and open the upper and lower dampers all the way. When the temperature reaches 300° F, place the wood chunks around the fire and add any accessories necessary for smoking on your particular grill, along with the grill rack. Close the dome, let the temperature build back to between 200° and 250° F, and wait for a little smoke to accumulate. Adjust the dampers to maintain the temperature in this range.

3. Place the ribs, bone side down, on the grill, close the dome, and cook until tender, about 2 hours. The ribs are done when they're tender when poked with a knife and droop significantly when picked up with tongs.

4. Place the racks on a cutting board and let rest for 10 minutes. Slice off a rib and enjoy your "chef's treat." When you taste the rib, it should be tender but it still should take some bite to pull it off the bone. Cut into individual ribs and serve with barbecue sauce.

Smoked Boneless Short Ribs with Hoisin Glaze and Kimchi

Serves 4

2 tablespoons canola oil

4 cloves garlic, finely chopped

1 (2-inch) piece fresh ginger, peeled and finely chopped

½ cup hoisin sauce

1 tablespoon maple syrup

Kosher salt and freshly ground black pepper

2 pounds boneless short ribs

Kimchi for serving

....

Recommended wood: Cherry

A good smoking (especially in a kamado, which traps moisture) can yield a result almost as tender as a long braise. This recipe is a perfect example, taking a cut of beef normally braised and giving it a low-temperature smoke to break down the meat fibers. *Voila*, tender short ribs with a nice crusty glaze and succulent interior. You can convert this recipe to any flavor profile you like—barbecue, Thai, Indian—just by changing the glaze. Be sure to try this recipe with kimchi (look for it in your supermarket's Asian foods aisle). The sweetness of the meat offset by the spicy cabbage is a twist on Korean barbecue and is flavor heaven.

1. Heat the oil in a small saucepan over medium-high heat until it shimmers. Add the garlic and ginger and stir-fry for about 2 minutes. Remove the pan from the heat, stir in the hoisin sauce and maple syrup, and season to taste with salt and pepper. The glaze is ready to use (or you can refrigerate it in an airtight container for 2 to 3 days; let it come to room temperature before using it).

2. Light a fire in the kamado grill using your favorite method. After about 10 minutes, close the dome and open the upper and lower dampers all the way. When the temperature reaches 300° F, place the wood chunks around the fire and add any accessories necessary for smoking on your particular grill, along with the grill rack. Close the dome, let the temperature build back to between 200° and 250° F, and wait for a little smoke to accumulate. Adjust the dampers to maintain the temperature in this range.

3. Place the meat on the grill, close the dome, and smoke for about 45 minutes. At this point, brush the beef with the glaze on both sides, close the dome, and cook until the internal temperature reaches 140° F. Brush again on both sides with glaze, close the dome, and cook another 5 minutes.

4. Transfer the ribs to a platter, brush both sides with the glaze, and serve, passing any remaining glaze at the table along with the kimchi.

Lou's Grilled Meat Loaf

Serves 6 to 8

1½ cups seasoned (your choice of flavor) bread crumbs

3 tablespoons finely chopped onion

2 cloves garlic, minced

½ teaspoon kosher salt

½ teaspoon dried oregano

½ teaspoon dried thyme

½ teaspoon crushed dried rosemary

¼ teaspoon freshly ground black pepper

½ cup half-and-half

1 pound *each* ground beef, veal, and pork (or any combination you prefer)

Your favorite marinara sauce for serving

● ●

Recommended wood: Hickory

One of the great demises in New York City was the loss of the original Balducci's store on the corner of Sixth and Ninth avenues. Many fancy food stores have tried to imitate Balducci's but none have quite succeeded. The one facet that made Balducci's special was the quality of the people that worked there. And nowhere was that more evident than at the butcher counter. Lou was my favorite meat cutter. He had already worked as a butcher for 30 years at A&P before he started his second career at Balducci's. He made an incredible meat loaf for the store, and one day he was kind enough to share his recipe with me. Then I got to thinking, what would happen if you took one of the best meat loaves that you've ever had and combined it with the sensual nature of a grill? The result? Comfort food with sophistication and sass.

1. In a large bowl, combine the bread crumbs, onion, garlic, salt, oregano, thyme, rosemary, and pepper and stir well to combine. Pour in the half-and-half and stir to combine. Add the meat and, using your hands, mix until thoroughly combined.

2. Spray a 9- x 13-inch disposable aluminum-foil pan with cooking spray. Place the meat mixture in the pan and form into a loaf around 3 inches wide and 8 inches long.

3. Light a fire in the kamado grill using your favorite method. After about 10 minutes, close the dome and open the upper and lower dampers all the way. When the temperature reaches 300° F, place the wood chunks around the fire and add any accessories necessary for smoking on your particular grill, along with the grill rack. Close the dome, let the temperature build back to between 200° and 250° F, and wait for a little smoke to accumulate. Adjust the dampers to maintain the temperature in this range.

4. Put the pan on the grill, close the dome, and smoke for about 2 hours, until the internal temperature in the center reaches 150° to 160° F. The meat loaf is going to take on a pretty pinkish-brown hue as it smokes.

5. When done, remove from the grill and, using two spatulas, lift the meat loaf from the pan onto a platter. Tent with aluminum foil and let rest a good 30 minutes. Slice and serve with warm marinara sauce.

Smoke-Barbecued Bologna

Serves 4 to 6

1 (3-pound) log of bologna

Your favorite barbecue sauce
for serving

Dill pickle slices for serving

Cheap white buns for serving

. . . .

Recommended wood: Hickory

This one's for fun and a great addition to a Texas cookout with brisket and sausages. Smoke it right alongside the brisket. The kids will love it.

1. Light a fire in the kamado grill using your favorite method. After about 10 minutes, close the lid and open the upper and lower dampers all the way. When the temperature reaches 300° F, place the wood chunks around the fire. Now add any accessories necessary for smoking on your particular grill, along with the grill rack. Close the dome, let the temperature build back to between 200° and 250° F, and wait for a little smoke to accumulate. Adjust the dampers to maintain the temperature in this range.
2. Place the bologna on the grill, close the dome, and smoke for about 3 hours, until the internal temperature reaches 180° F.
3. Remove the bologna to a cutting board. Peel off the skin and cut into thick slices. Serve with the barbecue sauce, pickles, and buns.

Smoked Vitello with Tonnato Sauce

Serves 10 to 12 as a first course with leftovers

½ cup kosher salt

½ cup firmly packed light brown sugar

10 sprigs fresh thyme

10 sprigs fresh parsley

5 sprigs fresh rosemary

4 cups warm water

1 (3- to 4-pound) veal sirloin roast

1 (7-ounce) container tuna packed in olive oil, drained

½ cup good-quality mayonnaise

5 anchovy fillets

3 tablespoons capers, drained and rinsed

2 tablespoons fresh lemon juice

½ cup extra virgin olive oil

Freshly ground black pepper

Chopped fresh chives

Veal with tuna sauce? This is a classic dish from the Italian Piedmont area reimagined for the smoker. It makes a great first course. Any leftover veal can be frozen or used for sandwiches and the tuna sauce is a great topping for most any grilled vegetable.

1. In a medium bowl, combine the salt, brown sugar, and herb sprigs. Add the water and stir until the salt and sugar have dissolved. Place the veal roast in a 2½-gallon zip-top plastic bag. Pour the brine over the veal roast, seal the bag, and lay flat on a rimmed baking sheet. Place in the refrigerator for at least 24 hours but no more than 48 hours.

2. Remove the veal roast from the brine and discard the brine. Rinse the veal and pat dry. Leave at room temperature while you start your fire.

3. Light a fire in the kamado grill using your favorite method. After about 10 minutes, close the dome and open the upper and lower dampers all the way. When the temperature reaches 300° F, add any accessories necessary for smoking on your particular grill, along with the grill rack. Close the dome, let the temperature build back to between 200° and 250° F, and wait for a little smoke to accumulate. Adjust the dampers to maintain the temperature in this range.

4. Place the veal on the grill, close the dome, and smoke until it has an internal temperature of 145° F at its thickest point, about 3 hours.

5. While the veal is smoking, combine the tuna, mayonnaise, anchovies, capers, and lemon juice in a blender. Pulse to combine thoroughly. With the machine running, slowly pour in the oil, blending until you have a nice thick sauce. Add 5 to 10 grindings of pepper and stir into the sauce. Pour the sauce into an airtight container and refrigerate until needed.

6. When the veal is done, transfer to a platter and let cool to room temperature. Place in a 2½-gallon ziptop plastic bag and refrigerate for at least 4 hours.

7. When ready to serve, slice the veal as thinly as possible and arrange on a platter. Drizzle the tuna sauce over the veal and scatter chives over the top. Serve at once.

Smoked Vitello with Smoked Tonnato Sauce: For a double punch of smoke, substitute about 5 ounces of your own house-smoked tuna (breaking it up into small pieces before adding it to the blender) and a couple of tablespoons of extra-virgin olive oil for the canned tuna.

Brined Italian-Style Bone-In Pork Loin

Serves 8

1 (4- to 5-pound) bone-in pork loin (you may have to order this from your butcher in advance)

BRINE:

¾ cup kosher salt

¼ cup firmly packed light brown sugar

12 cups water

¼ cup fennel seeds

½ cup black peppercorns

2 tablespoons slightly cracked juniper berries

RUB:

¾ cup fresh sage leaves

⅓ cup firmly packed light brown sugar

¼ cup kosher salt

¾ teaspoon ground fennel seeds

2 tablespoons kosher salt

2 tablespoons olive oil

8 cloves garlic, peeled

GLAZE:

¾ cup cider vinegar

⅓ cup red currant jam

1 tablespoon dry mustard, like Colman's

1 tablespoon fennel seeds

. . . .
Recommended wood: Apple

Pork is widely used in the Umbria region of Italy and the folks there love to do spit roasting and open fire cooking with the noble beast. This recipe pulls some of the best of Umbria's flavor profiles together in a spectacular dish of porky goodness. You could also use a fresh ham for this preparation; just lengthen the cooking time and take the internal temperature to 180° F. You can also use boneless pork loin but you will miss the depth of flavor that the bones impart.

1. Lightly score the fat on the loin in a 1-inch crosshatch pattern.
2. Make the brine. In a medium saucepan, combine the salt, brown sugar, and 4 cups of the water and bring to a boil. Stir until the salt and sugar dissolve completely. Remove from the heat and stir in the fennel, peppercorns, and juniper berries, then stir in the remaining 8 cups water. Transfer the brine to a container large enough to hold the brine and pork loin. Let the brine cool completely. Once cooled, add the pork loin and refrigerate at least 12 hours and no more than 24 hours.
3. Combine the rub ingredients in a food processor and pulse until mostly smooth and paste-like.
4. Remove the pork from the brine and pat dry. Spread the rub over it and let sit for 1 hour before smoking to come to room temperature.
5. Light a fire in the kamado grill using your favorite method. After about 10 minutes, close the dome and open the upper and lower dampers all the way. When the temperature reaches 300° F, place the wood chunks around the fire and add any accessories necessary for smoking on your particular grill, along with the grill rack. Close the dome, let the temperature build back to between 200° and 250° F, and wait for a little smoke to accumulate. Adjust the dampers to maintain the temperature in this range.
6. Set the loin on a wire rack in a disposable aluminum-foil pan, place on the grill, close the dome, and smoke for 1 hour.
7. Meanwhile, combine the glaze ingredients in a small saucepan and simmer over medium heat, stirring occasionally, until the liquid is reduced by half and the mixture is syrupy. Transfer to a bowl until ready to use.
8. After an hour, brush the loin generously with the glaze and close the dome. Baste once more with the glaze after another 30 minutes, close the dome, and let smoke until the internal temperature reaches 145° F, about 2½ hours total time. If the loin takes on too much color before it's done cooking, tent with aluminum foil.
9. Transfer the loin to a cutting board and baste once more with the glaze. Let it rest for 30 minutes before carving. Serve warm or at room temperature.

Carolina-Style Pork Barbecue

Serves 10 to 12

1 bone-in pork shoulder
(5 to 7 pounds)

¾ cup apple cider

½ cup granulated sugar

¼ cup kosher salt, plus more for
seasoning and sprinkling

¼ cup warm water

2 tablespoons Worcestershire
sauce

1 tablespoon hot pepper sauce

Freshly ground black pepper

Lexington-Style "Dip"
(page 246) for serving

Coleslaw for serving

10 to 12 cheap hamburger buns

....

Recommended wood: apple,
hickory, or a mixture

There is no better excuse to own a kamado grill than to smoke
barbecue. To be perfectly transparent, I'm from North Carolina, where we make some of the best pork barbecue on the
planet. With your kamado grill, now you can too!

1. At least 1 hour before you plan to cook, remove the pork from the
   refrigerator. Combine the cider, sugar, salt, water, Worcestershire, and
   hot pepper sauce in a jar, close, and shake vigorously until the sugar
   and salt have dissolved. Load a flavor injector with the cider mixture
   and inject it into the pork in several places (see Using a Flavor Injector,
   page 241). As you inject and push on the plunger, pull the injector
   toward you so that the cider mixture doesn't pool in just one place.
   Season the pork on all sides with salt and pepper.

2. Light a fire in the kamado grill using your favorite method. After about
   10 minutes, close the dome and open the upper and lower dampers all
   the way. When the temperature reaches 300° F, place the wood chunks
   around the fire and add any accessories necessary for smoking on
   your particular grill, along with the grill rack. Close the dome, let the
   temperature build back to between 200° and 250° F, and wait for a little
   smoke to accumulate. Adjust the dampers to maintain the temperature
   in this range.

3. Place the pork on the grill, close the dome, and smoke for about 6
   hours.

4. Working quickly, remove the pork from the grill and double wrap it in
   aluminum foil. Place it back on the grill, close the dome, and cook for
   another 4 hours, maintaining the temperature between 200° and
   250° F. The pork is ready when you can easily slide out the bone with
   a pair of tongs.

5. Move the pork to a cutting board and let it cool for about 30 minutes.
   Using tongs, remove the fat cap and discard. With the tongs and a fork,
   pull and shred all the meat. Sprinkle with a little additional salt and
   about ½ cup of the Lexington-Style "Dip". Toss to blend. Pile on a platter and serve with slaw, buns, and additional dip, letting diners make
   their own pulled-pork sandwiches.

Cuban Pork Butt

Serves 10 to 12

1 (7-pound) bone-in pork butt

½ cup fresh orange juice

⅓ cup fresh lime juice

¼ cup red wine vinegar

3 tablespoons olive oil

¼ cup chopped fresh flat-leaf parsley

1 tablespoon chopped fresh oregano

1 tablespoon chopped fresh thyme

1 teaspoon ground cumin

2 teaspoons grated orange zest

1 teaspoon grated lime zest

6 cloves garlic, finely minced

½ teaspoon kosher salt

½ teaspoon freshly ground black pepper

. . . .
Recommended wood: Apple

There's more to a pork shoulder or butt than Southern-style barbecue. Pork combined with the fresh herb and citrus juice mixture known as mojo results in a seductive melody of vibrant flavors. In Cuba, mojo is made with sour orange juice, which you can find in Hispanic markets. I've replicated the flavor by souring the juice with a little vinegar. You can also buy ready-made mojo in the Hispanic section of your supermarket. This is traditionally served with plantains and rice and beans.

1. Lightly score any fat or skin on the pork butt. Place in a 2½-gallon zip-top plastic bag.

2. In a small bowl, whisk the citrus juices, vinegar, oil, herbs, cumin, zest, garlic, salt, and pepper together. Pour the marinade over the pork. Seal and refrigerate for at least 12 hours (24 hours is better). Turn the bag occasionally. Remove from the refrigerator 45 minutes before smoking.

3. Light a fire in the kamado grill using your favorite method. After about 10 minutes, close the dome and open the upper and lower dampers all the way. When the temperature reaches 300° F, place the wood chunks around the fire and add any accessories necessary for smoking on your particular grill, along with the grill rack. Close the dome, let the temperature build back to between 200° and 250° F, and wait for a little smoke to accumulate.

4. Remove the pork from the marinade and pat dry. Reserve the marinade. Place the pork on the grill, close the dome, and smoke, basting occasionally (no more than once an hour) with the marinade, for about 6 hours, until the bone can easily be pulled out with a pair of tongs and the internal temperature is 190° F. Stop basting during the last 10 to 15 minutes of cooking.

5. Transfer the pork to a cutting board and let rest for 15 minutes. Pull off the skin and as much fat as possible and either slice across the grain or pull apart with two forks.

Easy Cuban Sandwich: Here's a good plan for any leftovers. Layer slices of the pork, smoked ham, Swiss cheese, dill pickle slices, and yellow mustard on a crusty sub roll. Grill or griddle the sandwich, pushing or weighting it down to flatten it. The sandwich is so good it's worth the effort of smoking the pork butt.

Smoke-Roasted Suckling Pig

Serves 12 to 16
with leftovers

1 cup olive oil

Juice of 3 lemons

½ cup tamari

¼ cup dry sherry

¼ cup firmly packed light brown sugar

3 cloves garlic, chopped

2 tablespoons chopped fresh thyme

2 tablespoons chopped fresh flat-leaf parsley

1 teaspoon crushed fennel seeds

Freshly ground black pepper

1 (15-pound) suckling pig, cleaned and dressed (have the butcher do this for you)

Wooden skewers soaked in water for an hour

2 oranges

2 maraschino cherries

. . . .

Recommended wood: A mix of apple and hickory

This will knock your friends over. And the kamado makes it so easy once it's on the grill. The work is in the prep. First, you will need to preorder the pig; your best bet is the local butcher or a hog producer at a farmers' market. Second, you need to marinate your pig, which is a bit of an undertaking but the end result will astound your guests and make you the barbecue king of the neighborhood. Oh yeah, and it eats mighty nice too!

1. In a large bowl, whisk the oil, lemon juice, tamari, sherry, brown sugar, garlic, thyme, parsley, and fennel seeds together. Season generously with pepper and whisk again.

2. Using your hands, rub the pig with the marinade, inside and out, working it into the meat. Transfer the pig to a large plastic bag (such as a garbage bag), pour any remaining marinade over the pig, and seal the bag. Put this bag inside another bag and fold closed. Refrigerate for at least 8 hours or overnight. Let the pig come to room temperature in the marinade at least 2 hours but not more than 3 hours before smoking.

3. Light a fire in the kamado grill using your favorite method. After about 10 minutes, close the dome and open the upper and lower dampers all the way. When the temperature reaches 300° F, place the wood chunks around the fire and add any accessories necessary for smoking on your particular grill. Close the dome, let the temperature to come back to between 200° and 250° F, and wait for a little smoke to accumulate. Adjust the dampers to maintain the temperature in this range.

4. Wrap the pig's tail, feet, ears, and snout with aluminum foil to prevent burning. Put an orange in the pig's mouth to hold it open during cooking. Skewer the hind legs into a forward position under the pig. Place the pig in a kneeling position on the grill. Pierce the skin behind the neck several times to prevent the skin from cracking. Put the largest foil pan that will fit between the heat deflectors and the grill grate to catch excess fat. Close the dome and smoke the pig for about 20 minutes per pound, roughly 4 to 5 hours, until an instant-read thermometer reads 165° F when tested in the rump. After 1 hour, begin basting the pig hourly with the pan drippings, closing the dome after each baste. When close to the end of the cooking time, remove all the foil from the pig.

5. Transfer the pig to a cutting board and let it rest for at least 30 minutes before serving. Replace the orange with a fresh one and put the cherries in the eye cavities, securing them with toothpicks. Remove the skewers from the hind legs. Carve from back to front. When you have cut as much meat as possible this way, tear the rib cage apart into ribs and slice what meat there is from the ribs. Serve immediately.

Caribbean Baby Back Ribs with Guava Barbecue Sauce

Serves 4

2 racks baby back ribs
(6 to 8 pounds total)

2 tablespoons chili powder

1 tablespoon smoked paprika

1 tablespoon Chinese five-spice
powder (found in the Asian or
spice section of the supermarket)

1 (11-ounce) jar guava preserves
(found in the Hispanic section)

2 tablespoons Worcestershire
sauce

2 tablespoons balsamic vinegar

2 tablespoons ketchup

2 tablespoons fresh lime juice
(about 1 lime)

2 cloves garlic, run through a
garlic press

. . . .

Recommended wood: Apple

Much of Caribbean cooking contrasts flashes of sweet with more assertive flavors. This recipe carries that theme nicely. Let me remind you of two things. Don't sauce it too soon (or you'll have a burnt mess). Second, monitor how the bones are pulling away from the meat. You only want ¼ inch and definitely no more than ½ inch of bone showing when the ribs are done. Serve these with black beans and rice.

1. Remove the membrane from the bone side of the ribs by grabbing it with a kitchen towel and ripping it off.
2. In a small bowl, combine the chili powder, paprika, and Chinese five-spice powder. Liberally sprinkle this mixture over both sides of the ribs and massage it into the meat. Cover and refrigerate the ribs overnight.
3. Make the barbecue sauce. In a small saucepan, combine the preserves, Worcestershire, vinegar, ketchup, lime juice, and garlic. Bring to a simmer over medium heat and cook until the flavors have blended and the sauce has thickened slightly (about 5 minutes), stirring frequently. Reserve until ready to use.
4. Light a fire in the kamado grill using your favorite method. After about 10 minutes, close the dome and open the upper and lower dampers all the way. When the temperature reaches 300° F, place the wood chunks around the fire and add any accessories necessary for smoking on your particular grill, along with the grill rack. Close the dome, let the temperature to come back to between 200° and 250° F, and wait for a little smoke to accumulate. Adjust the dampers to maintain the temperature in this range.
5. Place the ribs on the grill, close the dome, and smoke for about 1 hour and 45 minutes. Baste the ribs on both sides with the sauce and close the dome. The ribs should be done after about 2 hours or when about ¼ inch of the bone is exposed and the ribs flop easily when lifted with tongs.
6. Remove the ribs to a platter, cut into serving pieces, and serve with the remaining sauce alongside.

Don't Let Your Ribs Become Shrinking Violets

If the meat on your ribs is pulling away from the bone to where you're seeing more than $1/2$ inch of bone, you've got what is known as "shiners." Immediately remove the ribs from the grill, and get the temperature of the grill down, because you're way too hot. Shiners look cute in a photograph but they don't win championships at the barbecue contest for good reason—they're tough and dry. Just a little bit of bone should be exposed by the end of the cooking process.

Fred's Damn Good Ribs

Serves 6 to 8

6 racks baby back ribs (8 to 10 pounds total, though it's the number of racks that's important)

¼ cup coarse-grain Dijon mustard

2 tablespoons granulated sugar

2 tablespoons paprika (smoked paprika is a nice choice for this)

2 teaspoons chili powder

1 teaspoon ground cinnamon

1 teaspoon cayenne pepper

1 teaspoon kosher salt

Freshly ground black pepper

1 cup or more Righteous Memphis-Style Sauce (page 247) or your favorite barbecue sauce

2 tablespoons honey or more as needed

· ·

Recommended wood: Apple

You want finger-licking good? Then you want this recipe. These baby backs are one of the most requested recipes from my newspaper column—usually in a panic from someone who's lost the clipping for it. I've adapted it to the kamado, and the results are juicy, smoky perfection. Many times I will smoke the ribs to about 90% done the day before I'm going to serve them and then finish them over direct heat, which builds a little more caramelization and tasty flavor. Either way, they're damn good.

1. Remove the ribs from the refrigerator, rinse, and pat dry. Pull off the membrane from the back of the ribs. Place the ribs on a baking sheet and brush them generously with the mustard. Use enough to totally coat both sides of the ribs. Combine the sugar, paprika, chili powder, cinnamon, cayenne, and salt in a small bowl. Sprinkle this mixture over both sides of the ribs, working it into the meat, then grind fresh pepper onto both sides.

2. Light a fire in the kamado grill using your favorite method. After about 10 minutes, close the dome and open the upper and lower dampers all the way. When the temperature reaches 300° F, place the wood chunks around the fire and add any accessories necessary for smoking on your particular grill, along with the grill rack. Close the dome, let the temperature build back to between 200° and 250° F, and wait for a little smoke to accumulate. Adjust the dampers to maintain the temperature in this range.

3. Place the ribs on the grill, meat side down, close the dome, and cook for 15 minutes. Turn the ribs, close the dome, and cook for about 1 hour and 15 minutes.

4. Now start brushing the ribs with sauce. Nicely coat the meaty side, close the dome, and let the sauce cook to a glaze, about 15 minutes, then turn the ribs and coat the bone side. Do that two more times. Now, take a pair of tongs and pick up a rack. It should droop immediately; that's a sure sign that the ribs are done. With the meaty side up, generously drizzle the honey over each rack, close the dome, and let sit for 5 minutes.

5. Remove the ribs from the grill and let rest about 10 minutes. Whack the slabs into two- or three-rib portions, serve with additional barbecue sauce, and be ready to graciously accept the praises of all who eat at your table. The one problem with this recipe is that now you're the only one in the neighborhood who gets to cook ribs.

Southern Peach Country-Style Ribs

Serves 6

1 cup peach nectar

1 cup mango nectar

¼ cup dry sherry

1 teaspoon kosher salt

1 teaspoon finely grated peeled fresh ginger

6 country-style pork ribs

½ cup peach preserves, slightly melted

2 tablespoons balsamic vinegar

2 tablespoons finely chopped fresh chives

. . . .

Recommended wood: Apple or pecan

There's just something about peaches and pork (maybe it's their Southern upbringing) that makes a perfect pairing. Meaty, almost pork chop–like, country-style ribs have the highest meat-to-bone ratio and the lowest fat content of the rib types. With modern butchery, don't be surprised to get strips of pork with very little bone. Smoking these ribs is the way to go.

1. In a small bowl, stir the nectars, sherry, salt, and ginger together. Place the ribs in a 1-gallon zip-top plastic bag, add the marinade, seal the bag, and refrigerate for 2 days, turning the bag several times.

2. An hour before you want to smoke them, remove the ribs from the marinade, pat dry, and leave at room temperature. Discard the marinade.

3. Light a fire in the kamado grill using your favorite method. After about 10 minutes, close the dome and open the upper and lower dampers all the way. When the temperature reaches 300° F, place the wood chunks around the fire and add any accessories necessary for smoking on your particular grill, along with the grill rack. Close the dome, let the temperature build back to between 200° and 250° F, and wait for a little smoke to accumulate. Adjust the dampers to maintain the temperature in this range.

4. Place the ribs on the grill, close the dome, and smoke for about 1½ hours.

5. Meanwhile, in a small bowl, combine the preserves and vinegar.

6. When the internal temperature of the ribs hits 140° F, baste them with the peach glaze on both sides. Close the dome and continue to smoke until the internal temperature of the ribs reaches 150° F.

7. Transfer the ribs to a platter. Pour the remaining glaze over them and sprinkle with the chives. Serve warm or at room temperature with plenty of napkins.

Whiskey Sour Country Pork Ribs

Serves 6

6 country-style pork ribs

½ cup orange marmalade, melted

¼ cup Tennessee whiskey or bourbon

2 tablespoons dark brown sugar

2 tablespoons fresh orange juice

1 tablespoon fresh lemon juice

2 cloves garlic, very finely minced

4 whole cloves

Freshly ground black pepper to taste

....

Recommended wood: Hickory or apple

This is an ode to my father, who loved his Jack Daniel's Tennessee sipping whiskey, preferably in an old-fashioned glass with a splash of 7-Up. This marinade has the flavor notes of a whiskey sour, a nice contrast to the rich taste of the pork. Country-style pork ribs are a cross between a bone-in pork chop and a true rib, with much more meat and less fat than a sparerib—they're also a lot easier on the pocketbook. Most folks try to grill this style of rib almost like a pork chop, and the results are usually sketchy. Use a kamado and you'll have a super-moist result.

1. Place the ribs in a 1-gallon zip-top plastic bag.
2. In a small bowl, whisk the marmalade, whiskey, brown sugar, citrus juices, garlic, cloves, and pepper together. Pour the mixture over the ribs, seal the bag, and refrigerate 6 to 8 hours or overnight, turning the bag several times.
3. One hour before you plan to smoke them, remove the ribs from the marinade, squeezing the marinade off the ribs; reserve the marinade. Pat the ribs dry with paper towels. Let them sit at room temperature to develop a pellicle; this helps with smoke penetration.
4. Light a fire in the kamado grill using your favorite method. After about 10 minutes, close the dome and open the upper and lower dampers all the way. When the temperature reaches 300° F, place the wood chunks around the fire and add any accessories necessary for smoking on your particular grill, along with the grill rack. Close the dome, let the temperature build back to between 200° and 250° F, and wait for a little smoke to accumulate. Adjust the dampers to maintain the temperature in this range.
5. Place the ribs on the grill, close the dome, and smoke for about 1 hour, until the internal temperature of the ribs reaches 140° F.
6. Meanwhile, place the remaining marinade in a small saucepan. Bring it to a boil, reduce the heat to a simmer, and cook until slightly thickened, about 10 minutes. Baste the ribs with the mixture on both sides, close the dome, and continue to smoke. Baste the ribs several more times, until they are done, with an internal temperature of 150° F, about 30 minutes after the first basting. Be careful not to baste too early or you will end up with nasty burnt ribs. When done, the ribs should have a nice brown glaze and be fork tender.
7. Transfer the ribs to a platter and pass the remaining basting sauce on the side. These are good right off the grill or at room temperature.

Apple Pie Spice Spareribs with Applesauce Barbecue Glaze

Serves 6

4 pounds spareribs

4½ cups apple cider or apple juice

4 tablespoons apple pie spice

1 cup ketchup

1 cup applesauce

½ cup cider vinegar

¼ cup Worcestershire sauce

1 tablespoon yellow mustard

3 cloves garlic, chopped

½ teaspoon ground cinnamon

. . . .

Recommended wood: Apple

Using apple pie spice as the rub and adding applewood chunks to the fire gives these ribs a sweet-and-sour finish, American style. The apple note is repeated in the barbecue sauce, which my neighbor Barry Johnson shared with me. This combination also works nicely with pork chops, chicken, and salmon.

1. Remove the membrane from the bone side of the ribs by grabbing it with a kitchen towel and ripping it off. Place the ribs in a 2½-gallon zip-top plastic bag. Pour 4 cups of the cider over the ribs and add 1 table-spoon of the apple pie spice. Seal the bag and refrigerate at least overnight (2 days is better), turning the bag several times.

2. Meanwhile, make the sauce. In a small saucepan, whisk the ketchup, applesauce, vinegar, Worcestershire, mustard, garlic, cinnamon, and remaining ½ cup cider together. Slowly bring the mixture to a boil over medium heat. Reduce the heat to a simmer and let bubble for about 20 minutes. Remove from the heat and let cool completely if not using right away. Refrigerate in an airtight container up to 2 weeks.

3. Light a fire in the kamado grill using your favorite method. After about 10 minutes, close the dome and open the upper and lower dampers all the way. When the temperature reaches 300° F, place the wood chunks around the fire and add any accessories necessary for smoking on your particular grill, along with the grill rack. Close the dome, let the temperature build back to between 200° and 250° F, and wait for a little smoke to accumulate. Adjust the dampers to maintain the temperature in this range.

4. Remove the ribs from the marinade; discard the marinade. Place the ribs on a rimmed baking sheet and sprinkle with the remaining 3 table-spoons apple pie spice, rubbing it into both sides of the ribs.

5. Place the ribs on the grill, bone side down, close the dome, and smoke 2½ to 3 hours, until the bones are just beginning to show and the ribs bend easily when lifted with tongs. After about 1½ hours, baste with the sauce. Continue to baste every 20 minutes until the ribs are until done, closing the dome after each baste.

6. Transfer the ribs to a platter. Cut into 3-rib serving pieces and serve with the remaining sauce (reheat it if necessary before serving) passed at the table.

Smoked Spareribs with Adobo and Garlic Butter

Serves 4

6 ancho chiles
(about 2 ounces)

6 cloves garlic, chopped

Grated zest of 1 lime

¼ cup fresh lime juice
(about 3 limes)

1 tablespoon maple syrup
(grade B preferred)

2 teaspoons dried oregano

Kosher salt and freshly ground
black pepper

1 (4- to 5-pound) rack of spareribs

1 cup (2 sticks) unsalted butter,
softened

4 cloves garlic, finely chopped

••••••••••••••••••••••••••••••••
Recommended wood: A mix of
apple and hickory

Ribs! Ribs! Ribs!

Want to pull off a summer cookout that your friends will talk about till fall? Throw a rib party! Take several of the recipes here and cook a rack of each type. It's easy with a rib rack and you will be the grill master of the neighborhood!

S avory goodness topped with garlicky, buttery richness highlight this recipe, which not only is transformative with spareribs, but also delicious with pork chops, chicken, and boneless short ribs. Want more heat? Use a hotter dried chile. The ancho is a dried poblano chile and packs a lot of flavor without much heat. Because the kamado is so good at maintaining a low temperature, the most common problem experienced with cooking ribs—the meat getting tough and pulling away from the bones because the ribs have been cooked over too hot a fire—is never an issue. But be vigilant—you can still ruin ribs by leaving them on the grill too long.

1. Fill a 3-quart saucepan halfway with water. Bring to a boil, add the chiles, remove from the heat, and let steep until the chiles are soft and flexible, about 1 hour.

2. Drain the chiles, reserving 1 cup of the soaking water, then remove the stems and seeds from the chiles. Place the chiles in a blender along with the garlic, lime zest and juice, maple syrup, oregano, and the reserved soaking water. Blend until smooth and season to taste with salt and pepper.

3. Remove the membrane from the bone side of the ribs by grabbing it with a kitchen towel and ripping it off, then cut the rack in half. Place the ribs in a 2½-gallon zip-top plastic bag and add the marinade. Seal the bag and refrigerate for 4 hours, turning the bag once.

4. Light a fire in the kamado grill using your favorite method. After about 10 minutes, close the dome and open the upper and lower dampers all the way. When the temperature reaches 300° F, place the wood chunks around the fire and add any accessories necessary for smoking on your particular grill, along with the grill rack. Close the dome, let the temperature build back to between 200° and 250° F, and wait for a little smoke to accumulate. Adjust the dampers to maintain the temperature in this range.

5. Place the ribs in the grill, close the dome, and smoke until the racks bend immediately when picked up with tongs, 2 to 2½ hours.

6. While the ribs are smoking, make the garlic butter. Using a fork, mash the softened butter with the finely chopped garlic in a small bowl until well mixed. Cover and refrigerate until needed.

7. When the ribs are done, transfer the racks to a baking sheet and rub the garlic butter liberally over the ribs. Cut into portions and drizzle any melted butter from the pan over the ribs. Serve immediately.

Smoked Fresh Ham with Cherry Cola Glaze

Serves 12 to 18

1 cup cherry-flavored cola, like Cheerwine or Dr. Pepper

1 cup firmly packed light brown sugar

1 (10-ounce) jar hot pepper jelly (I like jalapeño jelly for this)

1 (8- to 10-pound) fresh ham

2 tablespoons olive oil

....

Recommended wood: Cherry

If you're ever near Piney Flats, Tennessee, be sure and check out The Ridgewood, a barbecue joint that smokes hams instead of the whole hog or shoulders. You can make this ham part of a barbecue, but I really like to serve it sliced for an elegant dinner. It's perfect for the holidays and, quite frankly, better than any store-bought spiral-sliced ham you'll come across. Yes, you'll have leftovers, but they freeze nicely. The cherry cola glaze is outstanding on any pork product as well as on chicken breasts and wings. This is also an excellent ham to stick in a biscuit.

1. Combine the cola, brown sugar, and jelly in a small saucepan over low heat. Cook, stirring, until the sugar melts and the ingredients are well combined. Remove from the heat and set aside.

2. Light a fire in the kamado grill using your favorite method. After about 10 minutes, close the dome and open the upper and lower dampers all the way. When the temperature reaches 300° F, place the wood chunks around the fire. Now add any accessories necessary for smoking on your particular grill, along with the grill rack. Close the dome, allow the temperature to come back to between 200° and 250° F, and wait for a little smoke to build.

3. Brush the ham with the olive oil and place on the grill. Close the dome and smoke for about 6 hours.

4. Over the next hour, brush the ham all over with the cherry cola glaze every 15 minutes, closing the dome after each application.

5. Check the internal temperature of the ham; it should be around 190° F. If not, continue cooking and glazing every 15 minutes until it reaches 190° F.

6. Transfer the ham to a cutting board and let it rest for about 15 minutes. Slice thinly and serve. Any remaining glaze can be passed with the ham.

Old South Holiday Corned Ham

Serves 12 to 16,
with leftovers

1 (10 pound) corned ham

2 tablespoons olive oil

Coarse-grain hot-sweet mustard
for serving

....

Recommended wood: Hickory

orned ham is a traditional Southern food that has come back into vogue. Especially around Thanksgiving and through the New Year, corned hams are easy to get in the South, although you might want to check with your butcher and have one ordered. Think of a corned ham much like you would corned beef. It's been salted and brined with a few flavorings and you don't really need to do much to it. Typically they're oven roasted to finish but by adding the dimension of smoke you can elevate this simple piece of pork to a new level.

1. Take a cooler large enough to hold the ham, place the ham inside, and fill the cooler with water. Let soak for at least 4 hours but not much more. This helps to rid the ham of a little excess salt. If you like your ham salty, skip this step. Remove the ham from the cooler, rinse under cold running water, and pat dry.

2. Light a fire in the kamado grill using your favorite method. After about 10 minutes, close the dome and open the upper and lower dampers all the way. When the temperature reaches 300° F, place the wood chunks around the fire and add any accessories necessary for smoking on your particular grill, along with the grill rack. Close the dome, let the temperature build back to between 200° and 250° F, and wait for a little smoke to accumulate. Adjust the dampers to maintain the temperature in this range.

3. Brush the ham completely with the oil, place on the grill, close the dome, and smoke until the internal temperature reaches 190° F, 6 to 8 hours. Remove to a cutting board, let rest for 30 minutes, and slice very thinly. Delicious at room temperature or even slightly chilled, served with mustard.

Salt Calculation

If your pork belly is short of 5 pounds or more than 5 pounds, use this formula suggested by Ruhlman to calculate the amount of salt you need for the cure. Multiply the weight of the belly in ounces (there are 16 ounces in a pound) by .025 and that's how much salt you should use. Many times after I trim a piece of pork belly, I wind up coming closer to four pounds than to five, so I'll do the math for you. That's 1.6 ounces of kosher salt for about 4 pounds, and ¼ cup kosher salt is 2 ounces. If you don't have a scale, find a neighbor who does. Guesstimating invariably leads to over-salting.

DIY Bacon

Makes roughly 4 to 5 pounds

1 (5- to 6-pound) slab fresh pork belly (order this from a specialty market, butcher shop, or the pork guy at the farmers' market)

¼ cup firmly packed light brown sugar

¼ cup coarsely ground black pepper

¼ cup kosher salt (I prefer Morton's for this)

2 teaspoons pink curing salt (available online and where canning items are sold)

2 tablespoons dried juniper berries, lightly crushed with the edge of a heavy skillet

1 teaspoon freshly grated nutmeg

10 cloves garlic, smashed with the flat side of a knife

10 sprigs fresh thyme

4 bay leaves, crumbled

. . . .

Recommended wood: Hickory, apple, or cherry

I thank Michael Ruhlman at least once a week for his wonderful book *Charcuterie*. Had it not been for Michael, I would never have started making my own bacon. But I'm here to tell you that once you've done it, you will be hard pressed to ever pick up another pound of processed store-bought bacon again. The added attraction here is that the kamado is perfect for a no-fuss finishing smoke that keeps the bacon moist and imparts just the right amount of smoke flavor. I encourage you to try this recipe: bacon, great bacon, is best made at home.

1. Place the pork belly on a cutting board and trim the edges to square it up. Freeze the trimmings.
2. In a small bowl, combine the brown sugar, pepper, both salts, juniper berries, nutmeg, garlic, thyme, and bay leaves. Rub this mixture on all sides of the belly. Place it in a 2½-gallon zip-top plastic bag. Pour any remaining spice mixture into the bag and give it all one last rub. Seal the bag, forcing out as much air out as possible. Place the belly flat on a shelf in the refrigerator for 4 days.
3. Open the bag and rub the spices back into the pork. Close the bag, again forcing out as much air as possible, and refrigerate for 3 days.
4. Press on the pork belly—it should be somewhat firm, but not solid; to be ready for smoking, it should still give but be much firmer than it was at the start of this process. If it's still a little mushy, put it back in the refrigerator for another couple of days.
5. Remove the belly from the bag and completely rinse off all of the cure under cold running water. Pat the belly completely dry. Some suggest placing the belly, unwrapped, back in the refrigerator to dry out and develop what's called a pellicle, a tacky surface that allows a meat to absorb more smoke. For making bacon, I find this unnecessary.
6. Light a fire in the kamado grill using your favorite method. After about 10 minutes, close the dome and open the upper and lower dampers all the way. When the temperature reaches 300° F, place the wood chunks around the fire and add any accessories necessary for smoking on your particular grill, along with the grill rack. Close the dome, let the temperature build back to between 200° and 250° F, and wait for a little smoke to accumulate.
7. Put the belly on the grill rack. Adjust the dampers to get the temperature right at 200° F, close the dome, and smoke the belly for 1½ to 2 hours, until the internal temperature is 150° F. Guess what? You now have bacon. Let it cool a bit and then go ahead and slice off a piece and cook it in a heavy skillet over low heat, turning often. It will keep up to 2 weeks in the refrigerator and 3 months in the freezer.

Homemade Canadian Bacon

Makes about 3 1/2 pounds

1 gallon water

1½ cups kosher salt
(I prefer Morton's)

½ cup granulated sugar

½ cup firmly packed light
brown sugar

8 teaspoons pink curing salt
(look for it online or where
canning items are sold)

1 tablespoon dried juniper berries,
lightly crushed

8 sprigs fresh thyme

8 sprigs fresh sage

4 cloves garlic, smashed with the
flat side of a knife

1 (4-pound) boneless pork loin

....

Recommended wood: Apple

Canadian bacon is another one of those products that is so much better when you make it at home. This style of bacon is actually a smoked cured pork loin, the curing accomplished with a wet brine. It's simple and will do wonders for your breakfast sandwich. Also try it as a topping for pizza or burgers.

1. Combine all the ingredients, except the pork, in a pot and bring to a simmer over medium heat, stirring to dissolve the salt and sugars. Remove from the heat, let cool to room temperature, then refrigerate until cold.

2. Remove all the fat and silverskin from the pork loin. Place it in a container large enough to hold the loin and brine. Pour the brine over and put a plate or other weighted object on top to hold the pork completely submerged in the brine. Refrigerate for 48 hours.

3. Remove the loin and discard the brine. Rinse the loin under cold running water and pat dry. Place on a rack set over a tray or sheet pan and refrigerate, uncovered, for 24 hours. This allows the loin to dry, creating a tacky surface called a pellicle, which enables the smoke to penetrate the loin more fully.

4. Light a fire in the kamado grill using your favorite method. After about 10 minutes, close the dome and open the upper and lower dampers all the way. When the temperature reaches 300° F, place the wood chunks around the fire and add any accessories necessary for smoking on your particular grill, along with the grill rack. Close the dome, let the temperature build back to between 200° and 250° F, and wait for a little smoke to accumulate. Adjust the dampers to maintain the temperature in this range.

5. Place the pork on the grill, close the dome, and smoke to an internal temperature of 150° F, usually around 2 hours, but it could take as many as 3. Let cool completely, then cover and refrigerate for up to 2 weeks or freeze for up to 3 months.

Homemade Smoked Sausage

Makes about 5 pounds

Hog casings, cleaned and soaked in cold water for about 1 hour

5 pounds boneless pork shoulder, cut into large cubes and thoroughly chilled (you'll get a better consistency if the meat is very cold when you grind it)

1 cup ice water

SEASONING MIX:

2 tablespoons granulated garlic

2 tablespoons dried marjoram

1 tablespoon cracked black peppercorns

1 tablespoon kosher salt

1 teaspoon mustard seeds, lightly crushed

1 teaspoon dry mustard

½ teaspoon pink curing salt (optional)

· ·

Recommended wood: Apple or cherry

Making your own smoked sausage is a lot of fun. To do it, though, you need a meat grinder and a sausage stuffer. If you have a stand mixer, like a KitchenAid, you are halfway there; purchase the meat grinder and sausage stuffer attachments and this recipe becomes a snap. Whether using a stand mixer or a meat grinder, use the coarse die (with larger holes) to grind the meat. Hog casings can be bought at butcher shops; I get mine at Whole Foods Market. They must be soaked and cleaned before using.

This recipe takes its flavor cues from traditional Polish sausages, a nod to my back-door neighbors, Barry and Linda Johnson, who both have Polish ancestry.

1. Clean the hog casings by running cold water through them for several minutes, then let them soak in cold water for an hour. ("Cleaning" is kind of a misnomer; the casings are usually sold packed in salt and what you're doing here is removing some of that salt before using them.)

2. In a small bowl, combine the ingredients for the seasoning mix.

3. Coarsely grind the meat. Sprinkle the seasoning mixture over the meat and pour in the water. Use your hands to combine everything well, working quickly.

4. Attach the hog casing to the sausage stuffer. Working in small batches, begin stuffing the casing with the sausage meat, making sure not to pack it too tightly, because the casing can burst. Continue until all the meat is stuffed in the casing. Tie off the end of the casing with a knot. If you want links, gently press into the casing about every 6 inches, and twist it around 3 or 4 times. Refrigerate the sausage until ready to smoke.

5. Light a fire in the kamado grill using your favorite method. After about 10 minutes, close the dome and open the upper and lower dampers all the way. When the temperature reaches 200° F, place the wood chunks around the fire and add any accessories necessary for smoking on your particular grill, along with the grill rack. Close the dome and let the temperature build back to between 200° and 225° F. Adjust the dampers to maintain the temperature in this range.

6. Place the sausage on the grill rack, close the dome, and smoke until an instant-read thermometer inserted in the center registers 140° F, about 1½ hours. This ready-to-eat sausage will keep, tightly wrapped, in the refrigerator for about a week or, vacuum-packed, in the freezer 6 to 9 months.

Smoked Spam

Serves 6 to 8

3 (12-ounce) cans Spam

. . . .

Recommended wood: Apple

That lovely amalgamation of canned mystery meat reaches new heights of flavor when smoked—it always surprises folks when you tell them what it is. This is something that I tend to do when there is another item on the grill to smoke. Once smoked, you can slice the Spam and sauté it to serve with eggs or in a really tasty sandwich, or turn it into pressed spam sushi, a popular preparation in Hawaii (see below). All I can say is, don't knock it until you've tried it.

1. Open and remove the meat from the cans.
2. Light a fire in the kamado grill using your favorite method. After about 10 minutes, close the dome and open the upper and lower dampers all the way. When the temperature reaches 300° F, place the wood chunks around the fire and add any accessories necessary for smoking on your particular grill, along with the grill rack. Close the dome, let the temperature build back to between 200° and 250° F, and wait for a little smoke to accumulate. Adjust the dampers to maintain the temperature in this range.
3. Place the spam on the grill, close the dome, and smoke for 1½ to 2 hours.
4. Remove the spam to a cutting board. If using right away, slice into ½-inch-thick pieces. Otherwise, leave whole and refrigerate until ready to use; it will keep for a week.

Smoked Spam Sushi: Make some sushi rice or buy some from a sushi bar. Shape the rice, slice the Spam into ¼-inch pieces, and dab each with wasabi. Place the Spam, wasabi side down, on the rice, brush with teriyaki sauce, sprinkle with sesame seeds, and garnish with a radish sprout. You will never look at Spam the same way again.

Smoked Seasoning Ham Hocks

Makes 6 smoked ham hocks

4 quarts warm water

1 cup kosher salt

½ cup firmly packed light brown sugar

1 tablespoon crushed juniper berries

1 bay leaf

6 fresh ham hocks, front leg preferred, about 3 pounds total

. . . .

Recommended wood: Hickory

Smoked ham hocks are an indispensable seasoning in Southern soul food cooking. If you can't find fresh hocks at your grocery store, order them from a local butcher or seek them out at farmers' markets. Even though already-smoked ham hocks are easy to find at the supermarket, smoking your own is so much better—more smoke and less salt.

1. In a large bowl, combine the water, salt, brown sugar, juniper berries, and bay leaf, stirring to dissolve the sugar and salt.
2. Place the ham hocks in a 2½-gallon zip-top plastic bag. Pour the brine over the hocks. Seal the bag and refrigerate for 2 days, turning the bag occasionally.
3. Remove the hocks from the brine, rinse, and pat dry. Place on a wire rack and let sit at room temperature for at least 1 hour.
4. Light a fire in the kamado grill using your favorite method. After about 10 minutes, close the dome and open the upper and lower dampers all the way. When the temperature reaches 300° F, place the wood chunks around the fire and add any accessories necessary for smoking on your particular grill, along with the grill rack. Close the dome, let the temperature build back to between 200° and 250° F, and wait for a little smoke to accumulate. Adjust the dampers to maintain the temperature in this range.
5. Place the ham hocks on the grill, close the dome, and smoke for 4 to 6 hours, depending on how smoky you want them.
6. Enjoy your ham hocks immediately or refrigerate for up to a week or freeze for up to a year.

Astoria Greek Easter Leg of Lamb with Roasted Potatoes

Serves 8

4 cloves garlic, minced

¼ cup fresh rosemary leaves

¼ cup fresh oregano leaves

¼ cup fresh mint leaves

2 tablespoons sugar

2 tablespoons coriander seeds

1 tablespoon red pepper flakes

Kosher salt and freshly ground black pepper

1 (6-pound) leg of lamb

4 pounds medium Yukon Gold potatoes, sliced ½ inch thick

1 large lemons, sliced ½ inch thick

1 head garlic, split in half

4 small sprigs fresh rosemary

Olive oil

Mint jelly for serving (optional)

....
Recommended wood: Hickory

If you want your nose to get a pleasurable workout, just hang around Astoria, Queens, as Easter approaches. When I've been part of these Greek gatherings, I took note of how they cooked the potatoes that always accompany the lamb—right over the fire and bathed with lamb drippings. The outline of this recipe comes from the owners of a Greek diner, with a few of my own twists. You can either put the potatoes under the grill grate on a ceramic smoking stone or use a grill extender.

1. The day before you intend to smoke the lamb, combine the minced garlic, rosemary, oregano, and mint leaves, sugar, coriander, red pepper flakes, and a good amount of salt and black pepper in a food processor and pulse until it forms a paste. Score the fat around the leg in a criss-cross pattern to allow the paste to penetrate the meat. Rub all of the paste into the leg. Wrap the leg tightly with plastic wrap and refrigerate overnight.
2. Remove the lamb from the refrigerator, rinse the paste off, pat dry, and let the chill come off of it for about 1 hour. Season the lamb with salt and black pepper.
3. In the meantime, arrange the potato slices in layers in a large cast-iron skillet or sheet pan in as even a layer as you can get. Place the lemon slices on top along with the split head of garlic and rosemary sprigs. Season generously with salt and black pepper and give it a drizzle of olive oil.
4. Light a fire in the kamado grill using your favorite method. After about 10 minutes, close the dome and open the upper and lower dampers all the way. When the temperature reaches 300° F, place the wood chunks around the fire and add any accessories necessary for smoking on your particular grill, along with the grill rack. Close the dome, let the temperature build back to between 200° and 250° F, and wait for a little smoke to accumulate. Adjust the dampers to maintain the temperature in this range.
5. Place the pan of potatoes under the grill grate and position the lamb directly above the potatoes, or, if you have a grill extender, place the lamb on the extender and the potatoes on the grill grate directly under the lamb. Close the dome and smoke for 2½ to 3 hours, letting the juices from the meat drip down onto the potatoes, until the internal temperature of the lamb at the thickest point reaches 140° F.
6. Transfer the lamb to a cutting board, tent with aluminum foil, and let it rest for at least 20 minutes. Check the doneness of the potatoes and, if needed, let them continue to cook. Slice the lamb thinly and serve with the potatoes and a lemon slice and mint jelly if desired.

Texas Goat

Serves 10-12

4 Anaheim chiles, chopped (leave the seeds in)

2 serrano chiles, chopped (leave the seeds in)

1 (3-inch) piece fresh ginger, peeled and chopped

10 cloves garlic, peeled

Leaves from 1 bunch fresh flat-leaf parsley

Leaves from 5 sprigs fresh oregano

2 tablespoons kosher salt

1 cup olive oil

1 bone-in goat shoulder (about 5 pounds)

. . . .

Recommended wood: Mesquite

Goat ropings (the goat version of a pig roast) are huge social events in Texas. In this version, I use a goat shoulder because a whole goat is simply too big for a backyard smoker. You'll likely need to special order the goat from your butcher or a Middle Eastern, Hispanic, or halal market, or you might find it at a farmers' market. The goat needs to marinate for at least 24 hours and will require 5 to 7 hours in the kamado. I was never happy with cooking goat on my other grills and smokers but the results in the kamado have been fantastic. I have routinely had coals burn for 10 to 12 hours or longer, maintaining a steady 200° F inside the grill with the initial load of hardwood lump charcoal. This recipe is a tried-and-true method used by ranchers.

1. Combine the chiles, ginger, garlic, parsley, oregano, and salt in a food processor and pulse 8 to 10 times. With the motor running, slowly pour in the oil, processing until the mixture forms a loose paste. Rub the goat shoulder all over with the chile paste, cover with plastic wrap, and refrigerate for 24 hours.

2. Light a fire in the kamado grill using your favorite method. After about 10 minutes, close the dome and open the upper and lower dampers all the way. When the temperature reaches 300° F, place the wood chunks around the fire and add any accessories necessary for smoking on your particular grill, along with the grill rack. Close the dome, let the temperature build back to between 200° and 250° F, and wait for a little smoke to accumulate. Adjust the dampers to maintain the temperature in this range.

4. Scrape the flavor paste off the goat and reserve it. Pat the goat dry with paper towels, then place it on the grill, close the dome, and smoke for about 3 hours.

5. Brush the goat with the leftover flavor paste and continue to brush it once an hour. Also, test for doneness every hour. Wiggle the leg bone, and when you get the sense that if you pulled just a bit harder you could tear it from the joint, it's ready. Total time will probably be between 5 and 6 hours. Transfer the goat to a rimmed baking sheet, hand your guests a fresh beer, and let them go at the goat, pulling at it with their fingers or tongs. Have lots of paper towels on hand.

Smoked-Roasted Any-Day Chicken

Each chicken serves 4 or 5

Olive oil

2 (3- to 4-pound) chickens, giblets removed

2 to 3 tablespoons dried herbes de Provence

Kosher salt and freshly ground black pepper

. . . .

Recommended wood: Apple

This recipe is for you if you are a fan of rotisserie chicken. I always smoke two birds at a time—one for now and one to use later in a salad, stew, sandwich, or such. You can easily change out the herb blend for any flavoring you might enjoy, and there are plenty of good rotisserie chicken spice blends available. This is a perfect Sunday-afternoon endeavor.

1. Drizzle olive oil over both birds and use your hands to rub it all over them. Liberally season both the cavities and outside of the birds with the herbes de Provence, salt, and pepper. Let sit at room temperature for about 30 minutes before smoking.

2. Light a fire in the kamado grill using your favorite method. After about 10 minutes, close the dome and open the upper and lower dampers all the way. When the temperature reaches 300° F, place the wood chunks around the fire and add any accessories necessary for smoking on your particular grill, along with the grill rack. Close the dome, let the temperature build back to between 200° and 250° F, and wait for a little smoke to accumulate. Adjust the dampers to maintain the temperature in this range.

3. Place the birds breast down on the grill or, if you would like to have pan juices for gravy, on a rack in a large disposable aluminum-foil pan and set that on the grill. Close the dome and smoke the birds for about 2 hours, until the internal temperature of the thigh is 165° F and the juices run clear.

4. Remove the chickens to a platter and let rest 15 to 20 minutes before carving. Serve hot or at room temperature.

Tandoori Chicken with Cucumber Raita

Serves 4 to 6

4 tablespoons Tandoori Seasoning (page 237)

1 (3- to 4-pound) chicken, cut into 8 pieces

3½ cups plain nonfat Greek yogurt

¼ cup fresh lemon juice (about 3 lemons)

¼ cup fresh lime juice (about 4 limes)

3 tablespoons chopped fresh cilantro

2 tablespoons minced garlic

2 tablespoons finely grated peeled fresh ginger

2 tablespoons canola oil

2 teaspoons ground coriander

2 teaspoons kosher salt

1 teaspoon hot paprika

½ teaspoon ground turmeric

1 English cucumber, peeled and cut into ½-inch dice

½ cup diced red onion

2 tablespoons honey

1 teaspoon curry powder

2 cups fresh cilantro leaves

1 cup fresh mint leaves

••••••••••••••••••••••••••••••••

Recommended wood: Any kind of fruitwood

The tandoori oven shares some similarities with a kamado grill. Usually made of brick and clay, it traps intense heat and can maintain that heat for a long period of time. This recipe can also be used with pork, lamb, and thick cuts of fish. Serve it with Kamado Naan (page 218) to complete the experience.

1. Sprinkle about 2 tablespoons of the tandoori seasoning over the chicken pieces, cover, and refrigerate while making the marinade.

2. In a large bowl, whisk 2 cups of the yogurt, the citrus juices, chopped cilantro, garlic, ginger, oil, coriander, salt, paprika, turmeric, and remaining 2 tablespoons tandoori seasoning together. Add the chicken and toss with the marinade to coat. Cover and refrigerate for at least 6 hours; overnight is better.

3. Light a fire in the kamado grill using your favorite method. After about 10 minutes, close the dome and open the upper and lower dampers all the way. When the temperature reaches 300° F, place the wood chunks around the fire and add any accessories necessary for smoking on your particular grill, along with the grill rack. Close the dome, let the temperature build back to between 200° and 250° F, and wait for a little smoke to accumulate. Adjust the dampers to maintain the temperature in this range.

4. Remove the chicken from the marinade and, using your hands, squeeze off as much of the marinade as possible. It's okay if a little remains on the chicken. Place the chicken on the grill, close the dome, and smoke for about 2 hours, until the internal temperature of the thighs reaches 165° F and the juices run clear.

5. Meanwhile, make the cucumber raita. Combine the cucumber, onion, honey, curry powder, and cilantro and mint leaves in a food processor. Pulse 2 or 3 times to combine but keep the mixture chunky. Transfer the mixture to a small bowl and stir in the remaining 1½ cups yogurt. Cover and refrigerate until needed.

6. When the chicken is done, transfer to a platter and serve with the cucumber raita passed on the side.

Smoke-Roasted Piri-Piri Chicken

Serves 4 to 6

1 (3- to 4-pound) chicken, giblets removed

¼ cup extra-virgin olive oil

¼ cup fresh lemon juice (about 2 lemons)

¼ cup fresh orange juice

¼ cup red wine vinegar

3 tablespoons piri-piri sauce or other hot pepper sauce

2 teaspoons paprika

½ teaspoon ground cumin

Kosher salt and freshly ground black pepper

2 tablespoons chopped fresh flat-leaf parsley

2 teaspoons finely grated peeled fresh ginger

2 teaspoons fresh thyme leaves

4 cloves garlic, minced

A trip to what is known as the Ironbound section of Newark, New Jersey, one of the largest enclaves of Portuguese immigrants, without sampling piri-piri chicken is just wrong. It's very simple to make at home now that piri-piri sauce can be found on most grocery store shelves alongside the other hot sauces. Traditionally the chicken is spit-roasted for this dish, and my friend Joseph Theresa, a native of Portugal, claims the best versions are always cooked outside over wood. The kamado works great, though, as the dome accumulates the woody, charcoal flavor that defines piri-piri chicken. In Swahili, *piri* means pepper.

1. Truss the chicken if desired. In a large, deep, nonreactive container, combine the oil, citrus juices, vinegar, piri-piri sauce, paprika, cumin, and salt and pepper to taste. Add the parsley, ginger, thyme, and garlic and stir to combine. Remove ⅓ cup of the marinade and reserve for basting. Place the chicken in the container, turn to coat it fully with the marinade, and refrigerate for 12 hours, turning the chicken a few times. Also refrigerate the reserved marinade. Remove from the refrigerator at least 30 minutes before smoking. Discard the marinade the chicken was soaking in.

2. Light a fire in the kamado grill using your favorite method. After about 10 minutes, close the dome and open the upper and lower dampers all the way. When the temperature reaches 300° F and add any accessories necessary for smoking on your particular grill, along with the grill rack. Close the dome, let the temperature build back to between 200° and 250° F, and wait for a little smoke to accumulate. Adjust the dampers to maintain the temperature in this range.

3. Place the chicken on the grill and close the dome. About every 30 minutes, brush the chicken with some of the reserved marinade, closing the dome again after each time. Cook until the internal temperature of the thigh meat is 165° F and the juices at the thigh run clear when pierced with a knife, about 2 hours.

4. Transfer the chicken to a cutting board and let rest 15 to 20 minutes. Cut the chicken into serving pieces and transfer to a platter. If you have any remaining basting marinade, drizzle that over the chicken pieces. Serve at once or at room temperature.

Smoked Chicken Wings with North Alabama White Sauce

Serves 4

3 pounds chicken wings

1 cup hot pepper sauce

2 tablespoons of your favorite barbecue rub

1 recipe North Alabama White Sauce (page 249)

....

Recommended wood: Hickory

Smoked chicken wings are a hot menu item in the South, from The Roosevelt in Richmond, Virginia, to Beasley's in Raleigh, North Carolina, to the food temples of Memphis. And what sauce are they serving with the smoked wings? Alabama white sauce. This little-known sauce was the private pleasure of North Alabamans for decades, but it's now gained a wider regional following. The acidic, horseradish-laden sauce is great with any smoked chicken, but particularly gratifying with wings. You can also use this method and substitute a more standard hot pepper butter sauce, an Asian-style sauce, or a milder barbecue sauce for the finish. The key is to marinate the wings in a heavy dose of hot sauce. What a wonderful treat!

1. Place the chicken wings in a 2½-gallon zip-top plastic bag. Add the hot sauce, squish it all around to coat the wings, seal the bag, and refrigerate for 3 days.

2. Light a fire in the kamado grill using your favorite method. After about 10 minutes, close the dome and open the upper and lower dampers all the way. When the temperature reaches 300° F, place the wood chunks around the fire and add any accessories necessary for smoking on your particular grill, along with the grill rack. Close the dome, let the temperature build back to between 200° and 250° F, and wait for a little smoke to accumulate. Adjust the dampers to maintain the temperature in this range.

3. Remove the wings from the hot sauce and place them on a rimmed baking sheet. You want a little of the hot sauce still clinging to the wings. Sprinkle them evenly with the barbecue rub. Place the wings on the grill, close the dome, and smoke for about 1 hour. Check for doneness by piercing the fat part of the wing with a knife. The juices should be clear and the meat tender, and the wings should have a lovely mahogany color.

4. Transfer the wings to a platter or bowl and give them a drizzle of the white sauce. If you wish, stir the wings to completely coat them with the sauce. Serve the remaining white sauce on the side.

Spicy and Sweet Smoked Chicken Thighs

Serves 4 to 6

8 bone-in skin-on chicken thighs

¼ cup Asian-Style Rub (page 236)

1 cup Asian sweet chili sauce

. . . .

Recommended wood: Apple or cherry

T highs are often overlooked in the chicken universe, but as far as I'm concerned, they should never play second fiddle to the breast. Bone-in, they are perfect candidates for smoking, and their dark, rich-tasting meat is a great foil for Asian flavors.

1. Place the chicken thighs on a rimmed baking sheet. Liberally season with the spice rub.

2. Light a fire in the kamado grill using your favorite method. After about 10 minutes, close the dome and open the upper and lower dampers all the way. When the temperature reaches 300° F, place the wood chunks around the fire and add any accessories necessary for smoking on your particular grill, along with the grill rack. Close the dome, let the temperature build back to between 200° and 250° F, and wait for a little smoke to accumulate. Adjust the dampers to maintain the temperature in this range.

3. Place the chicken thighs on the grill, close the dome, and smoke for about 1½ hours, until the internal temperature reaches 165° F and the juices run clear when pierced with a knife.

4. Before removing the chicken from the grill, brush the thighs liberally on both sides with the chili sauce. Close the dome and cook another 5 minutes to set the glaze.

5. Transfer the thighs to a platter and brush them again with the sauce. Serve any remaining sweet chili sauce on the side. These thighs are best served warm, but aren't at all bad at room temperature.

BBQ Turkey: A Leaner 'Que

Serves 10 to 12

1 cup apple cider

½ cup firmly packed light brown sugar

¼ cup kosher salt, plus more as needed

2 tablespoons Worcestershire sauce

1 tablespoon hot pepper sauce

Freshly ground black pepper

1 (12- to 14-pound) fresh turkey, giblets removed

2 to 3 tablespoons Best Ever Barbecue Rub (page 233)

Your favorite barbecue sauce for serving (I like Lexington-Style "Dip" on page 246 for this)

Coleslaw and buns if desired for serving

....

Recommended wood: A mix of apple and hickory

Turkey makes damn good barbecue when handled right—in fact, most people don't notice they're eating turkey, not pork shoulder. The keys to success are the flavor injection (you'll need to get yourself a flavor injector—they're available online) and a steady low temperature. I've made this recipe many times using a conventional grill, but when smoked in the kamado, the turkey was moister and had a deeper smoky flavor. With the kamado's unwavering consistent heat, the turkey luxuriates in the injection and its own natural juices. Don't skip the injection; it's key to overcoming the leanness of the turkey.

1. In a small bowl, combine the cider, brown sugar, salt, Worcestershire, pepper sauce, and several grindings of black pepper and stir until the salt and sugar have dissolved.

2. Fill a flavor injector with the mixture and inject the turkey all over, refilling the injector as needed until the mixture is all used up (see Using a Flavor Injector, page 241).

3. Sprinkle the rub on the turkey, both inside and out, and massage it into the skin. Let the turkey sit at room temperature for an hour.

4. Light a fire in the kamado grill using your favorite method. After about 10 minutes, close the dome and open the upper and lower dampers all the way. When the temperature reaches 300° F, place the wood chunks around the fire and add any accessories necessary for smoking on your particular grill, along with the grill rack. Close the dome, let the temperature build back to between 200° and 250° F, and wait for a little smoke to accumulate.

5. Put a rack in a disposable aluminum-foil pan and set the turkey on the rack. Now place the whole setup on the grill. Close the dome and smoke for 3 to 4 hours, until the juices run clear and an instant-read thermometer reads 170° F when inserted into the thigh.

6. Transfer the turkey to a cutting board and let rest for 15 minutes. Reserve the juices in the pan. Pull off the skin and, using tongs or a sturdy fork, pull the turkey apart as you would for pulled pork. Taste for seasoning and adjust by adding more salt or rub. Pour some of the pan juices over the turkey to moisten but not too much, since you will be saucing the turkey. Serve with barbecue sauce, slaw, and buns if desired. The leftovers can be frozen for 3 to 4 months or vacuum-packed and frozen for up to a year.

Thanksgiving Turkey

Serves 12 to 14

1 (12- to 14-pound) fresh turkey

½ cup dried herbes de Provence

¼ cup kosher salt

2 tablespoons freshly ground black pepper

1 large carrot, cut into thirds

1 rib celery, cut into thirds

1 medium onion, cut into quarters

1 lemon

. . . .

Recommended wood: Apple

Smoking your Thanksgiving turkey frees up an amazing amount of space in your kitchen when cooking a big holiday meal. But convenience isn't the real reason to take your turkey outdoors—it's the incredible flavor. One of the great beauties of kamado grilling is how the ceramics hold in the moisture, which means you can skip the messy wet brining that's so popular nowadays. Instead, we're going to "dry brine" the turkey before smoking it, a method favored by Europeans. It adds flavor without changing the texture of the meat. You'll need to start this process two days before you plan to cook, but I can assure you it will be one of the best turkeys you've ever eaten. And my guess is, turkey will start showing up on your menu a lot more often.

1. Remove the giblets and neck from the turkey and reserve for another use, such as making a giblet gravy, if desired. Rinse the turkey thoroughly with cold water and pat dry. In a small bowl, combine the herbes de Provence, salt, and pepper. Heavily coat the outside of the bird and the cavity with this mixture. Place on a rack, set the rack in a disposable aluminum-foil pan, cover with plastic wrap, and refrigerate 24 to 48 hours.

2. Remove the turkey from the refrigerator at least 1 hour before you plan to cook. Stuff the cavity with the carrot, celery, and onion pieces. Cut the lemon in half, squeeze the juices over the breast of the bird, and stuff the rinds into the cavity. Fold the wings under the bird and tie the legs together with kitchen twine.

3. Light a fire in the kamado grill using your favorite method. After about 10 minutes, close the dome and open the upper and lower dampers all the way. When the temperature reaches 300° F, place the wood chunks around the fire and add any accessories necessary for smoking on your particular grill, along with the grill rack. Close the dome, let the temperature build back to between 200° and 250° F, and wait for a little smoke to accumulate. Adjust the dampers to maintain the temperature in this range.

4. Place the roasting pan on the grill, close the dome, and smoke until an instant-read thermometer inserted into the thickest part of the thigh, away from the bone, registers 165° F, 3½ to 4 hours. The juices should run clear when the thigh is pierced with a skewer. Remove from the grill, tent with aluminum foil, and let rest for about 1 hour before carving. If desired, use the accumulated pan juices to make your gravy (see Making Gravy, page 27, but use turkey or chicken broth instead of beef broth). When ready to carve, remove the lemon, onion, celery, and carrot from the cavity. Carve however desired.

Smoked Duck with Spicy Plum Chutney Glaze

Serves 4

1 (5-pound) duck, neck and giblets removed

1 tablespoon Asian-Style Rub (page 236)

1 orange, quartered

1 red onion, quartered

4 cloves garlic, smashed with the flat side of a knife

½ cup spicy plum chutney

¼ cup Japanese-style steak sauce

....

Recommended wood: Cherry (my favorite for this), apple, or pecan

I want you to eat more duck. Duck is so rich and luxurious and takes to a wood fire like no other kind of poultry. In this preparation, we're going to give it some Asian flavor with a quick and easy glaze of store-bought spicy plum chutney and Japanese steak sauce. Look for the steak sauce in the Asian section of your supermarket (it's sometimes called hibachi sauce), and the chutney in or around the specialty cheese section. And don't hesitate to use any leftover chutney to spoon over brie.

1. Rinse the duck and pat dry. Sprinkle the Asian rub inside the cavity and all over the outside of the duck. Take the long piece of skin hanging off the breast, pull it up against the backbone, and then fold the wingtips under. Place the orange and onion pieces and garlic in the cavity and tie the legs together with kitchen twine. Set aside while you prepare the grill.

2. Light a fire in the kamado grill using your favorite method. After about 10 minutes, close the dome and open the upper and lower dampers all the way. When the temperature reaches 300° F, place the wood chunks around the fire and add any accessories necessary for smoking on your particular grill, along with the grill rack. Close the dome, let the temperature build back to between 200° and 250° F, and wait for a little smoke to accumulate.

3. Take a small knife or skewer and pierce the skin of the duck at ½-inch intervals. This will allow excess fat to drain off, creating a crisper skin. Place the duck on the grill, breast side up, and close the dome.

4. In a small saucepan, whisk the chutney and steak sauce together over low heat until liquidy and combined. Remove from the heat.

5. After 1 hour on the grill, brush the duck with the chutney glaze. Close the dome and continue cooking, brushing with glaze about every 15 minutes, until the internal temperature at the thickest part of the thigh (away from the bone) is 165° to 170° F. The duck should be mahogany brown and the juices should run clear when the thigh is pierced with a skewer.

6. Transfer the duck to a cutting board but do not tent with aluminum foil as you will lose the crispness of the skin. Let rest for 15 to 20 minutes. Carve the duck into 8 pieces and drizzle with a little of the glaze sauce. Serve immediately or at room temperature, passing any remaining sauce at the table.

Cold Smoked Salmon

Serves 8 to 12

2 skin-on salmon sides (3 to 4
pounds total), pin bones removed
(wild salmon is the best but farm-
raised works as well)

SALMON CURE:

½ cup granulated sugar

½ cup firmly packed light
brown sugar

⅓ cup kosher salt

2 tablespoons crushed black
peppercorns

FLAVOR RUB (OPTIONAL):

1½ tablespoons light brown sugar

1 tablespoon ground coriander

1 tablespoon paprika

1½ teaspoons freshly ground
black pepper

1½ teaspoons cayenne pepper

¾ teaspoon kosher salt

. . . .

Recommended wood: Alder or
cherry

A ny trip I take to New York City includes stops at Barney Green-
grass, Zabar's, Russ and Daughters—or, many times, all three—
for their excellent smoked salmon. The salmon at these
establishments is truly an art form, sliced with eagle-eye precision by
folks steeped in tradition and experience. I've never been able to find
that quality back home in North Carolina. My answer has been to
learn to smoke my own. It's actually pretty simple. Like making your
own pastrami, it requires a three-step process: curing, drying, and
smoking. Again, the kamado grill is your friend here, with its exceptional ability to maintain a steady low temperature, in this case 150° F,
which replicates cold smoking nicely.

Don't skip the drying step. This develops what is known as the pellicle, a thin, tacky film that aids in smoke absorption. The flavor rub is
optional; without it, you have the classic smoked salmon. Use the rub
if you want your smoked salmon to have a little kick.

Do not overcure the salmon. If you leave the cure on for more
than 12 hours, you will have a salty mess on your hands. In fact, if
your salmon is on the thin side, 8 hours of cure is more than suffi-
cient. So chop some red onions, get yourself some capers, a great
bagel and a smear, and enjoy!

1. In a small bowl, combine the ingredients for the salmon cure until well
   mixed.
2. Get out a baking sheet large enough to hold the salmon fillets. Lay a
   sheet of aluminum foil on the baking sheet, then lay plastic wrap on top
   of the foil. Sprinkle a third of the cure onto the plastic wrap, roughly the
   length of your fillet. Lay one fillet, skin side down, on the cure, then
   sprinkle half of the remaining cure over the fillet. Stack the second fillet,
   skin side down, on the coated flesh of the first fillet. Sprinkle the last of
   the cure on top of this fillet, then cover with another sheet of plastic
   wrap and more foil. Wrap the plastic wrap and foil tightly around the
   fish. This will contain any oils or juices that may escape during the curing process. Set another baking sheet on top of the foil-wrapped fish
   and weigh it down with something heavy, like a few cookbooks or
   canned goods. Refrigerate the salmon for 8 to 10 hours to cure. If your
   fillet is particularly thin (less than an inch), go for 8 hours; if it's thicker,
   you can go up to 10 hours. Never let the salmon cure for more than 12
   hours—it will get way too salty.
3. When the salmon has cured, remove the fish from the fridge and
   unwrap the foil and plastic. You should be greeted by a juicy, bright red
   piece of fish. Thoroughly rinse the fish off under cold running water,
   making sure to wash off any of the cure that hasn't been absorbed into
   the fish. Pat both fillets dry with paper towels.

4. In a small bowl, combine the flavor rub ingredients, if using. Pat the rub onto one of the fillets to form a thin layer. Dust off any excess. Repeat with the second fillet, or leave the second fillet unseasoned to give dinner guests an option. Allow the fillets to dry at room temperature for 1 to 3 hours to form the pellicle. It's hard to tell when this is done when the fish is covered with the dry rub, so use the unseasoned fish to judge when this process is complete or leave a small portion of one of the fillets clear of dry rub.

5. Light a fire in the kamado grill using your favorite method. After about 10 minutes, close the dome and open the upper and lower dampers all the way. When the temperature reaches 200° F, place the wood chunks around the fire and add any accessories necessary for smoking on your particular grill, along with the grill rack. Close the dome, let the temperature build back to between 150° and 175° F, and wait for a little smoke to accumulate. Adjust the dampers to maintain the temperature in this range.

6. Lay the salmon fillets side by side in the grill, skin side down, and close the dome. Depending on how many pounds of fish you're cooking and the thickness of the fish, the smoking process can take anywhere from 1 to 3 hours. Cooking is complete when the salmon registers 140° F on an instant-read thermometer inserted at its thickest point.

7. Once the fish reaches 140° F, take it off the grill and put it on a baking sheet. Tent with foil and allow the fish to rest for 20 to 30 minutes. This will allow the fish to warm up another 5 degrees and let the juices redistribute. Finally, remove the tented foil and let the salmon cool completely before serving. Letting it cool will make it easier to slice, plus the flavor can be a bit strong when the salmon is still warm. The unseasoned salmon is deliciously mild and delicate, with a clean, fresh salmon taste you can only get through smoking. The spice rub has a kick of pepper that's toned down by the sweetness of the brown sugar; it finishes nicely with an herbal note of coriander. Tightly wrapped, this will keep for a week in the refrigerator and can be frozen for a month

Smoked Tuna Steaks

Serves 4 to 6

4 cups water

¼ cup kosher salt

¼ cup firmly packed light brown sugar

2 to 3 pounds fresh tuna steaks

....

Recommended wood: Hickory

Karl Knudsen is a fishing and cooking buddy of mine. We routinely fish the Gulf Stream off the North Carolina coast for the abundant yellow-fin tuna. Karl butchers his own fish and uses every morsel. Tail sections he smokes and makes into a mouthwatering spread. Karl adds liquid smoke to the brine he uses to intensify the smoke flavor. I've left the liquid smoke out of this recipe because with the great seal on the kamado, you're going to end up with plenty of natural smoke flavor. Let the tuna sit out for an hour before putting it on the grill so it can develop a pellicle, which will help it capture more smoke.

You can use the smoked tuna to make Karl's spread (see below), or enjoy it for dinner. This treatment also works nicely with cobia, mackerel, and wahoo.

1. In a medium bowl, combine the water, salt, and sugar and stir until the salt and sugar dissolve. Place the tuna in a 2½-gallon zip-top plastic bag and add the brine. Refrigerate for at least 8 hours but no more than 24 hours.

2. Remove the tuna from the brine (discard the brine), pat dry, and place on a platter at room temperature for 1 hour.

3. Light a fire in the kamado grill using your favorite method. After about 10 minutes, close the dome and open the upper and lower dampers all the way. When the temperature reaches 300° F, place the wood chunks around the fire and add any accessories necessary for smoking on your particular grill, along with the grill rack. Close the dome, let the temperature build back to between 200° and 250° F, and wait for a little smoke to accumulate. Adjust the dampers to maintain the temperature in this range.

4. Place the tuna on the grill, close the dome, and smoke for about 1 hour, until the fish is just firm to the touch. Transfer the tuna to a platter.

Karl's Smoked Tuna Spread: In a medium bowl, beat 1 (8-ounce) package of cream cheese, softened, and ½ cup good-quality mayonnaise together using an electric mixer. Add 1½ to 2 cups flaked smoked tuna (use a fork to break the steaks into small flakes), 4 green onions (green and white parts), finely chopped, and freshly ground black pepper to taste. Run the mixer until the tuna is evenly dispersed through the cream cheese mixture but still chunky. Place in an airtight container and refrigerate for 1 day to allow the flavors to develop; the spread will keep up to 2 weeks. Serve with grilled toast or crackers. Serves 10 to 12.

Sweet and Spicy Smoked Bluefish

Serves 4

4 cups water

¼ cup tamari

¼ cup kosher salt

¼ cup firmly packed light brown sugar

4 bay leaves, crushed

2 tablespoons mustard seeds

1 tablespoon black peppercorns

2 sprigs fresh dill

4 fresh bluefish fillets (about 4 pounds total)

....

Recommended wood: Hickory or cherry

Another great fish to smoke is bluefish. The secret to success with bluefish is only using fresh (like just off the boat). This brine can also be used with Spanish mackerel and mountain trout, and you can use both to make the pâté below, which is adapted from the bluefish pâté served at Straight Wharf restaurant in Nantucket. Because of its oiliness, bluefish needs more time to develop a pellicle and benefits from a slightly lower smoking temperature than tuna.

1. In a medium bowl, combine the water, tamari, salt, brown sugar, bay leaves, mustard seeds, and peppercorns and stir until the sugar and salt dissolve. Add the dill.

2. Place the fillets in 2½-gallon zip-top plastic bag. Add the brine, seal the bag, and refrigerate overnight.

3. Pour off the brine, rinse the fillets, and put them on a wire rack set on a rimmed baking sheet. Refrigerate overnight so a pellicle can form.

4. Light a fire in the kamado grill using your favorite method. After about 10 minutes, close the dome and open the upper and lower dampers all the way. When the temperature reaches 300° F, place the wood chunks around the fire and add any accessories necessary for smoking on your particular grill, along with the grill rack. Close the dome, let the temperature build back to between 150° and 200° F, and wait for a little smoke to accumulate. Adjust the dampers to maintain the temperature in this range.

5. Place the fillets on the grill, close the dome, and smoke for about 3 hours, until they are slightly firm to the touch. Check after 2½ hours. The fillets should have a nice dark honey color to them.

6. Transfer the fillets to a platter and serve or let cool and freeze for up to 3 months.

Wonderful New England Bluefish Pâté: In a medium bowl, cream together 1 (8-ounce) package of cream cheese, softened, 1 tablespoon Worcestershire sauce, 1 tablespoon fresh lemon juice, 4 dashes hot pepper sauce, and ½ cup finely diced red onion. Gently fold in 1 cup flaked smoked bluefish, then sprinkle with ¼ cup minced fresh chives. It will keep in an airtight container in the refrigerator for up to a week. Serve with crackers or grilled toast points. Serves 10 to 12.

Smoked Oysters and Clams

Serves 4 to 6

1 quart shucked select oysters or cherrystone clams

Kosher salt and freshly ground black pepper

Cocktail sauce for serving (optional)

. . . .

Recommended wood: Alder or any kind of fruit wood; do not use a strong wood like hickory

Smoked Oyster Spread:

Take half the smoked oysters and chop. Mash together with 1 (8-ounce) package of cream cheese at room temperature, 2 tablespoons sour cream, and 1 green onion, finely chopped. Refrigerate for at least 1 hour to allow the flavors to meld; it will keep in an airtight container for about a week. Serve with crackers or toast.

Smoked Oyster Stew:

Use the smoked oysters and reserved oyster liquor in your favorite oyster stew recipe. Or, if you've smoked clams, substitute the clams and their liquor into your favorite clam chowder recipe.

My daddy loved smoked oysters. He would get so excited when he brought home a can or a tin from the grocery store and he passed that love on to me. I wish he were still alive to try these. Smoking oysters at home, like so many other things, just beats the pants off of store-bought. There are times when I get in the mood for oysters and do it just because I want them. But on many occasions when I'm having a party or friends over and plan to smoke something on the grill, I'll slide these mollusks on to have with cocktails and other munchies before I put on the main event. If you love smoked oysters or just oysters in general, this is a great recipe to have in your arsenal.

While you can do this by shucking your own oysters, I've found that I eat more raw oysters than I can reserve to smoke. So I tend to make this recipe with shucked selects, which hold up and absorb the smoke flavor and are also usually all about the same size. The exact same process can be used for clams.

1. Whether you are doing oysters or clams, the method is the same. Drain the mollusks, reserving their liquor for another use. Pour them in a large nonstick pan and place over low heat. Lightly cook them just until their edges begin to curl. This firms them up and helps them absorb more smoke once they're on the grill. Immediately remove them from the pan to stop the cooking.

2. Light a fire in the kamado grill using your favorite method. After about 10 minutes, close the dome and open the upper and lower dampers all the way. When the temperature reaches 300° F, place the wood chunks around the fire and add any accessories necessary for smoking on your particular grill, along with the grill rack. Close the dome, let the temperature build back to between 200° and 250° F, and wait for a little smoke to accumulate. Adjust the dampers to maintain the temperature in this range.

3. Pour the slightly cooked oysters or clams into a disposable aluminum-foil pan with holes poked through the bottom. Place the pan on the grill, close the dome, and smoke for at least 30 minutes but not much more than 45 minutes; taste the mollusks to check on their smoke flavor. Remove the mollusks from the grill and salt and pepper to taste. Serve immediately with cocktail sauce if desired, or refrigerate in an airtight container for up to 3 days and enjoy at your leisure.

Smoked Scallops with Bloody Mary Juice and Cilantro

Serves 6 to 8

4 cups water

¼ cup kosher salt

¼ cup firmly packed light brown sugar

2 pounds U-10 dry-pack sea scallops, side muscle removed if necessary

4 cups premium bloody Mary mix with horseradish

¼ cup coarsely chopped fresh cilantro

Short celery stalks for garnish

. . . .

Recommended wood: Pecan or cherry

Smoking tends to enhance sweetness and what shellfish has more sweetness than scallops? They get a short bath in a brine, and then are smoked just until almost cooked through. Do not overcook!

1. In a medium bowl, combine the water, salt, and brown sugar and stir until the salt and sugar have dissolved. Place the scallops in a 1-gallon zip-top plastic bag and add the brine. Seal the bag and refrigerate for 8 hours.

2. Remove the scallops from the brine; discard the brine. Set the scallops on a wire rack set in a rimmed baking sheet and refrigerate while you build the fire.

3. Light a fire in the kamado grill using your favorite method. After about 10 minutes, close the dome and open the upper and lower dampers all the way. When the temperature reaches 300° F, place the wood chunks around the fire and add any accessories necessary for smoking on your particular grill, along with the grill rack. Close the dome, let the temperature build back to between 200° and 250° F, and wait for a little smoke to accumulate.

4. Place the scallops on the grill, close the dome, and adjust the dampers to drop the temperature to no higher than 200° F. Smoke the scallops for about 45 minutes to 1 hour. They should feel slightly firm to the touch; if you're undecided about whether or not they're done, cut one in half. It should still be slightly translucent in the center. Of course, when I do this, I eat the scallop that I cut in half.

5. When the scallops are done, transfer them to a large bowl, add the bloody Mary mix and cilantro, and toss together. Let the scallops sit in that mixture at room temperature for about 30 minutes.

6. To serve, divide the scallops among 6 martini glasses. Pour some of the bloody Mary mixture into each glass, garnish with the celery stalks, and serve. You can also refrigerate the mixture overnight and serve cold.

Smoked Octopus with Warm White Beans

Serves 4 as a salad course or light lunch

1½ pounds frozen cleaned baby octopus

DRESSING:

2 tablespoons red wine vinegar

1 clove garlic, thinly sliced

1 tablespoon chopped fresh mint

1 tablespoon chopped fresh flat-leaf parsley

1 teaspoon Dijon mustard

Kosher salt and freshly ground black pepper to taste

2 cups cooked white beans, warmed and drained

Lemon wedges

The inspiration for this dish came from Frank and Jacky Bertoni. I have visited their home near Fort Bragg, California, many times and always come away with great recipes and a great education in sea critters. Frank has fished the north coast of California for decades and loves octopus only slightly less than he loves Dungeness crab. His trick to tenderizing octopus is to freeze it—no need for beating it to a pulp or simmering it for hours. Since most of us have access only to frozen octopus, this is good news.

When smoking octopus on the kamado, don't bother to thaw it. When thawed on the grill, the octopus smokes more slowly, picking up more flavor. The entire process (thawing and smoking) usually takes an hour but slide a knife into the octopus after about 45 minutes to check for tenderness. The knife should go in easily—that's the only sure way to check for doneness.

This is one of my favorite dishes—I like the contrast in textures between the beans and octopus.

1. Light a fire in the kamado grill using your favorite method. After about 10 minutes, close the dome and open the upper and lower dampers all the way. When the temperature reaches 300° F and add any accessories necessary for smoking on your particular grill, along with the grill rack. Close the dome, let the temperature build back to between 200° and 250° F, and wait for a little smoke to accumulate. Adjust the dampers to maintain the temperature in this range.

2. Place the frozen octopuses on the grill, close the dome, and smoke for about 1 hour, until they are tender; a sharp knife should slide through them easily.

3. Meanwhile, in a medium bowl, whisk the dressing ingredients together.

4. When the octopuses are done, transfer them to a cutting board and slice into bite-size pieces. Place the pieces in the bowl with the dressing and toss to coat. Refrigerate, covered, for at least 3 hours but not much longer before serving.

5. Divide the beans between four plates, then set the octopus pieces over the beans. Drizzle the remaining dressing on top and serve with lemon wedges.

Smoked Tomato Ragout over penne

Smoked Tomatoes

Makes about 1 quart

3 pounds summer-ripe tomatoes (heirlooms will yield the best flavor; an assortment of varieties is preferable)

Olive oil for drizzling

6 sprigs fresh oregano

6 sprigs fresh thyme

6 cloves garlic, finely minced

Kosher salt and freshly ground black pepper

· ·

Recommended wood: Apple

These will keep in the freezer for several months and you can use them all year round to make the recipes below.

1. Slice the tomatoes in half through the equator. Place on a sheet pan, cut side up. Drizzle with olive oil. Toss the herbs over the tomatoes and sprinkle with the garlic. Season with salt and pepper to taste.
2. Light a fire in the kamado grill using your favorite method. After about 10 minutes, close the dome and open the upper and lower dampers all the way. When the temperature reaches 300° F, place the wood chunks around the fire and add any accessories necessary for smoking on your particular grill, along with the grill rack. Close the dome, let the temperature build back to between 200° and 250° F, and wait for a little smoke to accumulate. Adjust the dampers to maintain the temperature in this range.
3. Using tongs, quickly place the tomato halves, cut side up, on the grill, close the dome, and smoke for about 2 hours. The tomatoes should have softened but still retain their shape.
4. Remove the tomatoes to a large bowl. If using right away, proceed with your recipe. If not, pack the tomatoes into clean glass jars. Cover with olive oil, place the lids on the jars, and refrigerate up to 4 weeks.

Smoked Tomato Salsa: Use these instead of fresh tomatoes in your favorite salsa recipe. They'll add a totally new flavor dimension.

Smoked Tomato Ragout: Place a large skillet over medium heat and brown ⅓ pound *each* ground beef, ground veal, and ground pork. Add 1 cup chopped onion and 1 large carrot and 1 rib celery, each cut into small dice. Cook, stirring a few times, until the vegetables are soft and lazy. Add 3 cloves garlic, finely minced, and cook until the garlic is fragrant, about 1 minute. Stir in 3 tablespoons double-concentrated tomato paste into the pan and sauté with the mixture for a minute or two. Add 2 cups smoked tomatoes, breaking them up with your hands as you add them to the skillet. Stir to combine, cover, and cook over low heat at a very gentle simmer for 30 to 45 minutes to allow the flavors to blend. Remove the lid and add ¼ cup whole milk or half-and-half and simmer for 15 minutes. Serve over pasta or use in making lasagna. Makes at least 4 cups.

Smoked Tomato and Basil Soup: Puree 2 cups smoked tomatoes and push through a fine-mesh strainer into a medium saucepan. Add 1 cup vegetable broth and bring to a boil. Reduce the heat to simmer. Add a pinch of dried oregano and ¼ cup heavy cream. Let simmer over low heat 10 to 15 minutes. Season with salt and white pepper to taste. Pour into warm bowls and toss torn fresh basil leaves over the top. Serves 4.

Smoking Vegetables

There is little difference between smoking vegetables and proteins. Your kamado grill is set exactly the same as it would be for a pork shoulder. And just as it does for pork and other animal proteins, the smoke of the kamado adds volumes of flavor to vegetables. You can smoke practically any vegetable you can think of and the method on the grill is the same.

Smoked Broccoli or Cauliflower

Makes about 4 cups

2 heads broccoli or cauliflower, cut into florets

Olive oil for drizzling

Kosher salt and freshly ground black pepper

Both of these good-for-you vegetables take on smoke beautifully and just might make a broccoli or cauliflower lover out of a hater. Also try the wonderful cheesy soup below—or combine them with softened cream cheese and a little shredded cheddar, and warm it all up in the microwave for a hot dip for crudités.

1. Place the florets on a disposable aluminum-foil baking sheet. Drizzle with oil and sprinkle with salt and pepper.
2. Light a fire in the kamado grill using your favorite method. After about 10 minutes, close the dome and open the upper and lower dampers all the way. When the temperature reaches 300° F and add any accessories necessary for smoking on your particular grill, along with the grill rack. Close the dome, let the temperature build back to between 200° and 250° F, and wait for a little smoke to accumulate. Adjust the dampers to maintain the temperature in this range.
3. Set the baking sheet on the grill, close the dome, and smoke; cauliflower will take about 1½ hours, broccoli about 2 hours. They will be soft and slightly charred.
4. Remove the vegetables from the pan and serve at once or place in an airtight container and reserve for another use. Enjoy within a couple of days.

Creamy Smoked Broccoli or Cauliflower Soup: Place 2 cups smoked broccoli or cauliflower in a medium saucepan. Add 2 cups vegetable broth and bring to a boil. Reduce the heat to low and simmer for 20 minutes. Add 1 cup heavy cream and a few gratings of nutmeg. Stir and let simmer for another 10 to 15 minutes. If desired, stir in ½ cup of your favorite cheese. Stir until melted and serve. For a more elegant presentation, you can puree the broccoli or cauliflower before adding it to the pot, which I prefer.

Smoked Corn on the Cob

Yield varies

Fresh ears of corn, husked and silks removed

Olive oil

Kosher salt and freshly ground black pepper

Some people like to smoke corn on the cob in its husk. I prefer to go ahead and husk and silk the corn. Once the ears are smoked, I take the kernels off the cob. Here's a tip—take a Bundt pan, place one ear of corn, small end down, into the hole of the pan. Take your knife and slice down the ear. The Bundt pan will catch the kernels. Be sure to take your knife and rub down each empty cob to get all the "milk" from the cob. Try smoked corn in the recipe below or in your favorite corn pudding recipe

1. Light a fire in the kamado grill using your favorite method. After about 10 minutes, close the dome and open the upper and lower dampers all the way. When the temperature reaches 300° F and add any accessories necessary for smoking on your particular grill, along with the grill rack. Close the dome, let the temperature build back to between 200° and 250° F, and wait for a little smoke to accumulate. Adjust the dampers to maintain the temperature in this range.
2. Brush the ears of corn with olive oil and give them a sprinkling of salt and pepper. Place the ears on the grill rack, close the dome, and smoke for about 1 hour. Take one ear of corn off and taste a kernel it to see if it's developed enough smoke flavor for you. If so, remove the ears from the grill; if not, continue smoking.

Smoked Corn Stew: This is one of my favorite uses for smoked corn. Place a Dutch oven over medium heat and melt ½ cup (1 stick) unsalted butter in it. Add 6 cups smoked corn; 2 cups finely chopped onions; and 1 jalapeño pepper, seeded, deveined, and thinly sliced. Cook, stirring a few times, until the vegetables are soft, about 10 minutes. Add 2 garlic cloves, finely minced, and 4 sprigs fresh cilantro. Cook until the garlic is fragrant, about 1 minute. Add 2½ to 3 cups water and a pinch of kosher salt. Bring to a boil, cover, reduce the heat to a simmer, and cook for 10 minutes. Remove the cilantro sprigs and discard. Place the soup in a blender or food processor and pulse until roughly pureed. If you like, place a small pile of crabmeat in each soup bowl, then ladle in the soup and top with a dollop of sour cream, if desired. Serve at once.

Smoked Corn Stew

Smoked French Onion Soup

Smoked Onions

Yield varies

Any kind of onion, left whole and unpeeled

These onions are delicious alongside steak or other beef entrees, but if you want something really magnificent, cut them up and use them to make your next batch of French onion soup. Killer! I usually do a 3-pound bag of onions at a time.

1. Light a fire in the kamado grill using your favorite method. After about 10 minutes, close the dome and open the upper and lower dampers all the way. When the temperature reaches 300° F and add any accessories necessary for smoking on your particular grill, along with the grill rack. Close the dome, let the temperature build back to between 200° and 250° F, and wait for a little smoke to accumulate. Adjust the dampers to maintain the temperature in this range.

2. Place the onions, unpeeled, on the grill rack, close the dome, and smoke for at least 2 hours but not more than 3 hours. Remove from the grill and, when cool enough to handle, cut off the roots and remove the skins. They keep for about a week in the refrigerator and up to 2 months in the freezer.

Smoked French Onion Soup: Melt ¼ cup (½ stick) unsalted butter in a Dutch oven over medium heat. Add 6 cups sliced smoked onions, tossing them in the butter to coat. Sprinkle 2 tablespoons all-purpose flour over the onions and stir. Cook for about 2 minutes, then add 1 (32-ounce) container (4 cups) reduced-sodium beef broth, 1 tablespoon Worcestershire sauce, 2 bay leaves, 8 sprigs fresh flat-leaf parsley, and 1 sprig fresh thyme. Bring to a boil, and then reduce the heat and simmer for about 15 minutes. Add 1 tablespoon red wine vinegar, cook for another 2 minutes, then pull out the thyme, parsley, and bay leaves. The soup can be prepared up to this point in advance and refrigerated for up to 2 days or frozen for up to 1 month. When ready to serve, divide equally among six ovenproof bowls. Top each with a toasted baguette slice and a slice of Swiss or provolone cheese or a generous layer of freshly grated Parmesan. Run under a broiler until the cheese is bubbly and beginning to crust. Serve immediately.

Smoke-Roasted Garlic

Makes about 1 1/2 cups

3 large, heavy heads of garlic

2 tablespoons olive oil, plus more to pour over the smoked cloves

....

Recommended wood: Cook's choice

Roasted garlic is one of those secret ingredients that great chefs use to add volumes of flavor to many dishes. Using roasted garlic will give almost any recipe a sweeter, deeper flavor than using raw garlic. Throw some heads of garlic on the grill to smoke whenever you're smoking something else. It will keep, covered with olive oil, 2 to 4 weeks in the refrigerator.

1. Light a fire in the kamado grill using your favorite method. After about 10 minutes, close the dome and open the upper and lower dampers all the way. When the temperature reaches 300° F, place the wood chunks around the fire and add any accessories necessary for smoking on your particular grill, along with the grill rack. Close the dome, let the temperature build back to between 200° and 250° F, and wait for a little smoke to accumulate. Adjust the dampers to maintain the temperature in this range.

2. Rub each head of garlic between your hands lightly to remove the outer layer of papery skin. Cut about ½ inch off the top of each head. Place the garlic in a disposable aluminum-foil pie plate and drizzle the olive oil over. Place the plate on the grill, close the dome, and smoke until the heads are soft when you poke them with your finger, about 1½ hours. You don't want to oversmoke the garlic, as the flavor can become harsh.

3. Remove from the grill and squeeze the cloves out of their skins. Put in an airtight container, cover with olive oil, and refrigerate. By the way, the olive oil left over when the garlic is gone makes for a superb vinaigrette.

Smoke-Roasted Garlic Compound Butter: This is one of the simplest ways to add bodacious amounts of extra flavor to any dish. Take 3 or 4 of the cloves of smoked garlic and mash them into a paste. Combine them with ½ cup (1 stick) room-temperature unsalted butter, along with a little salt and pepper and even additional herbs if you like. A fork is a good tool to use here. Place in a container and throw in the freezer. The next time you cook a steak, put a spoonful of this mixture on top while it rests.

Jack Stack's Kansas City Smoked Beans

Serves 8 to 10

4 slices bacon

1 (40-ounce) can regular pork and beans, drained

¾ cup firmly packed light brown sugar

1 tablespoon minced onion

1 tablespoon chili powder

1 tablespoon dry mustard

1 cup Kansas City–style barbecue sauce, homemade (page 248) or store-bought

¼ cup molasses

· ·

Recommended wood: Hickory

When on book tour for my cookbook *Barbecue Nation,* I ate at Jack Stack's—the food was awesome and the baked beans out of this world. The manager kindly gave me a tour of the kitchen and smokehouse, and I asked for the baked bean recipe. He laughed and said, "Sure, I'll give you the recipe but I doubt they will taste the same when you make them." I soon found out why—when he opened the smokers there were the pans of the beans being smoked, set under the briskets to catch all their drippings. That's the secret! With an extender rack, available from kamado manufacturers, and the high dome of the grill, this is easy to do at home. Even without the drippings, these are very tasty beans.

1. Cook the bacon until almost done but still a bit fatty. Combine the remaining ingredients in a large disposable aluminum-foil pan set inside another one. Add the bacon, laying the strips across the top.
2. Light a fire in the kamado grill using your favorite method. After about 10 minutes, close the dome and open the upper and lower dampers all the way. When the temperature reaches 300° F, place the wood chunks around the fire and add any accessories necessary for smoking on your particular grill, along with the grill rack. Close the dome, let the temperature build back to between 200° and 250° F, and wait for a little smoke to accumulate. Adjust the dampers to maintain the temperature in this range.
3. Place the beans under a grill holding a beef brisket that you are smoking so that the drippings fall into the beans. Close the lid and smoke for 1½ to 2 hours; the beans are done when they're tender and flavorful. Stir the drippings into the beans and serve.

Smoked Acorn Squash with Italian Sausage

Serves 4; can be doubled

2 acorn squash on the small side

2 teaspoons ground cinnamon

4 tablespoons maple syrup (grade B preferred)

1 to 1½ pounds bulk Italian sausage (sweet works better)

Olive oil spray

2 cups pasta sauce of your choice, warmed, for serving

. . . .
Recommended wood: Hickory

This is a really great side dish or a nice fall dinner when paired with a salad. If you are smoking a small turkey or pork roast, let it smoke right alongside.

1. Cut the acorn squash in half though the equator and scrape out the seeds. Cut a small slice off the bottom of each half so it will sit upright. Sprinkle each half with ½ teaspoon of the cinnamon, then drizzle each with 1 tablespoon of maple syrup. Divide the sausage into four hunks and roll each into a ball. Place one ball in each acorn half. Spray with the olive oil.

2. Light a fire in the kamado grill using your favorite method. After about 10 minutes, close the dome and open the upper and lower dampers all the way. When the temperature reaches 300° F, place the wood chunks around the fire and add any accessories necessary for smoking on your particular grill, along with the grill rack. Close the dome, let the temperature build back to between 200° and 250° F, and wait for a little smoke to accumulate. Adjust the dampers to maintain the temperature in this range.

3. Place the squash on the grill, close the dome, and smoke for about 2 hours, until a paring knife can easily be inserted into the flesh.

4. Transfer the squash to four serving plates. Pour sauce over each and serve.

Yes, You Can Smoke Macaroni and Cheese with Bacon

Serves 8 as a side

1 pound elbow macaroni

½ cup (1 stick) plus 1 tablespoon unsalted butter

1 cup shredded Muenster cheese (about 4 ounces)

1 cup shredded mild cheddar cheese (about 4 ounces)

1 cup shredded sharp cheddar cheese (about 4 ounces)

1 cup shredded Monterey jack (about 4 ounces)

2 cups half-and-half

8 ounces Velveeta, cubed

4 ounces smoked farmer's cheese or smoked mozzarella, shredded

8 slices smoked bacon (try the DIY Bacon on page 55), chopped and cooked until almost done but not crispy

2 large eggs, lightly beaten

¼ teaspoon seasoned salt

Freshly ground black pepper

. . . .

Recommended wood: Hickory or apple

Why not add a little smoked cheese and bacon to a classic and bake it in the kamado to add even more smoke? Slide this dish on the grill when you're smoking a protein that cries out for a rich and creamy side dish. Thanks to Linda Johnson, my back-door neighbor, for sharing the original mac and cheese recipe this is based on.

1. Light a fire in the kamado grill using your favorite method. After about 10 minutes, close the dome and open the upper and lower dampers all the way. When the temperature reaches 300° F, place the wood chunks around the fire and add any accessories necessary for smoking on your particular grill, along with the grill rack. Close the dome, let the temperature build back to between 200° and 250° F, and wait for a little smoke to accumulate. Adjust the dampers to maintain the temperature in this range.

2. Butter a deep 2½-quart casserole dish (cast-iron is best).

3. Cook the macaroni according to package directions just until tender. Don't overcook it, as it will be cooked further when it goes on the grill. Drain the pasta and return it to the pot.

4. Melt the ½ cup butter. Stir into the macaroni. Blend the shredded cheeses together. Pour the half-and-half into the pot with the macaroni and add 2 cups of the shredded cheese, the Velveeta, all of the farmer's cheese, bacon and the eggs. Sprinkle with the seasoned salt and 5 to 6 grindings of pepper. Stir all the ingredients to combine. Pour into the prepared casserole dish and sprinkle with the remaining cheese. Cut the remaining 1 tablespoon butter into little bits and dot those over the top of the cheese.

5. Place the pan on the grill, close the dome, and smoke until it's bubbling around the edges and just slightly browned on top, about 1 hour. Serve hot.

Smoked Almonds

Makes 2 pounds

2 pounds raw natural almonds

About 1½ tablespoons hot sauce

1 tablespoon of your favorite barbecue rub, or to taste (optional)

. . . .

Recommended wood: Hickory

What better snack is there than smoked almonds? Instead of paying a king's ransom for them at the supermarket, smoke them at home! I'm not going to set up the kamado just to smoke almonds; usually I slide them on the grill rack when I'm doing a pork shoulder or brisket to maximize the efficiency of my grill. But there are those times when I decide to make several batches at once so that I never run out of these enjoyable nuggets of healthy goodness.

1. In a medium bowl, toss the almonds, hot sauce, and rub (if using) together until the nuts are well coated with the sauce and rub. Pour into a disposable 9- x 13-inch aluminum-foil pan in an even layer.

2. Light a fire in the kamado grill using your favorite method. After about 10 minutes, close the dome and open the upper and lower dampers all the way. When the temperature reaches 300° F, place the wood chunks around the fire and add any accessories necessary for smoking on your particular grill, along with the grill rack. Close the dome, let the temperature build back to between 200° and 250° F, and wait for a little smoke to accumulate. Adjust the dampers to maintain the temperature in this range.

3. Set the pan on the grill, close the dome, and smoke until the nuts are crisp, about 3 hours

4. Let cool completely and store in an airtight container; they will keep at room temperature for up to a week but, believe me, they won't last that long! They also will freeze nicely for a couple of months.

Smoked Salt and Pepper

Makes 2 ½ cups salt and 1 cup pepper

1 (22-ounce) container coarse sea salt

1 (4.2-ounce) container black peppercorns

. . . .

Recommended wood: Hickory

Don't buy expensive smoked salts and peppers in the store when you can make them yourself in the kamado! The taste of smoke may not be evident to you if you take a little taste of the salt or pepper, but the flavor really blooms when you cook with them.

1. Using a paring knife, cut small slits in the bottom of a 9 x 13-inch disposable aluminum-foil pan. You are trying to create a perforated surface. Pour the salt in one end of the pan. Pour the pepper in the other end of the pan. Level them out but keep them separate.

2. Light a fire in the kamado grill using your favorite method. After about 10 minutes, close the dome and open the upper and lower dampers all the way. When the temperature reaches 300° F, place the wood chunks around the fire and add any accessories necessary for smoking on your particular grill, along with the grill rack. Close the dome, let the temperature build back to between 200° and 250° F, and wait for a little smoke to accumulate. Adjust the dampers to maintain the temperature in this range.

3. Place the pan on the grill, close the dome, and smoke for 4 to 6 hours. The longer you leave it in, the smokier the taste.

4. Remove the pan from the grill and put the pepper and salt in separate airtight containers. They will retain their smoky flavor for about 6 months when stored in a cool, dark place. Use in place of salt and pepper in any recipe.

Bacon-Wrapped Pork Tenderloin with Rosemary (page 116)

3

Grilling in the Kamado

Grilling, by definition, is cooking over direct heat, and it's no different on a kamado. Direct grilling is fast and hot, with full exposure of the food to the charcoal fire. The result is beautifully seared and caramelized surfaces and a juicy interior.

Yes, you need a hot fire to grill. No, it doesn't need to be 700° F. Great grilling can be accomplished anywhere from 400° to 700° F. I've found that 500° F works well for most all foods and is a good starting point. Some items, like pork and poultry, prefer a lower temperature, around 400° F; any higher and they'll likely toughen. Please follow the target temperatures I give you in each recipe.

Not every kind of food is cut out for direct heat. Pick foods that are naturally tender and generally no more than two inches thick, and that would cook within 20 minutes or less in any cooking circumstance. Steaks, chops, burgers, poultry parts, fish (both fillets or steaks and small whole fish), small whole cuts like a pork tenderloin, and vegetables fit into this category.

When grilling in a kamado, the dome must be closed. Remember the kamado mantra: "If it ain't closed, it ain't cooking." Everything about the superior results that come from a kamado is about keeping the dome closed, so when you do open it (to turn or baste your food or put cheese on burgers), work quickly.

For grilling, you want a very hot fire and there are several things to keep in mind in that regard. First, only use lump charcoal; it burns hotter, longer, and, most importantly, is ready to cook on faster than briquettes. With lump charcoal, you're good to go just as soon as you see a little gray.

Don't be bashful about the amount of charcoal you use; any unused charcoal will relight the next time you use the kamado. Start with larger pieces on the bottom, with the pieces getting progressively smaller as you build the pile. Have the upper and lower dampers open all the way open and within 5 to 10 minutes of lighting your fire, insert the grill grate and close the dome. Then let the kamado take over; once you hit your target temperature, adjust the dampers to maintain it. If you find your fire has gotten a bit out of control, the quickest way to adjust the temperature downward is to carefully open the dome for a moment, adjust the dampers, and then close the dome.

You may not have bought the kamado with grilling in mind, but my kamado has outperformed every grill I own, both gas and charcoal, in this task of direct heat. The food always has a pleasant extra nuance of smoke, stays moister, and has a proper char. It really is the go-to grill for all forms of outdoor cooking

The Perfect Steak

6 T-bone steaks, 1½ inches thick (about 10 ounces each)

Kosher salt and freshly ground black pepper

4 to 6 tablespoons olive oil

6 tablespoons (¾ stick) salted butter, cut into 1-tablespoon pats

Growing up, there was a serious ritual in my house every Saturday night. Dad would mix some Jack Daniels and 7-Up, then fire up his little brazier grill and cook four rib-eye steaks. We all looked forward to Saturday night. It made every weekend seem a little bit like a celebration. And I still to this day have to have at least one steak a week. Other than burgers and hot dogs, collectively we grill steaks more than any other item.

1. At least 30 minutes before you plan to grill, remove the steaks from the refrigerator. Season them generously on both sides with salt and pepper.

2. Light a fire in the kamado grill using your favorite method. After about 10 minutes, place the grill rack in position, close the dome, and open the upper and lower dampers all the way. When the temperature reaches between 600° and 700° F, adjust the dampers to maintain the temperature in that range. Remember, even when grilling, the dome should be closed as much as possible.

3. Brush the steaks on both sides with the oil. Place the steaks on the grill rack, close the dome, and cook for about 3 minutes. Using tongs or a wide spatula (never a fork, please—you'll lose precious juices through the puncture marks), rotate each steak 90 degrees. This will give you those beautiful crisscross grill marks that will impress your friends and neighbors and add flavor. Cook another 2 to 3 minutes, then flip the steaks. Cook until well marked and done to your liking, another 5 minutes for medium rare (135° F on an instant-read thermometer).

4. Transfer the steaks to a warm platter. Put a pat of butter on each steak and let the steaks rest for 5 to 10 minutes before serving. You should get plenty of oohs and aahs.

New York Strip with Summer Tomato and Blue Cheese "Salsa"

Serves 6

6 New York strip steaks, 1½ inches thick (8 to 10 ounces each)

Kosher salt and freshly ground black pepper (or substitute Canadian-Style Steak Seasoning, page 234)

Olive oil

2 cups sliced cherry tomatoes or chopped regular tomatoes

½ cup sliced red onion

¼ cup crumbled blue cheese

¼ cup garlic-flavored olive oil

2 tablespoons fig-infused balsamic vinegar

2 tablespoons finely chopped fresh basil

A sprinkling of sea salt

To me, there is no better steak than a New York strip, but feel free to substitute your favorite cut. The stout flavor and aroma of blue cheese are great foils to the sensuous flavor of the flame-lashed beef. If you're not a blue cheese fan, you can use another strong cheese such as an aged Gruyère or Parmesan.

1. At least 30 minutes before you plan to grill, remove the steaks from the refrigerator. Generously salt and pepper both sides and brush with oil.

2. In a medium bowl, combine the remaining ingredients and toss to mix. Let sit at room temperature until the steaks are ready.

3. Light a fire in the kamado grill using your favorite method. After about 10 minutes, place the grill rack in position, close the dome, and open the upper and lower dampers all the way. When the temperature reaches between 500° and 600° F, adjust the dampers to maintain the temperature in that range. Remember, even when grilling, the dome should be closed as much as possible.

4. Place the steaks on the grill, close the dome, and cook 2 to 3 minutes. Rotate the steaks 90 degrees. Cook for another 2 minutes. Flip the steaks and cook until well marked and cooked to your liking, about another 5 minutes for medium rare.

5. Remove the steaks to a warm platter and let rest 5 to 10 minutes before serving. Spoon the "salsa" over the steaks and serve.

5 Secrets of a Perfectly Cooked Steak

1. *Always buy good meat*—at least USDA choice and, if you can, step up to grass-fed or grass-finished beef; its bold flavor seems to love being licked by the flames of the grill.

2. *Don't go too nuts on seasoning.* Salt and pepper are generally all a steak needs. Many chefs have different opinions about salting. Some salt a steak the night before, others only salt after the steak is cooked. I've found that salting right before you cook is the best way.

3. *Help the grill do its job.* Brush steaks with olive oil, which will accelerate the transfer of heat to the steak. This is important because a big part of steak's flavor comes from the crusting (caramelization) that occurs when it's exposed to high temperature, converting the natural sugars in the beef into tasty bits of flavor. That doesn't mean burnt. You're looking for a crusty mahogany brown.

4. *Timing is crucial.* Nothing is worse than an over-cooked steak. Steak is best when cooked from rare to medium rare. That's the point where you will be able to enjoy all the juiciness and tenderness that comes with a good piece of beef.

5. *When it's done, let it rest.* This is critical. Let your steak rest for at least 5 to 10 minutes before cutting into it. This allows the juices to be reabsorbed into the muscle so that each bite you take is full of moisture and flavor. If you cut into a steak too soon, you'll have a puddle of juice all over your plate instead of in your mouth.

Bourbon-Glazed Bone-in Rib-Eye Steak

Serves 4

4 bone-in rib-eye steaks, 1½ inches thick (about 10 ounces each)

Canadian-Style Steak Seasoning (page 234) or kosher salt and freshly ground black pepper

Olive oil

¼ cup (½ stick) unsalted butter

¼ cup diced red onion

½ cup dark steak sauce, like A-1

2 to 4 tablespoons bourbon

1 tablespoon molasses

2 teaspoons yellow mustard

Being a Southern boy, bourbon has passed my lips more than once and I find it to be a delightful seasoning ingredient with a good piece of beef. The sweet honey vanilla of bourbon picks up on that flavor and intensifies it during the cooking process. Sweetening the glaze with molasses adds another Southern touch as well as greater depth of flavor. (See photo on page 19.)

1. At least 30 minutes before you plan to grill, remove the steaks from the refrigerator. Generously season both sides and brush with oil.

2. In a small saucepan over medium heat, melt the butter. Add the onion and cook, stirring a few times, until it wilts or, as a friend of mine says, "gets lazy," about 3 minutes. Add the steak sauce, bourbon, molasses, and mustard and stir to combine. Bring to a simmer and cook for 3 to 5 minutes. Remove from the heat. This sauce can be made up to a couple of days in advance and refrigerated. (Let it come to room temperature or gently reheat before using it.)

3. Light a fire in the kamado grill using your favorite method. After about 10 minutes, place the grill rack in position, close the dome, and open the upper and lower dampers all the way. When the temperature reaches between 500° and 600° F, adjust the dampers to maintain the temperature in that range. Remember, even when grilling, the dome should be closed as much as possible.

4. Place the steaks on the grill, close the dome, and cook for about 3 minutes. Rotate the steaks 90 degrees and cook for another 3 minutes. Flip the steaks and cook until well marked and cooked to your liking, about another 5 minutes for medium rare. During the last couple minutes of cooking, brush the steaks on both sides with the sauce and let it form a glaze.

5. Transfer the steaks to a warm platter and let rest for 5 to 10 minutes. Serve with the remaining bourbon steak glaze passed at the table.

Hanger Steak with Grilled Onions

Serves 6

¼ cup extra-virgin olive oil

¼ cup sherry vinegar or balsamic vinegar

¼ cup tamari

2 tablespoons coarse-grain mustard

1 tablespoon Dijon mustard

1 tablespoon yellow or brown mustard seeds

2 teaspoons grated peeled fresh ginger

6 cloves garlic, finely minced

Kosher salt and freshly ground black pepper

6 hanger steaks (8 to 10 ounces each)

3 large red onions, thickly sliced

3 tablespoons balsamic vinegar

Skewer Savvy

To keep the onion slices from coming apart on the grill, thread two bamboo or metal skewers through each slice lengthwise. Be sure to soak the bamboo skewers in water for 30 minutes before using.

In the days of real butcher shops, the hanger was the piece of meat that employees took home for their families and has lovingly been nicknamed the butcher's tenderloin for that reason. It is the traditional cut found on bistro and brasserie menus, and is increasingly easy to find in this country. The steak is extremely flavorful but a bit chewy. It's not that it's tough, it's just not tender. After a New York strip, I'd rather have a hanger steak above all other cuts. This recipe also works nicely with flat iron steak.

In this preparation, the steak gets a marinade, which helps tenderize it a bit, but you can skip that step and go straight to the grill. The grilled onions are a tip of the hat to the caramelized shallots usually served with hanger steaks in France. It's a delightful combination not to be missed.

1. In a glass baking dish large enough to hold the steaks in a single layer, whisk the oil, sherry vinegar, tamari, both mustards and mustard seeds, ginger, garlic, and salt and pepper (to taste) together. Add the steaks and turn to coat. Cover with plastic wrap and refrigerate for at least 4 hours and no more than 8 hours, turning them once or twice.

2. About an hour before you plan to grill, remove the steaks from the marinade. Discard the marinade and pat the steaks as dry as possible with a paper towel.

3. Light a fire in the kamado grill using your favorite method. After about 10 minutes, place the grill rack in position, close the dome, and open the upper and lower dampers all the way. When the temperature reaches 600° F, adjust the dampers to maintain the temperature. Remember, even when grilling, the dome should be closed as much as possible.

4. Place the steaks on the grill along with the onion slices, close the dome, and cook for about 5 minutes per side. This cut of meat really should be served medium rare or medium at most (125° to 140° F). Turn the onions when you turn the steaks.

5. When the steaks are done, remove to a warm platter and let rest for 5 to 10 minutes. Meanwhile, slide the onions off the skewers into a medium bowl, separating the rings. Toss with the balsamic vinegar while the onions are still warm. After the steaks have rested, spoon the onions over the steaks and serve.

Applewood Bacon–Wrapped Filet Mignon with Tarragon Butter

Serves 4

½ cup (1 stick) unsalted butter, softened

2 tablespoons chopped fresh tarragon

½ teaspoon tarragon vinegar

Kosher salt and freshly ground black pepper

8 slices thick-cut applewood-smoked bacon

4 filets mignon, 1½ inches thick (about 10 ounces each)

Kitchen twine

Canadian-Style Steak Seasoning (page 234)

Olive oil for brushing

The filet mignon is cut from the center portion of the beef tenderloin. It is a relatively lean but extremely tender cut of meat. But for all its buttery tenderness, I believe the filet mignon benefits from a little help in the flavor department. So for this recipe, we'll wrap our filets with bacon and serve them with tarragon butter.

1. At least 2 hours before you plan to grill, combine the butter, tarragon, vinegar, and a sprinkling of salt and pepper in a small bowl, using a fork to mash everything together thoroughly. This compound butter will keep, in an airtight container, in the refrigerator for up to a week and up to 3 months in the freezer.

2. Bring a saucepan half full of water to a boil over high heat. Add the bacon, reduce the heat to medium, and blanch for about 5 minutes. Remove using tongs or a slotted spoon and transfer the bacon to paper towels to drain and dry out a bit.

3. At least 30 minutes before you plan to grill, remove the filets from the refrigerator and wrap each with 2 slices of bacon, securing them in place with kitchen twine. Season both sides of the steak generously with steak seasoning, then brush both sides with olive oil.

4. Light a fire in the kamado grill using your favorite method. After about 10 minutes, place the grill rack in position, close the dome, and open the upper and lower dampers all the way. When the temperature reaches between 500° and 600° F, adjust the dampers to maintain the temperature in that range. Remember, even when grilling, the dome should be closed as much as possible.

5. Place the filets on the grill, close the dome, and cook for about 4 minutes. Rotate the steaks 90 degrees and cook for another 2 minutes. Flip the filets and cook for another 6 minutes. Your bacon should be getting crisp at this point and the filets should be medium rare. Filets are always best when served medium rare.

6. Transfer the filets to a platter, place a knob of the tarragon butter on each, and let rest for 5 to 10 minutes before serving.

Carne Asada

Serves 4

1 tablespoon chipotle chile powder

2 teaspoons hot paprika

1 teaspoon ground cumin

1 teaspoon dried oregano

½ teaspoon kosher salt

⅛ teaspoon cayenne pepper

2 cloves garlic, finely chopped

¼ cup olive oil

2 tablespoons fresh lime juice (about 1 lime)

1½ pounds skirt steak

Taco or fajita fixings as desired

The name of this Mexican specialty simply translates as "grilled meat" but that's an understatement. While every town and village has its own version of carne asada, all of them share the inclusion of an exciting mix of pure chile powders and assertive spices. This recipe will rival that of any taco truck or street stand. It is important to use a pure chile powder and not a blended chili powder. Use the grilled meat in tacos or burritos, or throw some peppers and onions on the grill to char as the meat cooks for an outstanding fajita. Or simply serve it with rice and beans.

1. Combine the chipotle powder, paprika, cumin, oregano, salt, cayenne, and garlic. Stir in the olive oil and lime juice. Place the skirt steak in a 1-gallon zip-top plastic bag, add the marinade, and squish around to coat the steak well. Seal the bag and let stand at room temperature for at least 30 minutes (an hour is better) and up to 4 hours.

2. Light a fire in the kamado grill using your favorite method. After about 10 minutes, place the grill rack in position, close the dome, and open the upper and lower dampers all the way. When the temperature reaches 500° F, adjust the dampers to maintain the temperature. Remember, even when grilling, the dome should be closed as much as possible.

3. Place the steak on the grill grate, close the dome, and cook for about 4 minutes per side for medium rare or to your desired degree of doneness.

4. Transfer the steak to a cutting board and let rest for about 5 minutes. Thinly slice the steak across the grain and serve as desired.

When to Turn

When it comes to proteins of any sort, they know when it's time to turn. The protein will relax its grip on the grate when it has taken on the right amount of heat. If you try to turn steak or a piece of chicken and it's having none of it, leave it be until you can turn it without tugging it.

Stupid Easy London Broil

Serves 4 to 6

1 (3- to 3½-pound) flank steak or thick sirloin tip

2 cups Italian salad dressing (homemade is great but store-bought is fine)

2 tablespoons dry sherry

2 teaspoons Worcestershire sauce

1 Granny Smith apple, cored, peeled, and thinly sliced

London broil is not a cut of meat but instead a recipe for marinated flank steak or sirloin tip. Most grocers now have started labeling sirloin tip roast as London broil, and it's a good choice for this recipe—but an even better choice is a flank steak, which seems to absorb the marinade better and, I think, is a little more tender. The apples may seem an odd addition, but they help blend the flavors while the meat is marinating.

I've been preparing this dish since I was in college and it still gets raves whenever it hits the grill. It is imperative that you slice flank steak and sirloin tip thinly, against the grain. Otherwise, you will wind up with a very chewy piece of meat.

1. Cut shallow diagonal slits into one side of the steak. This helps it absorb the marinade better. Combine the dressing, sherry, Worcestershire, and apple slices in a 1-gallon zip-top plastic bag. Add the beef, close the bag, and squish the marinade around the meat. Marinate in the refrigerator for at least 24 hours, but 3 days is optimal.

2. Light a fire in the kamado grill using your favorite method. After about 10 minutes, place the grill rack in position, close the dome, and open the upper and lower dampers all the way. When the temperature reaches 600° F, adjust the dampers to maintain the temperature. Remember, even when grilling, the dome should be closed as much as possible.

3. Remove the meat from the bag; discard the marinade and apples. Pat the meat completely dry with paper towels. Place the steak on the grill, close the dome, and cook for about 8 minutes per side or until the steak gives slightly to the touch and the internal temperature is 140° F for medium doneness, which is best for this tougher cut of meat. Transfer to a warm platter and let rest for 5 to 10 minutes. Slice very thinly across the grain and serve.

Grilled Boneless Short Ribs with Peanut Sauce

Serves 4

1 Serrano chile, seeded

2 shallots, roughly chopped

2 cloves garlic, peeled

2 teaspoons lemongrass paste (available in the produce section of most large supermarkets)

2 tablespoons Asian fish sauce

2 tablespoons fresh lime juice

1 tablespoon toasted sesame oil

2 tablespoons water

¼ teaspoon freshly ground black pepper

1½ to 2 pounds boneless beef short ribs

Metal skewers or wooden skewers soaked in water

PEANUT SAUCE:

1 cup smooth peanut butter

¼ cup tamari

¼ cup fresh lime juice (about 2 limes)

2 tablespoons dark brown sugar

1 teaspoon Asian chili sauce, or more to taste

½ cup hot tap water, or as needed

¼ cup chopped peanuts for garnish

Think Vietnamese satay with big beef flavor. The kamado does a first-rate job of grilling the short ribs, preserving their juiciness while allowing a great char to develop. This comes from the kamado's ability to seal everything inside the dome. Throw in the exciting flavors of Southeast Asia and you've got some heady eating in store. These ribs are delicious both hot and at room temperature.

1. Place the chile, shallots, garlic, and lemongrass in a food processor or blender and pulse 3 to 4 times. Add the fish sauce, lime juice, sesame, oil, water, and black pepper and pulse 2 to 3 times, then blend until the mixture forms a thick paste, about 1 minute.

2. Slice the short ribs lengthwise into ½-inch-thick slabs. Place in a large shallow nonreactive dish and spread the paste over the top, then turn all the pieces to coat well with the paste. Cover and refrigerate overnight.

3. Combine all the peanut sauce ingredients, except the hot water, in a clean food processor or blender. Pulse to combine, then, with the motor running, slowly add the hot water until the sauce is thinned to your liking. You may not need all of the hot water. Pour the sauce into an airtight container and cover until needed, up to several hours.

4. Light a fire in the kamado grill using your favorite method. After about 10 minutes, place the grill rack in position, close the dome, and open the upper and lower dampers all the way. When the temperature reaches 500° F, adjust the dampers to maintain the temperature. Remember, even when grilling, the dome should be closed as much as possible.

5. Remove the meat from the marinade and pat dry. Thread the meat onto the skewers. Place the skewers on the grill grate, close the dome, and cook for about 4 minutes per side for medium rare. The meat should feel like the tip of your nose when pressed.

6. Transfer the skewers to a cutting board and let rest for 10 minutes. Thinly slice the beef against the grain and arrange on a platter. Sprinkle with the chopped nuts and serve with the peanut sauce.

Bacon-Infused Cheeseburgers

Serves 6

1 pound 80% lean ground chuck

½ pound 90% lean ground sirloin

½ pound sliced bacon, cooked to 80% done (don't let it get crispy), drained on paper towels, and finely chopped

Kosher salt and freshly ground black pepper

3 tablespoons unsalted butter, at room temperature

6 hamburger buns

6 slices Swiss cheese

1 ripe avocado, peeled, pitted, thinly sliced, and sprinkled with a little lemon juice

Lettuce, tomato, onion, and condiments of your choice for serving

You've probably seen it on a restaurant menu—the 50/50 burger—where the restaurant has taken raw bacon and ground it together with their beef to form a patty. Works fine for them, not so easy for the home grill master. But I've found a better way of doing it. Cook your bacon until it's about 80% done, then chop it very finely and add it to your ground meat. The smokier the bacon, the better your result will be.

1. Using a light hand, work the meats and bacon together gently. Divide into 6 equal portions and carefully form into six 1-inch-thick patties. Take your thumb and make a good ¼-inch depression in the middle of each patty; this will keep them from puffing up on the grill. Sprinkle the patties on both sides with salt and pepper. Butter the cut sides of the buns.

2. Light a fire in the kamado grill using your favorite method. After about 10 minutes, place the grill rack in position, close the dome, and open the upper and lower dampers all the way. When the temperature reaches 600° F, adjust the dampers to maintain the temperature. Remember, even when grilling, the dome should be closed as much as possible.

3. Place the burgers on the grill and close the dome. Cook 4 to 6 minutes and flip over. Place the cheese on the burgers, close the dome, and cook another 4 to 5 minutes for medium; add a few more minutes for medium well. The burger's internal temperature should be between 140° and 160° F. About a minute or two before the burgers are done, place the buns on the grill, cut side down, to toast.

4. Transfer the burgers to a warm platter. Keep the buns on a separate platter. Let your diners construct their own burgers with the fixings and condiments.

A Better Buffalo Burger

If you use ground buffalo, which is leaner and healthier, instead of ground beef, insert a small piece of ice into the center of eah patty. This will help prevent it from drying out as it cooks, and make your buffalo burger a more satisfying treat.

Gilding The Perfect Beef Burger

For those times when perfect just isn't good enough.

- *Australian Heart Attack*: Australians have been putting over-easy fried eggs on burgers for years. When you bite into a burger topped with a fried egg, the richness of the yolk against the flavor of the beef will drive you crazy.

- *Spicy Bacon-Avocado Burger*: Mix ¼ cup mayonnaise with 1 tablespoon *each* of chopped fresh mint, pure ground chipotle powder, and adobo seasoning. Stir in a squeeze of lemon. Slather your bun with the mayo, top with a burger, and crown with slices of ripe avocado and crisp bacon.

- *New Mexico Green Chile Cheeseburger*: While still on the grill, top your burger with 1 tablespoon chopped roasted Hatch chiles (you can find them canned or frozen) and a slice of Monterey jack cheese and continue cooking until the cheese is melted.

- *Ham-and-Cheese Barbecue Burger*: Place 2 slices of deli ham and a slice of cheddar cheese on the burger when you turn it. Add your favorite barbecue sauce to complete the experience.

- *Paris Burger*: A couple minutes before it comes off the grill, top your burger with 2 slices of brie, then serve with grainy mustard and sliced cornichons.

- *Caramelized Onion Burger*: Thinly slice 2 red onions, then cook in 1 tablespoon unsalted butter over low heat, stirring occasionally, until caramelized, about 30 minutes. Season with a little salt and toss them on your burger.

The Perfect Beef Burger

Serves 6

1½ pounds 80% lean ground chuck

8 ounces 90% lean ground sirloin

Kosher salt and freshly ground black pepper

3 tablespoons unsalted butter, at room temperature

6 good-quality hamburger buns

6 slices of your favorite cheese

6 slices of dead-ripe tomato

6 romaine lettuce leaves

6 thin onion slices

Condiments of your choice

For the beef burger, the meat is key. And if you have a meat grinder and want to go down that road, knock yourself out. Most of us will be extremely satisfied with a mixture of high-quality 80% lean ground chuck and 90% lean ground sirloin. I'm also very big on using grass-fed and grass-finished beef. The flavor is more potent, with a richness that you can't get from chub ground beef.

If cheeseburgers are your thing, take care which cheese you choose—you want one that melts well. That runs the gamut from processed American cheese to cave-aged Gruyère. Let the cheese melt completely and enrobe the patty.

1. Put the meats in a medium bowl and season with salt and pepper. Don't go crazy with salt, because you're going to add more later. With a very light hand, work the meats and seasonings together. Form into patties that are least 1 inch thick and slightly wider than the buns you intend to use, about a third of a pound of meat per patty. Take your thumb and make a good depression about ¼ inch deep in the middle of each patty; this will keep them from puffing up on the grill. Season again with salt and pepper. Slather some butter on the cut sides of your buns.

2. Light a fire in the kamado grill using your favorite method. After about 10 minutes, place the grill rack in position, close the dome, and open the upper and lower dampers all the way. When the temperature reaches 600° F, adjust the dampers to maintain the temperature. Remember, even when grilling, the dome should be closed as much as possible.

3. Place the burgers on the grill and close the dome. Cook 4 to 6 minutes, then turn the burgers, close the dome, and cook for another 4 minutes, which will result in a medium pink doneness. If you want a more well-done burger, cook about 8 minutes per side. If you want to check doneness using an instant-read thermometer, insert it through the side of the patty, not through the top; be sure never to cook a burger to an internal temperature of more than 160° F.

4. If you're using cheese, place the cheese on the patties 1 or 2 minutes after you've turned them. During the last minute of cooking time, set the buns on the grill, cut side down, and grill until lightly toasted.

5. Transfer the burgers to a warm platter. Keep the buns on a separate platter. Let your diners construct their own burgers with the fixings and condiments.

Banh Mi "Burgers"

Serves 4

BURGERS:

1½ pounds ground pork

2 tablespoons finely chopped fresh basil

1 tablespoon grated lime zest

1 tablespoon minced garlic

3 green onions, finely chopped

1 tablespoon Asian fish sauce

1 tablespoon sugar

1 teaspoon freshly ground black pepper

1 teaspoon kosher salt

PICKLED CARROTS AND DAIKON:

½ cup shredded carrots

½ cup shredded daikon

¼ cup rice wine vinegar

¼ cup sugar

1 tablespoon fresh lime juice

1 teaspoon kosher salt

HOT CHILE MAYONNAISE:

1 cup good-quality mayonnaise

2 green onions, finely chopped

1 teaspoon to 1 tablespoon sriracha sauce, depending on how spicy you want it

TO FINISH:

4 (6-inch) Chicago rolls or 1 French baguette, cut into 6-inch pieces, sliced horizontally

Pickled jalapeño slices

Sprigs fresh cilantro

I am a big fan of the Vietnamese sandwich *banh mi,* with its unique fusion of French and Southeast Asian ingredients, and decided to "burgerize" its delicious combination of flavors. The pickled carrots and radishes are an important part of this burger experience and should not be skipped. Also, the quality of the bread has to be first rate. The flavors scream summer and yield a welcome cooling effect at the end of a hot day.

1. Two hours before you plan to grill, gently mix the burger ingredients together in a medium bowl. Divide the mixture into 4 equal hunks. Line a rimmed baking sheet with wax paper. Wet your hands and form each hunk of pork into an oblong patty. Just like with hamburgers, make an indention with your finger on each oblong burger. Cover with plastic wrap and refrigerate for 2 hours.

2. Meanwhile, in a small nonreactive bowl, combine the pickled carrots and daikon ingredients together. Let sit at room temperature until ready to use or cover and refrigerate up to 1 day.

3. In another small bowl, whisk the mayonnaise, green onions, and sriracha together. Cover and refrigerate for up to 1 day.

4. Light a fire in the kamado grill using your favorite method. After about 10 minutes, place the grill rack in position, close the dome, and open the upper and lower dampers all the way. When the temperature reaches 500° F, adjust the dampers to maintain the temperature. Remember, even when grilling, the dome should be closed as much as possible.

5. Remove the pork burgers from the refrigerator. Open the dome, allow the temperature to drop slightly, and adjust the dampers to maintain a temperature of 400° F. (Pork likes a little less heat than most grilled items.) Place the burgers on the grill grate and close the dome. Cook the burgers until an instant-read thermometer inserted in the center registers 160° F. This being pork, they need to be fully cooked. During the last couple of minutes, place the bread on the grill, cut side down, to toast a little. When done, remove the patties and bread to a platter.

6. To assemble the sandwiches, slather the bottom side of the bread with the mayonnaise. Top each with a pork patty, then top the pork patty with some drained pickled carrots and daikon, a few jalapeño slices, and sprigs of cilantro. Finish the sandwiches by placing the top bun on, and serve.

How Much Char Do You Like with Your Burger?

Do you like your burger right over the flames, cooking up a set of delicious grill marks? Or do you prefer the perfectly caramelized surface you get with a flat-top griddle? Can't decide? You can have them both with the kamado. Many kamado grill manufacturers offer a griddle accessory. A cast-iron skillet or griddle can acomplish the same result. Put the skillet on to preheat as you close the dome for the kamado to reach grilling temperature. The skillet needs to get super hot. If a drop of water sizzles and evaporates on it, you are ready. Perfect burger crust and charcoal flavor to boot, how great is that?

Sweet Tea-Brined Bone-in Pork Chops with Low Country Mustard Sauce

Serves 4

INJECTION:

¼ cup apple juice

¼ cup brewed sweet tea

¼ cup water

Juice of 1 lemon

2 teaspoons salt

4 bone-in pork chops,
1 to 1½ inches thick

Low Country Mustard Sauce
(page 245) for glazing

Pork chops are delicious on the grill, but they need some help to stay moist. Just cooking them on a kamado helps immensely, but a flavor injection of apple juice and sweet tea guarantees succulence.

1. In a small bowl, combine the injection ingredients, stirring until the salt dissolves. Using a flavor injector, inject the pork chops multiple times with the solution until it appears that they can hold no more (see Using a Flavor Injector, page 241). You'll know this when the solution starts pouring out of the holes where you've injected the pork previously. Set aside at room temperature until ready to grill, but no more than 1 hour.

2. Light a fire in the kamado grill using your favorite method. After about 10 minutes, place the grill rack in position, close the dome, and open the upper and lower dampers all the way. When the temperature reaches 450° F, adjust the dampers to maintain the temperature. Remember, even when grilling, the dome should be closed as much as possible.

3. Place the chops on the grill grate and close the dome. Grill the chops for about 10 minutes. Turn the chops and lightly brush with the mustard sauce. Close the dome and cook until the pork gives a little to the touch and the internal temperature is 140° F, about another 8 minutes.

4. Brush the chops lightly on both sides with the sauce again and transfer to a platter. Let rest for 5 to 10 minutes and serve.

Bacon-Wrapped Pork Tenderloin with Rosemary

Serves 4 to 6

1 tablespoon finely minced fresh rosemary

½ teaspoon kosher salt

½ teaspoon freshly ground black pepper

2 pork tenderloins (about 1 pound each)

12 slices thinly sliced hickory-smoked bacon (about ¾ pound)

It's the layering of lean meat, fatty smoked bacon, and assertive rosemary that makes this recipe special. Rosemary is a great herb to use with any pork cut, including pork chops, ribs, and pork roasts. The bacon is used here strictly for flavor, not to keep the pork moist. Please don't overcook the pork. A nice medium doneness is perfect, an internal temperature of 140° F when it is pulled off the grill. (See photo on page 96.)

1. In a small bowl, combine the rosemary, salt, and pepper. Set aside.

2. Trim the excess fat and silverskin from the tenderloins. Season with the rosemary mixture, rubbing it into the meat. Place 6 slices of the bacon on a cutting board. Place one of the tenderloins in the middle of the bacon slices and wrap the bacon slices around it. Repeat with the second tenderloin and remaining bacon. Let the pork sit at room temperature for about 15 minutes before grilling.

3. Light a fire in the kamado grill using your favorite method. After about 10 minutes, place the grill rack in position, close the dome, and open the upper and lower dampers all the way. When the temperature reaches 500° F, adjust the dampers to maintain the temperature. Remember, even when grilling, the dome should be closed as much as possible.

4. Place the pork on the grill grate, close the dome, and close the dampers halfway. You want to get a fast char, but because of the pork's longer cooking time, the grill temperature should be around 350° to 400° F. Grill the pork, turning it every 15 minutes, until the pork is firm but gives a little to the touch and the internal temperature is 140° F. The temperature will continue to rise while the meat rests.

5. Transfer the pork to a platter and let rest for about 10 minutes. Cut into 2-inch-thick slices and serve.

"Burnt Fingers" Lamb Rib Chops

Serves 4 to 6
as a main course

3 tablespoons stone-ground mustard

1 large clove garlic, peeled

2 tablespoons balsamic vinegar

½ teaspoon kosher salt

Freshly ground black pepper

½ cup extra-virgin olive oil

¼ cup slivered fresh basil

16 rib lamb chops, trimmed of excess fat (this is two half racks of lamb, about 4 pounds total)

Chopped fresh flat-leaf parsley for garnish

I must say that Italian Catholics really know how to throw a wedding, and that's how I first encountered this dish. At a wedding I attended in Ho-Ho-Kus, New Jersey, one of the hors d'oeuvres was single little grilled lamb rib chops that you ate with your fingers—thus the "burnt fingers."

These make for great party food as a first course or buffet selection, but why limit it to when company is coming? Buying racks of lamb and then cutting them into individual ribs is more cost effective than buying them already cut into ribs. And if my mother, the "cook-it-to-death queen," liked these ribs rare to medium rare, I know you will too. The meat is succulent and rich and the grill adds bunches of flavor. And yes, eat them with your fingers!

1. Place the mustard, garlic, vinegar, salt, and pepper to taste in a blender and pulse to combine. With the machine running, slowly pour in the olive oil. Pour the mixture into a small bowl and stir in the basil.

2. Place the chops in a 2½-gallon zip-top plastic bag. Add the marinade and squish around to evenly coat the chops. Seal the bag and refrigerate for 4 hours. Remove from the refrigerator at least 30 minutes before cooking.

3. Light a fire in the kamado grill using your favorite method. After about 10 minutes, place the grill rack in position, close the dome, and open the upper and lower dampers all the way. When the temperature reaches 500° F, adjust the dampers to maintain the temperature. Remember, even when grilling, the dome should be closed as much as possible.

4. Remove the chops from the marinade and wipe off any excess. Place the chops on the grill grate, close the dome, and cook until the chops feel like the tip of your nose when pressed, about 5 minutes per side. This will result in a medium-rare chop with an internal temperature of about 130° F.

5. Transfer the chops to a platter and let rest for 5 to10 minutes. Sprinkle with the parsley and serve.

Mediterranean Lamb Burgers

Serves 6

2 pounds ground lamb, preferably from the shoulder or leg

1 cup finely chopped fresh white mushrooms

1 tablespoon finely minced garlic

2 teaspoons finely minced fresh rosemary

1 tablespoon kosher salt

1 tablespoon coarsely ground black pepper

6 slices fontina cheese

3 tablespoons unsalted butter, at room temperature

6 whole-wheat buns or whole-wheat pita breads

Tzatziki Sauce
(optional; page 254)

Few things invigorate the senses more than the aroma of lamb being grilled—it's positively intoxicating. These burgers are a bit of a riff on the lamb burgers at San Francisco's famous Fog City Diner.

1. In a large bowl, using a light hand, gently work the lamb, mushrooms, garlic, rosemary, salt, and pepper together. Divide the mixture into 6 equal portions and gently form into 1-inch-thick patties. Take your thumb and make a good ¼-inch depression in the middle of each patty; this will keep them from puffing up on the grill. Refrigerate until ready to cook.

2. Light a fire in the kamado grill using your favorite method. After about 10 minutes, place the grill rack in position, close the dome, and open the upper and lower dampers all the way. When the temperature reaches 500° F, adjust the dampers to maintain the temperature. Remember, even when grilling, the dome should be closed as much as possible.

3. Place the patties on the grill, close the dome, and cook to your desired doneness. I'm a firm believer that lamb is best at medium, still nice and pink in the center. That should be 5 to 7 minutes per side, or an internal temperature of 140° F. When you turn the burgers, place a slice of cheese on top of each. With about 2 minutes left in the cooking time, butter the buns and place them, cut side down, on the grill to toast.

4. When done, transfer the burgers and buns to a warm platter. Place a burger on the bottom half of each bun and top with the tzatziki.

The 10 Secrets of Burger Nirvana

1. Buy the best quality meat you can find, no matter what kind of burger you're making.

2. Make good-size patties and handle them so they just hold together. The more you compact any burger, the greater the chances that it will end up tough. My patties are about ⅓ pound each and 1 inch thick.

3. Don't let your burgers suffer from "swollen belly syndrome," where they puff up in the middle on the grill, then shrink and cook unevenly. It's a simple fix: Shape your patty, then make an indention in the center of it with your thumb.

4. Refrigerate the patties for at least 30 minutes before putting them on the grill; 1 hour is even better. This helps the patties hold together and cook more evenly.

5. Burgers get a lot of their flavor from the caramelization that develops as they sit on a sizzling hot grill, so let the grill grate get really hot before putting the burgers on it.

6. Cook your burgers with the dome down.

7. Turn the burgers only once. Too much turning interferes with the caramelization and makes them dry.

8. *Never* press on the patties. All you're doing is pushing out flavorful juices.

9. Use good-quality buns; toasting them boosts the flavor of your burgers by a mile.

10. Don't overdo the condiments and fixings. Let the flavor of the burger shine, with just a few well-selected add-ons to elevate the overall experience.

Venison Steaks with Cranberry and Orange

Serves 4

4 boneless venison loin steaks, 1 inch thick (4 to 6 ounces each)

1 cup canned cranberry-orange crushed fruit for chicken (look for Ocean Spray), divided

½ cup dry red wine

2 tablespoons Dijon mustard

4 cloves garlic, minced

2 tablespoons fresh rosemary leaves, chopped

½ teaspoon freshly ground black pepper

This recipe hails from the areas north and west of Akron, Ohio, where there seems to be more deer-processing centers than grocery stores. It helps to know a deer hunter, but nowadays farm-raised venison is easy to find in specialty food stores and butcher shops. Venison is extremely lean, whether farm raised or wild, and a very healthy red meat. When cooking venison on other types of grills, you have to be very careful not to overcook it. With the kamado's moisture-lock seal, grilling venison has never been easier. The combination of sweet and tart really does the venison justice in this recipe. It's also delicious with pork and chicken.

1. Place the steaks in a 1-gallon zip-top plastic bag. Pour in ½ cup of the mixed fruit, the wine, mustard, garlic, rosemary, and pepper and squish around to coat the venison. Seal the bag and refrigerate for at least 4 hours or overnight, turning the bag several times.

2. Light a fire in the kamado grill using your favorite method. After about 10 minutes, place the grill rack in position, close the dome, and open the upper and lower dampers all the way. When the temperature reaches 400° F, adjust the dampers to maintain the temperature. Remember, even when grilling, the dome should be closed as much as possible.

3. Take the steaks out of the bag and discard the marinade. Lightly pat the steaks dry with paper towels, place them on the grill, and close the dome. Cook for 5 minutes, turn, close the dome, and cook 4 to 5 minutes longer. You don't want to overcook venison. A nice medium-rare to medium doneness is perfect. The steaks should give easily when touched but offer some resistance. An instant-read thermometer inserted at the thickest point should register 140° F. Transfer the steaks to a warm platter and serve with a dollop of the remaining fruit on top of each.

What Goes with Game?

For veggie pairings with grilled wild (or even farm-raised) game, try turnips, cabbage, chestnuts, mushrooms, and onions. In the South, a bowl of hot, generously buttered grits or rice is always welcome, and most any chutney or pepper relish is extremely good.

"Spineless" (Butterflied) Chicken with Lemon and Herbs

Serves 4

1 chicken (3 to 4 pounds)

Kosher salt and freshly ground black pepper

¼ cup chopped fresh flat-leaf parsley

1 tablespoon chopped fresh oregano

1 tablespoon chopped fresh rosemary

1 tablespoon chopped fresh thyme

1 tablespoon chopped fresh basil

4 cloves garlic, pressed

½ cup fresh lemon juice (from 2 to 4 lemons)

½ cup olive oil

This is my favorite way to cook chicken. When you remove the backbone and flatten the chicken, it cooks almost like a steak. Why buy a store-bought roast chicken when you can put this on your table? It's also delightful cold the next day, making it an excellent choice for a picnic or tailgate.

1. Place the chicken on a cutting board, breast side down. Using poultry shears or kitchen scissors, make a cut on one side of the backbone, from the neck to the tail. Duplicate that on the other side. Remove the backbone (put it in a zip-top plastic bag and throw it in the freezer; after you make this enough times, you can make chicken broth with them). Open the bird like a book and press down on each side. Turn the chicken over and press on both sides again. You will hear joints pop, but the chicken should be somewhat flat. Season it liberally on both sides with salt and pepper, and place in a 2½-gallon zip-top plastic bag.

2. In a small bowl, whisk the herbs, garlic, and lemon juice together, then whisk in the oil. Pour this mixture over the chicken and squish it around to coat the chicken. Seal the bag and lay the bag flat in the refrigerator to marinate for at least 24 hours and up to 48 hours. Be sure to turn the bag over several times. Remove the chicken from the refrigerator and its marinade at least 30 minutes before you plan to cook.

3. Light a fire in the kamado grill using your favorite method. After about 10 minutes, place the grill rack in position, close the dome, and open the upper and lower dampers all the way. When the temperature reaches 350° F, adjust the dampers to maintain the temperature. Remember, even when grilling, the dome should be closed as much as possible.

4. Pat the chicken dry and place the bird, skin side down, on the grill, close the dome, and cook for 12 to 15 minutes. Turn, close the dome, and cook about another 15 minutes or until the internal temperature at the thigh, away from the bone, registers 165° F on an instant-read thermometer. If the chicken begins to burn, remove it from the grill and adjust the heat downward, then return the chicken to the grill. Remove to a cutting board, let rest for 10 minutes, cut into serving pieces, and serve.

Boneless Chicken Breasts and the Kamado

I'm not a big fan of boneless, skinless chicken breasts, but I know many people are. Feel free to use your favorite recipes with the kamado. Build a 500° F fire, put the breasts on, close the dome, and they'll be done in about 10 minutes (be sure to turn them once).

Here's a time-saving tip. When I do grill boneless, skinless chicken breasts, I'll cook up a whole grill full of them. I let them cool, then vacuum-pack and freeze them. A quick dip of the bag in boiling water and they are as good as the day they were grilled, ready to be used in salads and sandwiches. For me, this maximizes the investment of my time and charcoal.

Bone-in Herbed Goat Cheese-Stuffed Chicken Breasts with Pear Preserves

Serves 4

4 ounces fresh soft goat cheese

1 tablespoon finely chopped fresh tarragon

1 tablespoon finely chopped fresh parsley

1 tablespoon finely chopped fresh chives

1 teaspoon finely chopped fresh oregano

1 tablespoon extra-virgin olive oil, plus more for brushing

Kosher salt and freshly ground black pepper

4 bone-in chicken breast halves

Kitchen twine or toothpicks

½ cup pear preserves or more as needed

Dash of vanilla extract

Friend and James Beard Award–winning chef Ben Barker routinely has a goat cheese-stuffed chicken breast on the menu at his Durham, North Carolina, restaurant, Magnolia Grill. I've simplified his method and serve it with vanilla-laced pear preserves. Goat cheese seems to have an affinity for chicken, and adding the smoke of a charcoal fire to the mix further enhances the pairing. It's fine to use store-bought pear preserves but, of course, homemade will make this even better, if you have them. This is quite an elegant dish—perfect for Mother's Day.

1. In a small bowl, mash the goat cheese, herbs, olive oil, and a sprinkling of salt and pepper together with a fork until thoroughly combined.
2. One at a time, take the chicken breasts and sit each one on its rib bones. Make an incision horizontally almost through the breast. Season the breasts with salt and pepper, then divide the goat cheese mixture among the breasts. Fold the breasts back together and tie a couple of loops around each breast or insert a toothpick or two to hold each breast together. Cover with plastic wrap and refrigerate for 24 hours.
2. In a small saucepan, heat the pear preserves over low heat until loose. Add the vanilla and taste, adding more if you like. Set aside. (Any leftovers are great on toasted bread.)
3. Light a fire in the kamado grill using your favorite method. After about 10 minutes, place the grill rack in position, close the dome, and open the upper and lower dampers all the way. When the temperature reaches 500° F, adjust the dampers to maintain the temperature. Remember, even when grilling, the dome should be closed as much as possible.
4. Remove the breasts from the refrigerator and brush both sides with olive oil. Place on the grill grate, skin side down, and close the dome. Cook for about 10 minutes, then turn over and cook another 10 minutes. When the chicken is pressed, it should feel somewhat firm, and an instant-read thermometer inserted in the center should read 165° F.
5. Transfer the breasts to a platter, pull out the twine or toothpicks, and serve with at least a tablespoon of pear preserves over the top of each breast.

Bone-in Chicken Thighs with Mexican Adobo and "Golf" Sauce

Serves 6

ADOBO:

6 ancho chiles
(about 2 ounces)

6 cloves garlic, chopped

Grated zest of 1 lime

¼ cup fresh lime juice
(about 2 limes)

2 tablespoons chopped fresh oregano

1 tablespoon maple syrup
(grade B preferred)

Kosher salt and freshly ground black pepper

6 bone-in, skin-on chicken thighs

Kitchen twine

GOLF SAUCE:

1 cup good-quality mayonnaise

¾ cup ketchup

1 tablespoon Worcestershire sauce

2 teaspoons yellow mustard

Kosher salt and freshly ground black pepper to taste

This is a bit of a Latin American mash-up; the chicken is marinated in a traditional Mexican seasoning mixture, then grilled and served with a Costa Rican sauce. The mildly hot adobo gets mellowed by the golf sauce. When I photographed Sandra Gutierrez's wonderful cookbook, *Latin American Street Food,* she explained the genesis of golf sauce to me. It seems the sweet and savory sauce started as a popular condiment for fries and tacos in the golf clubs of Costa Rica. This recipe will make more sauce than you need for this. It will keep up to two weeks in the refrigerator—and, in addition to chicken, fries, and tacos, it's also delicious with shrimp.

I like chicken thighs for grilling. They always result in a tender, moist bite and have enough personality to hold their own against stout seasonings. I like to tie them into bundles for even cooking.

1. Fill a small saucepan halfway with water and bring to a boil. Add the chiles, remove from the heat, and let steep until the chiles are soft and flexible, about 1 hour. Remove them from the pan, reserving the water; discard any stems and seeds. Place the chiles in a blender along with the garlic, lime zest and juice, oregano, maple syrup, and 1 cup of the chile soaking liquid. Blend until smooth; season to taste with salt and pepper.

2. Place the thighs in a 1-gallon zip-top plastic bag. Add the adobo and squish it around the chicken. Seal the bag and refrigerate at least 4 hours, or overnight.

3. In a small bowl, whisk the golf sauce ingredients together. Refrigerate in an airtight container until ready to use.

4. Remove the chicken from the refrigerator at least 30 minutes before cooking. Wipe off as much adobo as you can. Discard the adobo. For each thigh, tuck the meat around the bone and make two loops around each with kitchen twine to form a little trussed thigh.

5. Light a fire in the kamado grill using your favorite method. After about 10 minutes, place the grill rack in position, close the dome, and open the upper and lower dampers all the way. When the temperature reaches 400° F, adjust the dampers to maintain the temperature. Remember, even when grilling, the dome should be closed as much as possible.

6. Place the thighs on the grill grate and close the dome. Cook, turning once, until the skin is crisp and the internal temperature is 165° to 170° F, about 20 minutes total. Transfer the thighs to a platter and let rest for 5 minutes. Cut away the twine and serve with the golf sauce on the side.

Best Ever Turkey Burgers

Serves 6

1 pound ground turkey breast

1 pound ground dark-meat turkey

½ cup minced oil-packed sun-dried tomatoes

¼ cup minced pitted green olives

¼ cup balsamic vinegar

¼ cup dry red wine

Kosher salt and freshly ground black pepper

12 thin slices Parmesan cheese (use a vegetable peeler to get these slices)

3 tablespoons unsalted butter, at room temperature

6 onion or focaccia rolls, sliced in half

2 cups baby spinach, drizzled with a little extra-virgin olive oil and balsamic vinegar and tossed

'm not a big fan of turkey burgers. Most of the ones I've had are pretty dry and tasteless. But I know that I should be eating more ground turkey, so I set out to develop a turkey burger that's really awesome. My most avid haters of ground turkey love this burger. The mixture of the turkey, tomatoes, olives, vinegar, and red wine brings flavor and moisture to the patty. Also note that this burger cooks at a lower temperature to keep it from drying out.

1. Put the ground turkey, tomatoes, olives, vinegar, wine, and salt and pepper to taste in a large bowl. Using a light hand, work all the ingredients together. Divide into 6 equal portions and form into 1-inch-thick patties. Take your thumb and make a good ¼-inch depression in the middle of each patty; this will keep them from puffing up on the grill. Refrigerate until ready to cook.

2. Light a fire in the kamado grill using your favorite method. After about 10 minutes, place the grill rack in position, close the dome, and open the upper and lower dampers all the way. When the temperature reaches 450° F, adjust the dampers to maintain the temperature. Remember, even when grilling, the dome should be closed as much as possible.

3. Place the burgers on the grill, close the dome, and cook for about 6 minutes. Flip the burgers over, close the dome, and cook at least another 6 minutes. Turkey burgers must be thoroughly cooked but not overcooked, so use an instant-read thermometer to check their internal temperature, which needs to be at least 165° F and can go as high as 180° F without ruining the burger. Insert the thermometer into the side of the burger, not through the top. During the last 2 minutes of cooking, place two slices of Parmesan on each patty, then butter the rolls, and place them, cut side down, on the grill to toast.

4. Transfer the burgers and buns to separate platters. Place one burger on the bottom half of each bun. Top with the spinach mixture and serve immediately.

Black Cherry and Truffle Balsamic-Glazed Duck Breasts

Serves 4

4 skin-on boneless duck breasts (6 to 8 ounces each), any excess fat trimmed away

1 tablespoon kosher salt

1 teaspoon freshly ground black pepper

1 teaspoon chopped fresh thyme

1 teaspoon chopped fresh rosemary

1 bay leaf, crumbled

BLACK CHERRY AND TRUFFLE BALSAMIC GLAZE:

½ cup truffle-infused balsamic glaze (found in the vinegar section of most supermarkets)

½ cup black cherry preserves

Fruit, especially a dark, jammy fruit, is a natural pairing with duck. The meat itself is so rich and flavorful that a dark fruit like black cherry both complements and heightens the duck's flavor. Couple it with some truffle magic and the mellow sweetness of balsamic vinegar and you've got a dish that's a showstopper but easy enough to enjoy on a weeknight.

Grilling duck breast is all about letting the layer of fat under the skin render. Doing so yields a crispy, charred skin that contrasts deliciously with the rare, succulent duck meat. A word of warning: This is going to generate a lot of smoke and, on most grills, flare-ups. The kamado will contain the smoke and deposit that flavor on the duck, which is a good thing. The kamado's damper system will keep flare-ups to a minimum; simply close the dampers as needed. You want the skin of the duck to be a nice, rich dark brown, but not burnt. If you think the skin is browning too rapidly, move the breasts to the outside edges of the grill and adjust the temperature downward. If you have to take the breasts off the grill for a moment to wait for the fire to cool, that's perfectly okay. If you purchase *magret de canard* (duck breast from the Moulard breed), add 5 minutes to the skin-side-down cooking time.

1. Lightly score the skin side of the duck breasts in a crisscross pattern but be careful not to cut all the way into the meat. In a small bowl, combine the salt, pepper, thyme, rosemary, and bay leaf; rub the mixture on the skin of the duck breasts. Refrigerate the breasts for 2 to 4 hours or let stand at room temperature for about 1 hour.

2. Meanwhile, make the glaze. In a small saucepan, combine the balsamic glaze and preserves. Place over medium heat and cook until the preserves have just melted; stir to combine. Taste the glaze. If you feel it is too sweet, add a touch more vinegar, or if it's too acidic, a bit more preserves. Remove from the heat and keep warm.

3. Light a fire in the kamado grill using your favorite method. After about 10 minutes, place the grill rack in position, close the dome, and open the upper and lower dampers all the way. When the temperature reaches 400° F, adjust the dampers to maintain the temperature. Remember, even when grilling, the dome should be closed as much as possible.

4. Be prepared to adjust the dampers if you get flare-ups; you can also move the breasts to cooler areas of the grill. (By the way, I have found that spritzing the duck-fat flare-ups with water just seems to move the

flaming fat to a different location.) Place the duck breasts, skin side down, on the grill, close the dome, and cook for 8 to 10 minutes, then turn them 90 degrees and cook for another 3 minutes. (Cooking the duck breast skin side down for the greater portion of the total cooking time will render much of the fat between the skin and the meat and also make the skin crispy.) At this point, the duck breasts should yield easily to the touch. For me, duck is better rare or medium rare; these times should give you a medium-rare finish. Turn the breasts skin side up, completely close the dampers, and brush the skin lightly with the glaze. Close the dome for about 2 minutes.

5. Transfer the duck breasts to a platter, drizzle with more of the glaze, and pass any remaining glaze at the table.

Beach-Style Grilled Sardines

Serves 6 as a first course, or 8 to 10 as part of a tapas buffet

2 pounds fresh sardines (about 24), cleaned and dressed, but left whole

Olive oil

Kosher or coarse salt and freshly ground black pepper

2 tablespoons chopped fresh parsley, plus more for garnish

1 sprig fresh rosemary for each fish

1 cup halved cherry tomatoes (a mixture of different types is nice)

½ cup pitted olives (try Kalamata or a French or Greek blend)

3 tablespoons fruity extra-virgin olive oil

2 teaspoons sherry wine vinegar

2 lemons, quartered

Europeans have delighted in sardines forever. In this country, we think of a sardine as something packed in a tin. Boy, are we missing out! Fresh and frozen sardines have become widely available here, and I hope you will give them a try. They have a deep, rich flavor that makes them perfect for grilling over coals. My Portuguese friend Joseph Theresa got me believing in the beauty of a grilled sardine. When he was living in Portugal, he would cook them at the beach over a driftwood fire, skewered on a stick. This recipe is a mash-up of Joseph's method and a recipe from a fish house on the Amalfi Coast. Simplicity is the key to great sardines. Serve with very cold white Portuguese wine to complete the experience.

1. Arrange the sardines on a rimmed baking pan. Drizzle them with olive oil, then use your hands to coat them fully with it. Sprinkle with salt, pepper, and the parsley. Place a rosemary sprig in the cavity of each fish.

2. Light a fire in the kamado grill using your favorite method. After about 10 minutes, place the grill rack in position, close the dome, and open the upper and lower dampers all the way. When the temperature reaches 500° F, adjust the dampers to maintain the temperature. Remember, even when grilling, the dome should be closed as much as possible.

3. While the kamado is coming to temperature, toss the tomatoes, olives, fruity olive oil, and vinegar together; set aside.

4. Place the sardines on the grill, close the dome, and cook for 3 minutes. Gently roll them over and cook until the fish is firm and just thinking about flaking, about another 3 minutes. Look into the cavity to gauge the doneness. You can also take a cake tester and push into the thickest part of the fish. Remove the tester and touch it to your lip. If it is warm, the fish should be done.

5. Transfer the sardines to a warm platter. Squeeze the lemon quarters over the fish and top with the tomato mixture and parsley. The sardines can be served hot off the kamado or at room temperature.

Herb-Grilled Whole Mountain Trout

Serves 4

4 small whole rainbow, golden, or mountain trout, heads removed, scaled, and gutted

½ cup mayonnaise

8 sprigs fresh thyme

8 sprigs fresh oregano

4 sprigs fresh rosemary

8 (¼-inch-thick) lemon slices

2 teaspoons chopped garlic (optional)

Extra-virgin olive oil, as needed

Dreaming of sitting beside a mountain stream at sunset? This recipe will transport you there. The kamado is the perfect tool for grilling whole fish, delivering beautifully charred, crispy skin and succulent, moist flesh. If ramps are in season, sauté a mess of them to serve alongside for the perfect Smoky Mountain culinary "high."

1. Coat the outside of each trout with the mayonnaise. In the body cavity of each trout, stuff 2 thyme sprigs, 2 oregano sprigs, 1 rosemary sprig, and 2 lemon slices. Add a little garlic if you like. Refrigerate until ready to grill.

2. Light a fire in the kamado grill using your favorite method. After about 10 minutes, place the grill rack in position, close the dome, and open the upper and lower dampers all the way. When the temperature reaches 500° F, adjust the dampers to maintain the temperature. Remember, even when grilling, the dome should be closed as much as possible.

3. Place the trout on the grill grate, close the dome, and cook for 5 to 6 minutes on each side, depending on the thickness of the trout. To check doneness, take a cake tester and push it into the thickest part of the fish. Remove the tester and touch it to your lip. If it is warm, the fish should be done.

4. Transfer the trout to a platter and let them rest for 5 minutes. Serve with a drizzle of first-rate extra-virgin olive oil.

Grilled Whole Fish with Lemony Mint Drizzle

Serves 4

LEMONY MINT DRIZZLE:

¾ cup extra-virgin olive oil

3 tablespoons fresh lemon juice

2 tablespoons white wine vinegar

1 small clove garlic, finely chopped or run through a press

Sea salt or kosher salt

½ cup chopped fresh mint

1 (2½- to 3-pound) whole striped bass or red snapper, scaled and gutted

1 recipe of Karl's "Fish Bath" (page 133)

The kamado makes grilling whole fish a whole lot easier. It allows you to get the heat you need to char and crisp the fish's skin, and keeping the dome down as you cook guarantees a moist outcome. This recipe has vibrant flavors that don't mask the delicate taste of the fish. You can use this recipe for most any whole small to medium-size fish, and it's even good with thick-cut fillets like salmon, tuna, grouper, halibut, or cod.

1. At least an hour (but not more than 2 hours) before you plan to use it, make the mint drizzle. In a medium bowl, whisk the olive oil, lemon juice, vinegar, garlic, and salt to taste together. Stir in the mint and set aside at room temperature.

2. Light a fire in the kamado grill using your favorite method. After about 10 minutes, place the grill rack in position, close the dome, and open the upper and lower dampers all the way. When the temperature reaches 500° F, adjust the dampers to maintain the temperature. Remember, even when grilling, the dome should be closed as much as possible.

3. Rinse the fish in cold water and dry with paper towels. Brush both sides with the fish bath. Place the fish on the grill grate and close the dome. Grill for 8 to 10 minutes, brushing with the fish bath once about halfway through. Using a large metal spatula or two smaller ones, lift the fish from the grill and carefully turn it over. Brush it with the fish bath now and again once more, about halfway through cooking this side, which will probably take another 8 to 10 minutes in all. To check doneness, take a cake tester and push it into the thickest part of the fish. Remove the tester and touch it to your lip. If it is warm, the fish should be done.

4. Transfer the fish to a large serving platter and serve with the mint drizzle on the side.

Pick a Pack of Peppadews

The Peppadew is a sweet, piquant pepper originally cultivated in the Limpopo area of South Africa. About the size of a cherry tomato, it is sold pickled or brined, which is what you want for this recipe. Check the olive section of your supermarket and most all olive bars will have them. A word of warning, though: Once you taste one, you'll want to always have some on hand. Try stuffing them with goat or blue cheese for a fabulous nibble.

Grilled Swordfish with Karl's "Fish Bath" and Mediterranean Mélange

Serves 6

KARL'S "FISH BATH":

¼ cup (½ stick) unsalted butter

½ cup tamari

½ cup Worcestershire sauce

2 tablespoons toasted sesame oil

1 tablespoon garlic powder

1 tablespoon Italian seasoning blend

1 tablespoon cracked black peppercorns

1 teaspoon ground ginger

1 teaspoon dried basil

THE MÉLANGE:

2 tablespoons olive oil, divided

1 large red onion, cut into slivers

1 cup cremini mushrooms, julienned

½ cup Kalamata olives, pitted and cut into slivers

½ cup Peppadew chile peppers, seeded and cut into strips

1 (13.75-ounce) can artichoke hearts, drained and each heart cut into eighths

¼ cup capers, drained

¼ cup slivered oil-packed sun-dried tomatoes

6 (8-ounce) swordfish steaks

¼ cup crumbled feta cheese or to taste

I shared Karl Knudsen's recipe for smoked tuna in the smoking chapter (page 78), and this one is a keeper as well. I've made this dish many times and the most common reaction I get is, "This is the best meal I think I've ever eaten." I agree.

The "fish bath" is not a marinade, but more of a mop, layering an extra bit of flavor on the fish. The recipe makes more than you will need but it will keep in an airtight container in the refrigerator for several weeks (believe me, you'll use it up long before then). Just gently reheat it before you use it so the butter is liquid.

Serve this over pasta or risotto for a meal that you'll be sad to see the end of.

1. In a small saucepan over medium heat, melt the butter, then add the remaining "fish bath" ingredients and whisk to combine. Cook, stirring, for about 2 minutes. Remove from the heat and let cool.

2. Make the mélange. In a large skillet over medium heat, heat 1 tablespoon of the olive oil, then add the onion and cook until lightly caramelized, about 20 minutes, stirring frequently. Throw in the mushrooms and cook until soft, about 5 minutes. Add the olives, Peppadews, artichokes, capers, and sun-dried tomatoes, drizzle the mixture with the remaining 1 tablespoon olive oil, and cook until everything is heated through, 5 to 10 minutes, stirring every few minutes so nothing sticks. Remove from the heat. Reserve at room temperature if you'll be serving that day or refrigerate in an airtight container for up to 2 days. Rewarm before serving.

3. Light a fire in the kamado grill using your favorite method. After about 10 minutes, place the grill rack in position, close the dome, and open the upper and lower dampers all the way. When the temperature reaches 500° F, adjust the dampers to maintain the temperature. Remember, even when grilling, the dome should be closed as much as possible.

4. Brush the fish on both sides with the fish bath. Place the steaks on the grill grate, close the dome, and cook, basting every 2 minutes with the fish bath. Your grill temperature will drop but that's okay. Swordfish should be firm to the touch when done, but you can also test it by inserting a cake tester; remove it and touch it to your lip—if it is warm, the fish is ready to serve. It should take about 4 minutes per side.

5. Transfer the fish to a platter and cover with the mélange. Sprinkle with the crumbled feta cheese. Serve immediately.

Nancie's Thai-Inspired Grilled Salmon

Serves 4 to 6

FLAVOR PASTE:

3 tablespoons chopped garlic

3 tablespoons chopped fresh cilantro stems and leaves

2 tablespoons Thai fish sauce

2 tablespoons vegetable oil

1 tablespoon tamari

½ teaspoon sugar

½ teaspoon salt

½ teaspoon freshly ground black pepper

4 (6- to 8-ounce) skinless center-cut salmon fillets, 1 inch thick, pin bones removed

SAUCE:

¼ cup Thai fish sauce

3 tablespoons fresh lime juice

2 tablespoons sugar

1 teaspoon finely chopped garlic

1 teaspoon finely chopped fresh green chiles (leave the seeds in)

1 teaspoon finely chopped fresh cilantro

I love cookbook author and Asian cooking expert Nancie McDermott's combinations, based on her years in Southeast Asia with the Peace Corps. Her flavors always bring excitement to the table and this is one of my favorites. This recipe also works well with tuna, swordfish, and halibut.

1. In a small food processor or a blender, combine the flavor paste ingredients and grind into a fairly smooth paste, stopping now and then to scrape down the side, and adding a little water as needed to bring the ingredients together. Scrape the paste into a medium bowl, add the fish fillets, and toss to coat them well with the paste. Set aside at room temperature, covered, for 20 to 30 minutes or overnight in the refrigerator (I highly recommend letting it sit overnight. Don't let it go any longer than that, though, as the texture of the fish will change.)

2. Make the sauce. In a small bowl, combine the fish sauce, lime juice, sugar, and garlic, stirring until the sugar dissolves. Sprinkle with the chiles and cilantro. This sauce can be made up to 2 days in advance and refrigerated in an airtight container. Let come to room temperature before serving.

3. Light a fire in the kamado grill using your favorite method. After about 10 minutes, place the grill rack in position, close the dome, and open the upper and lower dampers all the way. When the temperature reaches 400° F, adjust the dampers to maintain the temperature. Remember, even when grilling, the dome should be closed as much as possible.

4. Place the salmon on the grill, close the dome, and cook, carefully turning once, until handsomely browned on both sides and done to your liking, about 4 to 5 minutes on each side. Salmon is at its best when medium, which means that it will look a little wet towards the center of the fillet. Serve hot or warm, with the bowl of sauce on the side.

Tidewater "Grilled" Sea Scallops

Serves 4 to 6

RÉMOULADE SAUCE:

½ cup good-quality mayonnaise

1 tablespoon capers, drained and minced

1 tablespoon sweet pickle relish

1 tablespoon finely chopped fresh tarragon

1 tablespoon finely minced shallot

1 teaspoon tarragon or champagne vinegar

1 teaspoon minced garlic

½ teaspoon Dijon mustard

Kosher salt to taste

A good sprinkle of paprika

20 to 24 large sea scallops, all about the same thickness (1½ to 1¾ pounds), side muscle removed if necessary

Canola oil

Kosher salt and freshly ground black pepper

Okay, this recipe may cause you to stop short, because the scallops actually never touch the grill grate. I've always been disappointed with grilled scallops. So much of their flavor comes from being nicely caramelized and even with a super-hot fire you would only get this over part of the surface of the scallop. The kamado allows me to take a different tack, which yields in a superior result. I use a cast-iron or carbon-steel pan that's been preheated on the kamado to cook the scallops. The kamado's excellent heat retention lets the pan get smoking hot and the dome captures all the smoky goodness from the charcoal. This is also a great way to prepare shrimp and thin fillets of fish like flounder.

1. Put the rémoulade ingredients in a blender and pulse several times until well combined. You can make this sauce up to 24 hours in advance and refrigerate in an airtight container.
2. Brush each scallop on all sides with canola oil and season with salt and pepper.
3. Light a fire in the kamado grill using your favorite method. After about 10 minutes, place the grill rack in position, set a cast-iron or carbon-steel skillet or griddle on the grate, close the dome, and open the upper and lower dampers all the way. When the temperature reaches 500° F, adjust the dampers to maintain the temperature. Remember, even when grilling, the dome should be closed as much as possible. Be sure to have an oven mitt handy to handle the pan, as it will be searingly hot.
4. Place the scallops in a single layer, flat side down, in the pan, close the dome, and cook until barely opaque in the center, about 2 to 3 minutes per side. The scallops should feel firm to the touch but with some give. Please don't overcook the scallops—they become hockey pucks.
5. Transfer the scallops to a platter and serve with the sauce on the side.

Dry-Pack vs. Wet-Pack Scallops

Scallops are sold both "dry" and "wet." Wet-pack scallops are put in a solution whose only purpose is to extend shelf life—never, ever buy wet-pack scallops. Dry packs brown well and develop a deep sweetness on the grill that is outstanding. Look for scallops that are different shades of white and beige to know you're getting dry packs (you can also ask your fishmonger).

Western Shore Grilled Oysters with Spicy Garlic Butter

Serves 4 as a main dish or 8 as an appetizer

½ cup (1 stick) unsalted butter

6 cloves garlic, finely chopped

½ cup Lexington-Style "Dip" (page 246)

48 oysters, opened and left on the half shell

I f you love oysters, head for the Western Shore of Maryland. It is oyster heaven, and host to multiple oyster festivals each year, the one in St. Michaels being the largest and most famous.

I got this recipe from a bunch of oyster ranchers who swear it can only be enjoyed with cold beer or bourbon neat. Regardless of your beverage, this is a damn good way to eat oysters!

1. Light a fire in the kamado grill using your favorite method. After about 10 minutes, place the grill rack in position, close the dome, and open the upper and lower dampers all the way. When the temperature reaches 400° F, adjust the damper to maintain the temperature. Remember, even when grilling, the dome should be closed as much as possible.

2. In a small saucepan over low heat, melt the butter, then add the garlic and barbecue sauce and whisk to combine. Let simmer for 5 minutes. Remove from the heat.

3. Place the oysters on the grill in a single layer (you'll need to cook them in several batches) and quickly spoon some of the butter sauce into each shell. Close the dome and grill for about 5 minutes or until the oysters are to your liking. Transfer to a platter and serve immediately.

Lobster Tails with Tarragon Butter

Serves 4

½ cup (1 stick) unsalted butter

2 cloves garlic, finely chopped

1 tablespoon finely chopped shallot

1 tablespoon chopped fresh tarragon

Grated zest of 1 lemon

Kosher salt

8 (8-inch) metal skewers

8 lobster tails (4 ounces each)

Truffle oil for drizzling (optional)

Lobster tails are delicious any way you serve them, but a turn on the grill brings out flavor dimensions well worth exploring. This simple tarragon butter conjures taste memories of béarnaise sauce, and the addition of the optional truffle oil makes it unforgettable.

1. Light a fire in the kamado grill using your favorite method. After about 10 minutes, place the grill rack in position, close the dome, and open the upper and lower dampers all the way. When the temperature reaches 400° F, adjust the dampers to maintain the temperature. Remember, even when grilling, the dome should be closed as much as possible.

2. Meanwhile, in a small saucepan over low heat, melt the butter, then stir in the garlic, shallot, tarragon, and lemon zest and let simmer for a few minutes, until fragrant. Salt to taste. Remove from the heat.

3. Run skewers down the length of each lobster tail. This will help them lie flat on the grill. Place them on the grill, meat side down, close the dome, and cook for about 3 minutes. Turn them over, spoon some of the tarragon butter over each, close the dome, and cook until the meat firms up, another 4 to 5 minutes. Check by pressing on the front part of the tail where the meat is exposed. Remove from the heat, remove the skewers, crack the tails, spoon some more of the butter over each tail, drizzle with truffle oil if using, and serve.

Grilled Romaine Salad with Blue Cheese and Bacon Dressing

Serves 8

½ cup good-quality mayonnaise

½ cup sour cream

½ cup crumbled blue cheese (the very best quality)

½ cup chopped crisp-cooked bacon, divided

½ teaspoon dried thyme

Freshly ground black pepper to taste

4 hearts of romaine lettuce, cut in half lengthwise

¼ cup white balsamic vinegar

Good, fruity extra-virgin olive oil for drizzling

Kosher salt

1 cup halved cherry tomatoes (Sungolds are fantastic)

This has become one of my favorite side dishes for a host of grilled foods, especially a good Porterhouse steak. While the steaks are resting, toss the lettuce halves on the grill—the timing will work out perfectly. Don't hesitate to change the vinegar or the oil to your liking, or even use a bottled dressing that your family enjoys. Caesar dressing is a good choice, topped with shaved Parmesan (this is how my daughter likes it, the blue cheese hater, favorite way). In other words, make this salad your own.

1. In a small bowl, whisk the mayonnaise, sour cream, blue cheese, ¼ cup of the bacon, the thyme, and lots of pepper together until nicely blended but still chunky. Cover with plastic wrap and refrigerate for a couple of hours to allow the flavors to marry.

2. Light a fire in the kamado grill using your favorite method. After about 10 minutes, place the grill rack in position, close the dome, and open the upper and lower dampers all the way. When the temperature reaches 500° F, adjust the dampers to maintain the temperature. Remember, even when grilling, the dome should be closed as much as possible.

3. In a large bowl, toss the lettuce with the vinegar. Place the lettuce, cut side down, on the grill, close the dome, and cook until you have some char and the lettuce has wilted slightly, 4 to 6 minutes.

4. Remove the lettuce from the grill to 8 individual salad plates. Drizzle liberally with olive oil and season well with salt and pepper. Pour some of the dressing over each, sprinkle with the remaining ¼ cup bacon, and divide the tomatoes among the servings. Get this to the table quickly.

Portobello Burgers with Basil Mayonnaise

Serves 6

6 medium portobello mushrooms, stems removed

¼ cup extra-virgin olive oil

Kosher salt and freshly ground black pepper

6 (¼-inch-thick) slices fresh mozzarella cheese

6 (¼-inch-thick) slices ripe heirloom tomatoes

½ cup good-quality mayonnaise

¼ cup chopped fresh basil

No bun and no meat, but who cares? Filled with umami goodness and a texture that chews like a tenderloin steak, this portobello burger will satisfy both the vegetarian and meat eater. Grill it during the height of tomato season to add the perfect acidic sweetness. If at all possible, use a local mozzarella made with grass-fed cows' milk.

1. Slice each mushroom cap in half horizontally. Brush each with the oil on both sides and place on a rimmed baking sheet, cut side up. Season to taste with salt and pepper.
2. Season the mozzarella and tomato slices with salt. Put one mozzarella slice on the bottom half of a mushroom and top with a tomato slice. Place the top of the mushroom over the tomato to form a "sandwich." Repeat with the remaining mushroom, mozzarella, and tomato slices.
3. Light a fire in the kamado grill using your favorite method. After about 10 minutes, place the grill rack in position and close the lid, then open the upper and lower dampers all the way. When the temperature reaches 500° F, adjust the dampers to maintain the temperature. Remember, even when grilling, the dome should be closed as much as possible.
4. While the grill heats, combine the mayonnaise and basil in a small bowl.
5. Place the mushrooms on the grill grate, top side down. Close the dome. Grill for 4 minutes and then turn over. Grill until the mozzarella shows signs of melting, about another 4 minutes.
6. Transfer to serving plates and serve with the basil mayonnaise.

Eggplant with Garlic, Basil, and Feta Cheese Dressing

Serves 4 to 6

¼ cup plain Greek-style yogurt

¼ cup crumbled Greek feta cheese

1 tablespoon good-quality mayonnaise

1 tablespoon fresh lemon juice

1 tablespoon chopped fresh mint

8 large fresh basil leaves, cut across into a thin chiffonade

3 cloves garlic, finely chopped

Kosher salt and freshly ground black pepper

2 tablespoons buttermilk or regular milk, or as needed

2 medium eggplant, cut into ½-inch-thick slices

2 tablespoons canola or olive oil

I love this dish, especially with grilled or grill-roasted lamb, but it pairs well with any recipe that takes its cue from the Middle East. The method here works with zucchini or yellow squash, as does the dressing. Even without the feta mixture, this is wonderful.

1. In a medium bowl, combine the yogurt, feta, mayonnaise, lemon juice, mint, basil, and garlic. Season to taste with salt and pepper. Use the buttermilk to thin the sauce to the consistency you prefer; I like it thick and chunky.

2. Light a fire in the kamado grill using your favorite method. After about 10 minutes, place the grill rack in position, close the dome, and open the upper and lower dampers all the way. When the temperature reaches 500° F, adjust the dampers to maintain the temperature. Remember, even when grilling, the dome should be closed as much as possible.

3. Generously brush the eggplant slices with the oil. Place the eggplant slices on the grill grate, close the dome, and cook until the eggplant is soft, but still retains its shape, about 6 minutes per side.

4. Transfer the eggplant to a platter and spoon the sauce over the top. Serve immediately or at room temperature.

Antipasto from the Grill

Putting together an antipasto platter is simple with the kamado. Almost any vegetable can be grilled quickly, and roasting peppers gives them a flavor you can't get from a jar. One of my favorite combinations is thinly sliced Smoked Vitello with Tonnato Sauce (page 38), "Burnt Fingers" Lamb Rib Chops (page 117), Eggplant with Garlic, Basil, and Feta Cheese Dressing, and a few purchased pickled onions—but don't stop there. You could substitute Tidewater "Grilled" Sea Scallops (page 137) or Smoked Tomatoes (page 85) for a different twist. Heck, combine them all for an awesome, show-stopping cocktail buffet.

A kamado-grilled antipasto platter: From left to right, Eggplant with Garlic, Basil, and Feta Cheese Dressing; "Burnt Fingers" Lamb Rib Chops (page 117); and thin slices of Smoked Vitello with Tonnato Sauce (page 38).

Grilled Asparagus with Sauce Gribiche

Makes about 2 cups of sauce and serves 6 to 8

SAUCE GRIBICHE:

1 cup good-quality mayonnaise

3 large hard-boiled eggs, peeled and finely chopped

Juice of ½ lemon

2 tablespoons chopped shallot

1 tablespoon capers, drained and rinsed

1 tablespoon chopped cornichons (you can substitute dill pickles)

1 tablespoon chopped fresh flat-leaf parsley

1 tablespoon chopped fresh chives

1 teaspoon chopped fresh dill

1 teaspoon Dijon mustard

2 bunches fresh asparagus (thicker is better; about 2 pounds), woody ends snapped off where they naturally break—you'll know

Garlic-infused oil or olive oil as needed

Kosher salt and freshly ground black pepper

I first ate sauce Gribiche alongside poached salmon in a Belgium bistro in New York City and it has been one of my go-to sauces ever since. As good as it is with salmon, it's even better with grilled, fresh spring asparagus. This is an easy dish to cook up while the meat you just took off the grill is resting.

This makes more sauce than you'll need for the asparagus. In fact, it's just enough sauce to toss with three pounds of warm cooked potatoes for an amazing potato salad.

1. In a medium bowl, whisk the sauce Gribiche ingredients together. Refrigerate in an airtight container for at least 3 hours (overnight is even better); it will keep 3 to 4 days.
2. Arrange the asparagus on a rimmed baking sheet. Drizzle with oil and season to taste with salt and pepper. Roll the asparagus around in the oil to coat evenly.
3. Light a fire in the kamado grill using your favorite method. After about 10 minutes, place the grill rack in position, close the dome, and open the upper and lower dampers all the way. When the temperature reaches 500° F, adjust the dampers to maintain the temperature. Remember, even when grilling, the dome should be closed as much as possible.
4. Place the asparagus on the grill, perpendicular to the grates so they won't fall through, and close the dome. Grill for 5 to 8 minutes, rolling the asparagus with a spatula, much like you would with hot dogs. When they pick up some char, they are done. You want the asparagus to be slightly crisp, so taste one to check on doneness.
5. Transfer the asparagus to a platter and serve hot off the grill or at room temperature with the sauce Gribiche on the side.

Dry-Brined Roast Turkey
(page 170)

4
Roasting in the Kamado

Roasting on a kamado grill is even better than using your indoor oven. Your oven can't give you that extra layer of woodsy flavor that you get from cooking outdoors, or the moist cooking environment the kamado grill is built to provide. When you roast in the kamado, food will cook quicker, with more even browning, and end up more moist and succulent than if you cooked it in your oven.

Roasting takes place anywhere from 350° to 500° F. You will be cooking indirectly; in other words, the heat will not make direct contact with the food. The key to success is the barrier between the fire and the food. You can set up your kamado just as you would for smoking, using a ceramic plate as that barrier, or you can place your food in a roasting pan (you can even use a disposable aluminum-foil pan), cast-iron skillet, or baking sheet. The advantage of roasting in a pan is that you'll end up with the makings for a nice pan gravy.

147

In many of the recipes in this chapter, you'll see that I initially start my food directly over the fire to get some tasty browning and caramelization, then move to indirect cooking and a lower grill temperature. You'll find the specific temperatures indicated in each recipe. And dropping from a higher temperature to a lower temperature isn't difficult to do. Let's say you are searing a beef tenderloin. When you open the dome to set it on the grill, the temperature starts dropping. By the time you are done searing and have inserted the ceramic plate or put the tenderloin in a roasting pan and returned it to the grill, the temperature may have dropped 100 degrees, getting you to your roasting temperature. Now all you need to do is close the dome and adjust the dampers to maintain this lower temperature. I strongly encourage you to invest in a probe thermometer, which will allow you to monitor the internal temperature of your food without opening the dome. Remember the kamado mantra: "If it ain't closed, it ain't cooking."

This is an exciting chapter with some really over-the-top flavors. Try them all, to the delight of your family and friends. While many of us think of the kamado as a smoker, I'm here to tell you it's also a roasting machine!

Japanese Negimaki Roll with Lemon Dipping Sauce

Serves 6

1 (3-pound) center-cut section beef tenderloin

2 tablespoons prepared wasabi paste

2 tablespoons good-quality mayonnaise

4 green onions, trimmed

4 pencil-thin asparagus spears, woody bottoms snapped off

½ cup shredded carrots

Kitchen twine

½ cup ponzu sauce

¼ cup fresh lemon juice

¼ cup tamari

¼ cup rice wine vinegar

¼ cup mirin (sweet rice wine)

1 teaspoon toasted sesame oil

Shichimi (Japanese pepper blend), homemade (page 235) or store-bought

Teriyaki sauce as needed to glaze

Toasted sesame seeds (toast yourself in a dry skillet over medium heat, or you can buy already-toasted sesame seeds)

This is a reworking of the classic Japanese appetizer into a main course, and it is doggone good eating. Serve it over Japanese noodles or sushi rice, if you like, with some pickled ginger on the side. Ponzu is a citrus-flavored soy sauce; you can find it and the other Japanese ingredients called for in the Asian sections of most large supermarkets.

1. Cut the tenderloin almost in half lengthwise. On each side of that cut do another cut so that the piece of meat begins to lay flat like a book.

2. In a small bowl, whisk the wasabi and mayonnaise together and spread over the cut surfaces of the meat. Arrange the green onions on top of the meat so that the white and green ends alternate. Do the same with the asparagus. Sprinkle the carrots over the top. Roll the meat up like a jellyroll and tie with kitchen twine at 1-inch intervals. Pour the ponzu into a 1-gallon zip-top plastic bag. Add the beef, seal, turn the bag over several times to coat the beef with the ponzu, and refrigerate overnight.

3. Remove the meat from the marinade and pat dry at least 1 hour before cooking. Make the dipping sauce by combining the lemon juice, tamari, vinegar, mirin, and sesame oil in a small bowl. Set aside at room temperature until ready to serve.

4. Light a fire in the kamado grill using your favorite method. After about 10 minutes, place the grill rack in position and close the dome, then open the upper and lower dampers all the way. When the temperature reaches 500° F, adjust the dampers to maintain the temperature.

5. Sprinkle the tenderloin generously with the Japanese pepper. Place the tenderloin on the grill, close the dome, and cook for about 5 minutes per side to get a good sear. If necessary, adjust the dampers to drop the temperature down to 425° F (it's likely already dropped down significantly during the searing) and maintain it there.

6. Insert the ceramic plate in the kamado and put the tenderloin on the grill, or put the tenderloin on a rack in a roasting pan and put the pan on the grill. Close the dome and roast to your desired degree of doneness, 1 hour to 1 hour and 15 minutes for medium rare (an internal temperature of 135° to 140° F).

7. Transfer the beef to a cutting board, brush generously with teriyaki sauce and sprinkle with the sesame seeds. Let rest for 10 minutes. Remove the kitchen twine and cut the roast into 1-inch-thick slices. Arrange on a platter and serve with the dipping sauce.

Charred Whole Beef Tenderloin with Romesco Sauce

Serves 8 to 10

½ cup roasted red peppers

⅓ cup natural almonds

2 tablespoons red wine vinegar

½ teaspoon red pepper flakes

2 cloves garlic, peeled

1 slice sourdough bread, crust removed

¼ cup extra-virgin olive oil

1 whole beef tenderloin (about 6½ pounds), silverskin removed (it's best to have your butcher remove this; unless you have a super-sharp knife, you're likely to lose some of the meat along with the silverskin)

6 cloves garlic, thinly sliced

Kosher salt and freshly ground black pepper

12 green onions, trimmed

Whole beef tenderloin is one of the simplest ways to feed a crowd. Spike it with slices of garlic that melt into the meat and use the kamado grill magic to keep the roast moist—there is no better way to prepare tenderloin. The tart Romesco sauce it's served with beats any steak sauce. And if there are any leftovers, you'll be able to enjoy the king of all roast beef sandwiches.

1. Place the roasted peppers, almonds, vinegar, red pepper flakes, whole garlic cloves, and bread in a blender and pulse to combine. With the machine running, add the oil slowly and process until you have a nice thick sauce. The Romesco sauce can be prepared a day ahead and refrigerated in an airtight container. Bring to room temperature before using.

2. Using a boning knife, cut small slits into the beef tenderloin and slide in the slices of garlic. Liberally season with salt and pepper. Let rest at room temperature for at least 45 minutes before cooking.

3. Light a fire in the kamado grill using your favorite method. After about 10 minutes, place the grill rack in position, close the dome, and open the upper and lower dampers all the way. When the temperature reaches 500° F, adjust the dampers to maintain the temperature.

4. Place the tenderloin on the grill, close the dome, and sear for 5 minutes per side.

5. Insert the ceramic plate in the kamado and put the tenderloin on the grill, or put the tenderloin on a rack in a roasting pan and put the pan on the grill. Throw the green onions on the grill as well. Close the dome. The temperature will have dropped to around 425° to 450° F; adjust the vents to maintain that temperature and continue to roast to your desired degree of doneness, 1 hour to 1 hour and 15 minutes for medium rare (an internal temperature of 135° to 140° F).

6. Transfer the tenderloin to a platter and let rest for at least 15 minutes. To serve, slice, arrange the green onions with the beef, and spoon the Romesco sauce over everything. This is delicious warm or at room temperature.

Mr. Payne's Pot Roast

Serves 6

1 (3-pound) boneless chuck roast

1 (16-ounce) bottle California French dressing

Kosher salt and freshly ground black pepper

1 tablespoon honey

1 tablespoon chopped fresh chives

Pumpernickel bread for serving (optional)

My high school sweetheart's dad is the force behind this recipe. His classic was fairly straightforward and simple, and I've made only a few tweaks. I added the honey and chives, making an already-tasty end result even more delicious. I've also changed up Mr. Payne's method. He would cook this roast over direct heat and I remember him fighting and cussing at his fire as he tried not to char the outside of the roast. Considering how much sugar is in the French dressing, it was hard not to do. I've taken a different approach by charring the roast slightly (which is key to this roast's great flavor) over direct flame and then finishing it over indirect heat.

1. Place the roast in a 1-gallon zip-top plastic bag. Pour off ¼ cup of the dressing and set it aside. Pour the rest of the bottle into the bag. Seal the bag and squish the dressing around the roast to coat it completely. Refrigerate for up to 24 hours.

2. Remove the roast from the bag and discard the marinade. Season liberally with salt and pepper. Let stand at room temperature for 30 minutes.

3. Light a fire in the kamado grill using your favorite method. After about 10 minutes, place the grill rack in position, close the dome, and open the upper and lower dampers all the way. When the temperature reaches 500° F, adjust the dampers to maintain the temperature.

4. Place the roast on the grill, close the dome, and sear for 5 minutes per side. Remove the roast from the grill.

5. Insert the ceramic plate in the kamado and put the roast on the grill, or put the roast on a rack in a roasting pan and put the pan on the grill. Close the dome and adjust the dampers for a grill temperature of 375° to 400° F. Roast until the internal temperature at the thickest point is 175° F, about 1½ hours.

6. Transfer the roast to a cutting board. Drizzle with the honey and sprinkle with the chives. Let rest for 15 minutes, then slice thinly across the grain. Serve on a platter or make sandwiches with it using the pumpernickel bread.

Steakhouse Roast

1 tablespoon Canadian-Style Steak Seasoning (page 234)

1 tablespoon garlic paste (about 8 cloves garlic, smashed and worked into a paste, or prepared garlic paste in a tube, which can be found in the produce section)

1 tablespoon Worcestershire sauce

1 teaspoon Dijon mustard

1 (3- to 4-pound) New York strip loin roast

Horseradish or steak sauce for serving

I grew up in a home where we "enjoyed" a dry, overcooked eye of round roast every Sunday for lunch. This is the antithesis of that roast. Garlicky and vibrant, with the unmatched flavor of a New York Strip steak, it's great for Sunday dinner or a party, and the leftovers make killer sandwiches, as well as being delicious served over a salad. This kind of roast is usually available at price clubs, but if not, ask your butcher to cut you one. Try it with Kamado 157 Steak Sauce (page 253) to complete the experience.

1. In a small bowl, combine the steak seasoning, garlic, Worcestershire, and mustard and massage the mixture into the roast. Set the roast on a rack in a roasting pan and let stand at room temperature for an hour.
2. Light a fire in the kamado grill using your favorite method. After about 10 minutes, place the grill rack in position, close the dome, and open the upper and lower dampers all the way. When the temperature reaches 500° F, adjust the dampers to maintain the temperatures.
3. Insert the ceramic plate in the kamado and put the roast on the grill, or put the roast on a rack in a roasting pan and put the pan on the grill. Close the dome and adjust the dampers for a grill temperature of 450° F. Roast to your desired degree of doneness, 1½ to 2 hours for medium rare (an internal temperature of 135° to 140° F).
4. Transfer the roast to a cutting board and let rest for 15 minutes. Slice as you prefer (I like ½-inch-thick slices), arrange on a platter, and serve with the sauces if desired.

Horseradish-Crusted Standing Rib Roast with Pan Gravy

Serves 6 to 8

1 (5- to 6-pound) bone-in standing rib roast, trimmed of excess fat

6 large cloves garlic, peeled

¼ cup grated, peeled fresh horseradish or well-drained prepared horseradish

2 tablespoons chopped fresh oregano

1 tablespoon chopped fresh rosemary

1 tablespoon kosher salt

1 tablespoon freshly ground black pepper

¼ cup extra-virgin olive oil

½ cup dry white wine

1 tablespoon gravy flour or all-purpose flour

2 cups low-sodium chicken broth

2 sprigs fresh thyme

¼ cup (½ stick) unsalted butter, cut into tablespoons

Few foods are as impressive as a standing rib roast—it's perfect for holidays and special occasions. I've taken its normal accompaniment, horseradish, and used it in a flavor paste that will turn into a tasty crust, giving the roast a smoky bite. Make sure you follow my method exactly; do it, and you'll be rewarded with a delicious, succulent roast. You can *only* use this method with a kamado grill because of its superior heat retention. And I'm serious—do not peek. If you open the dome midway through, all is lost. This would be a good time to invest in a probe thermometer if you have not done so already, which will allow you to monitor the roast's internal temperature without lifting the dome.

1. Let the roast stand at room temperature 30 to 45 minutes.
2. In a mini food processor or blender, finely mince the garlic, horseradish, oregano, rosemary, salt, and pepper together. Add the olive oil all at once and process into a paste. Smear the paste all over the roast. Set the roast on a rack in a roasting pan and let sit at room temperature for another hour.
3. Light a fire in the kamado grill using your favorite method. After about 10 minutes, place the grill rack in position, close the dome, and open the upper and lower dampers all the way. When the temperature reaches 500° F, adjust the dampers to maintain the temperature.
4. Place the roasting pan on the grill, close the dome, and roast at 450° to 500° F for 45 minutes.
5. Adjust the dampers to drop the grill temperature to 350° F and roast for another 30 minutes.
6. Close the dampers entirely and let the roast cook until it has an internal temperature of 125° to 130° F. Depending on the tightness of your seal, this will take anywhere from 30 to 70 minutes. No peeking! Trust your kamado grill. The key to success is the internal temperature. As soon as you hit it, remove the roast from the grill.
7. Transfer the roast to a cutting board, loosely tent with aluminum foil, and let rest for 20 to 30 minutes. The internal temperature will rise 5 to 10 degrees. Meanwhile, pour off some of the fat and place the pan over two burners on the stove set at medium heat. Pour in the wine and scrape up the browned bits from the bottom of the pan. Whisk in the flour, then whisk in the broth and add the thyme. Cook, stirring, until the gravy reaches the thickness you like. Remove the pan from the heat and whisk in the butter. Carve meat into slices and serve with the pan gravy.

Sunday-Best Pork Loin Roast with Thyme-Fig Balsamic Marinade

Serves 6 to 8

¾ cup fig balsamic vinegar

⅓ cup olive oil

6 cloves garlic, finely chopped

3 tablespoons chopped fresh thyme

1 tablespoon Dijon mustard

1 teaspoon kosher salt

1 teaspoon fennel seeds

Freshly ground black pepper

1 (3- to 4-pound) center-cut boneless pork loin roast

Okay, this isn't just for Sunday—make it anytime you have a hankering for a juicy piece of pork. The fig-flavored balsamic vinegar supplies a deep jamminess that nicely offsets the tart mustard and blends with the earthy thyme. This marinade is also good with pork chops and pork tenderloin.

1. In a small bowl, whisk the vinegar, oil, garlic, thyme, mustard, salt, fennel seeds, and 5 grindings of black pepper together. Place the pork roast in a 2½-gallon zip-top plastic bag. Add the marinade, seal the bag, and squish the marinade around the pork to coat. Refrigerate for at least 24 hours; 48 is better. Turn the bag frequently.

2. Remove the pork from the marinade at least 45 minutes before cooking; reserve the marinade. Let the pork stand at room temperature.

3. Light a fire in the kamado grill using your favorite method. After about 10 minutes, place the grill rack in position, close the dome, and open the upper and lower dampers all the way. When the temperature reaches 400° F, adjust the dampers to maintain the temperature.

4. Insert the ceramic plate in the kamado and place the roast on the grill, or set the pork roast on a rack in a roasting pan, and place the pan on the grill. Close the dome and adjust the dampers for a grill temperature of 375° F. Roast for about 20 minutes, then brush the pork with the reserved marinade. Cook for another 45 to 60 minutes for a medium doneness; the internal temperature should be between 145° and 150° F.

5. Transfer the pork to a cutting board and let rest for 15 minutes. Cut into ½-inch-thick slices and serve warm or at room temperature.

Crown Roast of Pork with Apple-Chestnut-Sausage Stuffing

Serves 6 to 8

Grated zest and juice of 2 oranges

Grated zest and juice of 1 lemon

1 tablespoon kosher salt

1 (8- to 10-pound) crown roast of pork

1 tablespoon unsalted butter

1 tablespoon olive oil

½ cup chopped onion

2 ribs celery, chopped

1 tart apple, peeled, cored, and finely chopped

1 pound bulk country pork sausage

8 ounces jarred or canned peeled chestnuts, drained and coarsely chopped

½ cup shelled unsalted pistachio nuts

8 cups cubed day-old French bread

3 to 4 cups low-sodium chicken broth or equal parts apple cider and broth

¼ cup finely chopped shallots

4 cloves garlic, run through a press

½ teaspoon ground fennel seeds

1 to 2 tablespoons all-purpose flour or gravy flour

Please resist the urge to put little "chop hats" on the bones of this roast, unless you're serving it up at a retro-themed dinner party. You will probably need to order the roast in advance. If a crown roast is a little over the top for you, or you don't have many folks to feed, order a bone-in pork loin (a crown roast is two bone-in pork loins tied together) and cook the stuffing alongside the roast.

This is an easy recipe to make you own. You can use whatever type of sausage you prefer, swap pecans and/or walnuts for the pistachios, and feel free to leave out the chestnuts entirely if you can't find them or don't like them.

1. In a small bowl, combine the zests and salt. Rub the mixture all over the roast, inside and out. Set the roast in a large cast-iron skillet.

2. In a large sauté pan over medium heat, heat the butter and oil. When the butter foams, add the onion, celery, and apple and cook until softened, about 5 minutes, stirring a few times. Crumble the sausage into the pan and cook until it is browned and no pink remains. Pour the sausage mixture into a large bowl. Add the nuts, bread, and citrus juices and toss to combine. Add 1 to 2 cups of the broth to moisten; the mixture should stay together when pinched. Let the stuffing cool off until no steam is rising from the bowl. Firmly pack the stuffing into the center of the crown roast.

3. Light a fire in the kamado grill using your favorite method. After about 10 minutes, place the grill rack in position, close the dome, and open the upper and lower dampers all the way. When the temperature reaches 450° F, adjust the dampers to maintain the temperature.

4. Place the skillet on the grill and close the dome. Roast for about 30 minutes.

5. Adjust the dampers to drop the grill temperature to about 325° F. Continue to roast the pork until internal temperature of the pork (not the stuffing) is 140° to 145° F.

6. Transfer the roast to a cutting board, loosely tent with aluminum foil, and let it rest for 25 to 30 minutes. Meanwhile, place the skillet over medium heat on the stovetop, add the shallots, garlic, fennel, and flour, and cook, stirring, until the shallots are slightly colored, 5 to 10 minutes. Pour in 2 cups broth and scrape the bottom of the pan to get up all the browned bits. Bring to a boil, then reduce the heat to a simmer and let bubble till the sauce has the desired thickness. Strain the sauce through a fine mesh strainer and keep warm. Carve the roast between the ribs and serve with the stuffing and pan gravy.

Roasted Pork Loin Stuffed with Bacon-Onion Jam, Mascarpone, Apricots, and Plums

Serves 6 to 8

1 (4- to 5-pound) boneless center-cut pork loin roast

½ cup Bacon-Onion Jam (page 256) or store-bought onion jam

½ cup mascarpone cheese

12 to 14 dried apricots

12 to 14 dried plums (prunes)

Kosher salt and freshly ground black pepper

Kitchen twine

Apricot jam, slightly melted so it's easy to brush

Pork with pork—how good does that sound? You need to start this recipe a day or two before you plan to serve it if you are going to make the bacon jam, which I highly recommend you do. This is a perfect dish for a holiday centerpiece or for whenever you have a taste for something out of the ordinary.

1. Slice the pork roast lengthwise but not all the way through. Open the roast up and then slice both sides in half so that the pork roast lies open like a book. Take care not to cut any of the meat all the way through.

2. Smear the insides of the pork roast with the bacon-onion jam. Spread the mascarpone over the jam and then top with the apricots and dried plums, spreading them evenly throughout the roast. Season with salt and pepper. Roll the roast tightly together lengthwise and tie at 1-inch intervals with kitchen twine. Let sit at room temperature while you start your fire.

3. Light a fire in the kamado grill using your favorite method. After about 10 minutes, place the grill rack in position, close the dome, and open the upper and lower dampers all the way. When the temperature reaches 400° F, adjust the dampers to maintain the temperature.

4. Insert the ceramic plate in the kamado or set the roast on a rack in a roasting pan and place the pan on the grill. Close the dome and adjust the temperature downward to 375° F. Roast for about 1 hour, then brush with the apricot jam. Continue to cook about another 20 minutes, brushing again with the jam toward the end of that time. The roast is ready when the internal temperature is between 140° and 150° F.

5. Transfer the pork to a cutting board and let rest for 15 minutes. Cut into ½-inch-thick slices and serve warm or at room temperature.

Porchetta

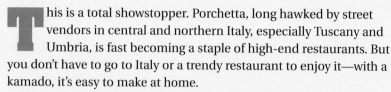

Serves 12 to 15

1 (5- to 6-pound) slab skin-on fresh pork belly

¼ cup chopped fresh sage

2 tablespoons finely chopped fresh rosemary

1½ tablespoons ground fennel seeds

1½ tablespoons finely minced garlic

Grated zest of 2 oranges

1 (3-pound) boneless center-cut pork loin

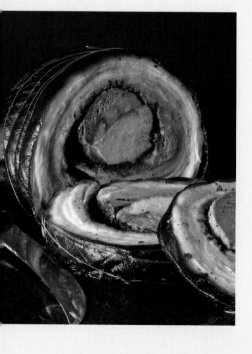

This is a total showstopper. Porchetta, long hawked by street vendors in central and northern Italy, especially Tuscany and Umbria, is fast becoming a staple of high-end restaurants. But you don't have to go to Italy or a trendy restaurant to enjoy it—with a kamado, it's easy to make at home.

To make porchetta, a layer of pork belly is rolled around a pork loin laced with sage, rosemary, citrus, and fennel, then slowly roasted until it is meltingly tender, with a crackling, crunchy, scrumptious skin. The results make every bit of the effort worth it.

You'll need a few days for this, so plan accordingly. Pork belly, or fresh bacon as it is sometimes referred to, is fairly easy to find at many of the new butcher shops cropping up around the country and at specialty markets. If need be, special order it.

1. Place the pork belly skin side down on a cutting board and trim it into a rectangle. Take the knife and, across the meaty side of the belly, make cuts about every inch, no more than ⅓ inch deep. Flip the belly and, with a meat tenderizer mallet, whack the skin several times. This will cause the skin to break during roasting and allow you to pull off awesome hunks of crispy skin to nibble.

2. In a small bowl, combine the sage, rosemary, fennel, garlic, and orange zest. Rub this mixture on the cut side of the pork belly. Place the pork loin at one end of the belly. If it overhangs, trim the meat so it is even (cook that trimmed piece of pork like a chop for a snack to sustain the cook!). Roll the belly around the pork loin, jelly-roll style. Tie the roll at about ½-inch intervals with kitchen twine. With an ice pick or a skewer, poke dozens of holes through the skin of the belly. Set the roll on a rack in a roasting pan. Refrigerate for 24 hours, uncovered. Remove the roll from the refrigerator at least 1 hour before cooking. Pat the roll dry with paper towels.

3. Light a fire in the kamado grill using your favorite method. After about 10 minutes, place the grill rack in position, close the dome, and open the upper and lower dampers all the way. When the temperature reaches 400° F, adjust the dampers to maintain the temperature.

4. Place the roasting pan on the grill and close the dome. Roast for 40 to 50 minutes.

5. Turn the roll over in the pan, close the dome, and adjust the dampers to drop the grill temperature to 300° F. Continue to cook until the internal temperature of the porchetta reaches 145° F, typically 1½ to 2 hours.

6. Transfer the porchetta to a cutting board and let rest for 30 minutes. Cut the porchetta into ½-inch-thick slices and enjoy. A serrated knife works best.

Marinated Herb-Mustard Leg of Lamb

Serves 6 to 8

1 (4- to 5-pound) boneless or 1 (6- to 8-pound) bone-in leg of lamb

¾ cup vegetable oil

½ cup red wine vinegar

½ cup chopped onion

2 cloves garlic, bruised

2 teaspoons Dijon mustard

2 teaspoons kosher salt

½ teaspoon dried oregano

½ teaspoon dried basil

1 bay leaf

⅛ teaspoon freshly ground black pepper

The scent of this dish on the grill is so mesmerizing that even lamb haters line up for a taste. Before my conversion to kamado, I used to grill this but would have to be very careful not to let it get too charred. In the kamado, that's no longer an issue. The method I use here yields a nice crust and, because of the unevenness of the butterflied piece of meat, an interior cooked to multiple degrees of doneness, which is a plus when you're cooking for a crowd. If desired, you could roll and tie the lamb for a more elegant presentation

1. If working with a bone-in leg, have your butcher bone the leg and butterfly it. Place the lamb in a 2½-gallon zip-top plastic bag.
2. In a medium bowl, whisk the oil, vinegar, onion, garlic, mustard, salt, oregano, basil, bay leaf, and pepper together. Add to the bag, seal, and squish the marinade all around to coat the lamb. Refrigerate for 48 hours, turning the bag over occasionally.
3. Remove the lamb from the marinade, reserving the marinade. Pat the lamb dry and let sit at room temperature for about 30 minutes. Bring the marinade to a full boil in a small saucepan over high heat. Reduce the heat slightly and cook for 5 minutes. Remove from the heat and let cool.
4. Light a fire in the kamado grill using your favorite method. After about 10 minutes, place the grill rack in position, close the dome, and open the upper and lower dampers all the way. When the temperature reaches 500° F, adjust the dampers to maintain the temperature.
5. Set the lamb on the grill, close the dome, and sear about 5 minutes per side. Remove the lamb from the grill.
6. Insert the ceramic plate in the kamado and put the lamb back on the grill, or set the lamb on a rack in a roasting pan and put the pan on the grill. Close the dome and adjust the dampers to drop the grill temperature to 350° F. Roast until the internal temperature at the thickest point of the lamb registers 135° F, about 1 to 1½ hours.
7. Transfer the lamb to a cutting board and let rest for 10 minutes. The lamb will be crusty on the outside and cooked to multiple levels of doneness, from rare to well done. Cut into slices and serve with the reserved marinade, reheated, as a dipping sauce.

Roasted Rack of Lamb with Thyme

Serves 4

⅓ cup Dijon mustard

2 tablespoons ketchup

1 tablespoon Worcestershire sauce

1 tablespoon fresh lemon juice

¼ cup chopped fresh thyme or lemon thyme (preferred)

2 (1½-pound) racks of lamb, Frenched if desired

¼ cup olive oil

Ketchup in a lamb marinade? When the recipe comes from a French chef, why not? This dish is based on one from Cyril Renaud, who was the chef-owner of one of my favorite New York City restaurants, Fleur de Sel, which unfortunately closed its doors during the last recession. It's an unusual take on rack of lamb but one well worth trying.

1. In a small bowl, whisk the mustard, ketchup, Worcestershire, lemon juice, and thyme together, then brush the mixture liberally over the lamb. Cover with plastic wrap and refrigerate overnight. Reserve the remaining marinade.
2. Wipe the marinade off the lamb, then brush the lamb with the olive oil.
3. Light a fire in the kamado grill using your favorite method. After about 10 minutes, place the grill rack in position, close the dome, and open the upper and lower dampers all the way. When the temperature reaches 500° F, adjust the dampers to maintain the temperature.
4. Place the lamb on the grill and sear for a couple of minutes on each side. Remove the lamb from the grill and brush on both sides with the reserved marinade.
5. Insert the ceramic plate in the kamado and put the lamb back on the grill, or set the lamb racks in a roasting pan and set the pan on the grill. Close the dome and roast until the internal temperature reads 125° F, 20 to 30 minutes, brushing with the marinade again halfway through.
6. Transfer the racks to a cutting board and let rest at least 10 minutes before cutting into individual or double chops. Serve at once.

Sweet and Spicy Glazed Lamb Ribs

Serves 6

4 racks lamb spareribs
(3 to 4 pounds total)

Seasoned salt

Freshly ground black pepper

Smoked paprika (optional)

1 (12-ounce) jar grape jelly

½ cup Worcestershire sauce

Lamb ribs are becoming increasingly available in supermarkets, specialty stores, and farmers' markets. Besides being a change from pork or beef ribs, they cook much faster and I like to serve them as an appetizer. Lamb ribs seem to take best to a semi-sweet thin vinegar sauce, like Lexington-Style "Dip" (page 246), but I'm suggesting here you mix up a simple sauce recipe based on grape jelly. No snickering—it's delicious!

1. Sprinkle the lamb ribs evenly and liberally on both sides with salt, pepper, and paprika if using. Place them in a shallow pan, cover with plastic wrap, and refrigerate overnight.

2. Remove the ribs from the refrigerator and let stand at room temperature for at least 30 minutes before cooking.

3. Light a fire in the kamado grill using your favorite method. After about 10 minutes, place the grill rack in position, close the dome, and open the upper and lower dampers all the way. When the temperature reaches 350° F, adjust the dampers to maintain the temperature.

4. Insert the ceramic plate in the kamado and place the ribs, meaty side down, on the grill. Close the dome and cook for about 10 minutes per side. Remove from the grill and wrap loosely in aluminum foil. Return to the grill and roast for 1½ hours.

5. When the ribs are close to being done, combine the jelly and Worcestershire in a small saucepan over medium heat. Slowly bring to a simmer, whisking, then cook until slightly reduced, about 5 minutes.

6. Remove the ribs from the grill and place in a disposable aluminum-foil pan. Pour the sauce over the ribs and cover tightly with foil. Set the pan on the grill, close the dome, and cook until they are extremely tender, about another 20 minutes.

7. Remove the pan from the grill and place the ribs on a platter. Pour the sauce into a separate bowl and pass at the table.

Everyday Roasted Chicken

Serves 4 to 6

1 (4-pound) chicken

No-salt-added seasoned "salt"

Kosher salt and freshly ground black pepper

OR

2 cups Herb Poultry Marinade (page 240)

Remember when we used to roast our own birds instead of buying a rotisserie one at the store? A roast chicken is ridiculously easy to do at home, and with a kamado grill you'll get extra flavor from the charcoal and a much moister bird than from the grocery store.

You can go at this recipe in two different ways: using a dry brine or a wet marinade. I encourage you to try both and see which you like the best. Always cook two chickens at a time, one for now and one to use later pulled apart in salads, soups, and sandwiches.

1. Remove the giblets and neck from the chicken's cavity and freeze for another use. Rinse the chicken thoroughly in cold water and pat dry with paper towels. Sprinkle inside and out liberally with the seasoned "salt," salt, and pepper, place on a rack in a roasting pan, and refrigerate overnight. OR, place the chicken in a 2½-gallon zip-top plastic bag and add the marinade. Seal the bag, turn it over several times to coat the chicken with the marinade, and refrigerate at least overnight and up to 2 days, turning the bag occasionally.

2. Remove the chicken from the refrigerator 30 minutes before cooking. Tie the legs together with kitchen twine, and flip the wing tips under the breast. If necessary, remove the chicken from the marinade.

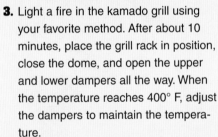

3. Light a fire in the kamado grill using your favorite method. After about 10 minutes, place the grill rack in position, close the dome, and open the upper and lower dampers all the way. When the temperature reaches 400° F, adjust the dampers to maintain the temperature.

4. Insert the ceramic plate in the kamado and set the chicken on the grill, or set the chicken on a rack in a roasting pan and place the roasting pan on the grill. Close the dome and roast until the juices run clear and the internal temperature at the thigh is 170° F, about 1 to 1½ hours.

5. Transfer to a platter and let rest for 10 minutes before cutting into serving pieces.

Cornish Game Hens with Jalapeño Pesto

Serves 4

2 jalapeño chiles, peeled (see below) and seeded

2 cups lightly packed fresh cilantro leaves

1 clove garlic, peeled

½ cup blanched almonds

¼ cup (about 1 ounce) crumbled cotija cheese (available at most supermarkets and Hispanic markets)

¼ cup extra-virgin olive oil

2 tablespoons fresh lemon juice

Kosher salt and freshly ground black pepper

4 (1½-pound) Cornish game hens, defrosted if necessary

Cornish game hens were a splurge food in my younger days. I always liked having my own little bird, and I still think that it's a wonderful way to make your guests feel special. This recipe puts some serious flavor in the hen—a spicy pesto is worked under the skin. It's a great choice in the summer—the heat from the birds seems to kill the heat and humidity of my native North Carolina.

1. In a food processor or blender, combine the chiles, cilantro, garlic, and almonds and pulse until chopped, scraping down the sides once or twice during the process. Add the cheese and puree. With the motor running, add the olive oil and lemon juice. Transfer the pesto to a bowl and taste for seasoning, adding salt and pepper if necessary. Cover and refrigerate until needed. This can be made several hours in advance.

2. When ready, remove about ⅓ cup of the pesto to a separate bowl. Using an iced tea spoon or other small spoon and your finger, loosen the skin around the breast and the thigh of the game hens. Take a spoonful of pesto and push it up under the skin of both the breast and thigh, repeating for the other side and the other birds.

3. Light a fire in the kamado grill using your favorite method. After about 10 minutes, place the grill rack in position, close the dome, and open the upper and lower dampers all the way. When the temperature reaches 400° F, adjust the dampers to maintain the temperature.

4. Insert the ceramic plate in the kamado and put the hens on the grill, or put the hens on a rack in a roasting pan and put the pan on the grill. Close the dome and roast the birds until the juice runs clear and the internal temperature at the thigh registers 165° F, 45 to 75 minutes.

5. Transfer the hens to a platter and let rest for 15 minutes before serving. Serve with the remaining pesto on the side.

Peeling Chiles

To remove the skin from any chile, you need to roast or blacken and blister the skin. You can do this by placing the chile over an open flame like a gas burner, broiling them, or grilling them. Turn the chiles so that all sides get charred, then put them in a zip-top plastic bag, seal, and let steam for 20 minutes. The skin will peel right off.

Cajun Turkey Breast

Serves 6 to 8

2 tablespoons chili powder

1 tablespoon sweet paprika

1 tablespoon dried thyme

2 teaspoons dried oregano

1 teaspoon granulated onion powder

1 teaspoon granulated garlic powder

1 teaspoon granulated sugar

1/8 teaspoon cayenne pepper

1 (4- to 5-pound) bone-in, skin-on turkey breast

2 tablespoons canola oil

Rémoulade, homemade (page 137) or store-bought, for serving (optional)

Put on a pot of red beans and get ready for some Zydeco music playing, because this recipe will make you dance! Turkey breast is normally a challenge to not cook to dryness, but not with the kamado. This nicely spiced version is from my New Orleans buddy Pableaux Johnson. Too bad he roasts it in an oven.

1. In a small bowl, combine the chili powder, paprika, thyme, oregano, onion and garlic powders, sugar, and cayenne together. Brush the turkey breast all over with the oil, then liberally coat the breast with the rub mixture, massaging it into the meat. Cover with plastic wrap and refrigerate for at least 4 hours; overnight is preferred. Remove the breast at least 30 minutes before you plan to cook.

2. Light a fire in the kamado grill using your favorite method. After about 10 minutes, place the grill rack in position, close the dome, and open the upper and lower dampers all the way. When the temperature reaches 500° F, insert the ceramic plate and set the turkey breast on the grill, or set the turkey on a rack in a roasting pan and place the pan on the grill. Close the dome and adjust the dampers to drop the temperature to 350° to 375° F. Cook the turkey breast until the internal temperature at the thickest point registers 160° F, 1 1/2 to 2 hours.

3. Transfer the turkey breast to a cutting board and let rest for at least 30 minutes but not longer than 45 minutes. Carefully cut each breast meat portion from the bone, slice across, and serve warm or at room temperature with rémoulade, if you like.

Dry-Brined Roast Turkey

Serves 8 to 12

1 (12- to 14-pound) turkey, giblets removed, rinsed, and patted dry

2 tablespoons kosher salt

1 tablespoon freshly ground black pepper

1 tablespoon dried herbes de Provence

1 tablespoon grated lemon zest

1 teaspoon dried sage

1 onion, quartered

1 rib celery, cut into chunks

6 cloves garlic, mashed with the back of your knife

½ cup (1 stick) unsalted butter, melted

Try this once and I'm certain it will become your preferred method for cooking turkey. Notice that I'm using a 12-pound bird. Turkeys in the 12- to 14-pound range roast much more evenly than larger birds. If you need more turkey than a 12- or 14-pound bird will provide, I strongly suggest you roast two birds rather than a 20-pound monstrosity. (See photo on page 146.)

1. Two days before you plan to roast the turkey, place it on a rack set in a rimmed baking sheet. In a small bowl, blend the salt, pepper, herbes de Provence, lemon zest, and sage and rub all over the turkey, including in the cavity. Refrigerate, uncovered, for 2 days.

2. Remove the turkey from the refrigerator at least 1 hour before you plan to roast it. Stuff the cavity with the onion, celery, and garlic. Tuck the wings under the breast and tie the legs together with kitchen twine. Brush the turkey with the melted butter.

3. Light a fire in the kamado grill using your favorite method. After about 10 minutes, place the grill rack in position, close the dome, and open the upper and lower dampers all the way. When the temperature reaches 400° F, insert the ceramic plate in the kamado.

4. Place the turkey on the grill and close the dome. Adjust the dampers to drop the grill temperature to 325° F. Roast the turkey until the juices run clear and the internal temperature at the thigh reaches 165° F, about 3 hours.

5. Transfer the turkey to a cutting board and loosely tent with aluminum foil. Let rest for 1 hour, then carve and serve.

Tea-Roasted Whole Duck

Serves 6

½ cup loose tea leaves

5 whole cloves

3 whole star anise

2 tablespoons grated orange zest

¼ cup thawed frozen orange juice concentrate

1 tablespoon tamari

1 tablespoon rice wine vinegar

½ teaspoon kosher salt

¼ teaspoon ground cinnamon

1 (5- to 6-pound) duck

Many Asian cultures use tea as a smoking medium, and I enjoyed a version of this duck smoked on a kamado during a trip to Tokyo. My method is far easier, using the tea as a rub ingredient, which my host in Japan suggested. The flavor is deep and sparkles with rich spice and citrus notes. Lay some halved bok choy on the grill for the last 5 minutes to serve alongside the duck. This rub is excellent on all sorts of poultry, but it particularly shines with duck and quail.

1. Using a spice grinder, coffee grinder, or mortar and pestle, grind the tea leaves, cloves, and star anise together into a fine powder, then stir in the orange zest. Pour the tea blend into a small bowl and whisk in the juice concentrate, tamari, vinegar, salt, and cinnamon. Let the mixture stand at room temperature for 30 minutes or cover and refrigerate for up to 2 hours.

2. Cut any excess fat from the duck cavity and pin any excess skin under the duck by folding the wing tips under. Smear the tea paste over the duck, including some in the cavity. Let stand at room temperature for 1 hour or cover with plastic wrap and refrigerate for up to 4 hours.

3. Light a fire in the kamado grill using your favorite method. After about 10 minutes, place the grill rack in position, close the dome, and open the upper and lower dampers all the way. When the temperature reaches 500° F, adjust the dampers to maintain the temperature.

4. Place the duck on a rack in a roasting pan, then set it on the grill. Close the dome, adjust the dampers to drop the grill temperature to 400° F, and roast until the duck is a beautiful mahogany and the internal temperature at the thigh registers 150° to 160° F, about 2 hours.

5. Transfer the duck to a cutting board and let rest for about 30 minutes. Cut into serving portions and serve hot or at room temperature.

Your Goose Is Cooked

Serves 6

1 (9- to 11-pound) goose

1 orange, cut in half

1 teaspoon ground allspice

Kosher salt and freshly ground black pepper

½ cup maple syrup (grade B preferred)

¼ cup orange-flavored liqueur

I guess too much Charles Dickens around Christmas prompted me to cook my first goose some twenty years ago. It was a change of pace from turkey and a big hit. Now I alternate between a standing rib roast and the goose for the holiday. Goose has a lot of fat, and you want to render much of it out while cooking. The magic is in what that rendering fat is doing for the flesh of the goose. Take a peek every so often to make sure the pan doesn't overfill with liquid fat. If it starts to get too full, carefully remove some with a ladle or turkey baster. Be sure to save that fat in the fridge, though. Potatoes are delicious fried up in goose fat.

1. Remove the giblets and any obvious fat from the goose. With an ice pick or metal skewer, puncture the skin of the goose all over. This will let excess fat render out of the goose. Rub the orange halves all over the goose, inside and out, squeezing the juice out as you do. Place the orange halves inside the cavity. Season the goose inside and out with the allspice and salt and pepper to taste. Cover with plastic wrap and refrigerate for 24 hours.

2. Remove the bird from the refrigerator at least 1 hour before you plan to roast. Cross the legs and tie them together with kitchen twine and put the wing joints under the bird. Place the bird on a rack in a roasting pan.

3. Light a fire in the kamado grill using your favorite method. After about 10 minutes, place the grill rack in position, close the dome, and open the upper and lower dampers all the way. When the temperature reaches 500° F, adjust the dampers to maintain the temperature.

4. Place the roasting pan on the grill, close the dome, and roast for about 30 minutes.

5. Adjust the dampers to drop the grill temperature to 350° F. Roast for 1 hour, then baste with the maple syrup. Roast for about another hour, basting every 30 minutes, alternating between the maple syrup and pan juices each time. The bird is done when the juices run clear and the internal temperature at the thigh is 165° F; figure on 20 minutes per pound.

6. Transfer the goose to a cutting board and let rest for 15 minutes before carving.

Roasted Side of Salmon with Herb Goat Cheese and Spinach

Serves 8

10 ounces fresh spinach leaves, well washed and trimmed of heavy stems

4 ounces herb-flavored goat cheese, at room temperature

Pinch of freshly grated nutmeg

Kosher salt and freshly ground black pepper

1 (4-pound) side of salmon

Olive oil for brushing

2 cups plain dry breadcrumbs

½ cup (1 stick) unsalted butter, melted

This is a very elegant family-style presentation of salmon. The flavors are bright and sweet, with a slight bitter afternote that complements the richness of the salmon. The breadcrumbs add a little crunch. Look for sides of salmon at your local price club.

1. Blanch the spinach in a pot of boiling salted water until wilted, about 30 seconds. Drain and rinse with cold water. Roll the spinach up in paper towels and squeeze to get out as much water out as possible. Finely chop the spinach and put in a bowl. Add the goat cheese, nutmeg, salt, and pepper and stir until well combined.

2. Cut a ½-inch-deep pocket along the top of the salmon, running its entire length. Use your fingers to open the pocket and stuff as much of the spinach mixture into the pocket as possible. Mound the rest on top of the salmon. Brush a rimmed baking sheet with olive oil. Place the salmon on the baking sheet.

3. Light a fire in the kamado grill using your favorite method. After about 10 minutes, place the grill rack in position, close the dome, and open the upper and lower dampers all the way. When the temperature reaches 400° F, adjust the dampers to maintain the temperature.

4. Toss the breadcrumbs and melted butter together and sprinkle over the top of the salmon to form a crust. Place the baking pan on the grill and close the dome. Roast until the tip of a cake tester stuck into the thickest part of the salmon is just warm when touched to your lip, about 12 minutes.

5. Remove the pan from the kamado and, using two long spatulas, transfer the salmon to a platter, and serve.

Shrimp, Chicken, and Sausage Paella

Serves 6 to 8

6 bone-in, skin-on chicken thighs

1 linguica sausage

1 pound bulk (raw) chorizo sausage

½ cup chopped red onion

½ cup chopped green bell pepper

¼ cup prepared sofrito (available in the Hispanic section of the supermarket)

1 cup long-grain rice

4 cups low-sodium chicken broth, divided

1 tablespoon chopped fresh thyme

1 teaspoon turmeric

½ teaspoon smoked paprika

½ teaspoon saffron threads, crushed between your fingers

2 cloves garlic, finely minced

1 pound 34/40-count shrimp, shells left on, cut down the back and veins removed (cooking the shrimp with their shells will add a ton of flavor to the paella)

½ cup green peas

1 tablespoon chopped fresh oregano

Paella is a snap to make in the kamado. I've simplified the recipe, but you will still get the authentic essence. You can purchase a paella pan in most Hispanic markets or use a 15-inch cast-iron skillet instead. Paella is a perfect patio party dish, but promise me you won't start drinking the sangria until it's done, okay?

1. Light a fire in the kamado grill using your favorite method. After about 10 minutes, place the grill rack in position, close the dome, and open the upper and lower dampers all the way. When the temperature reaches 500° F, adjust the dampers to maintain the temperature. The temperature is going to vary through this cooking process, so don't panic if you can't maintain 500° F. You'll find that you are going to stay in the 400° F range but if your first target temperature is 500° F and your dampers are set for that heat, the grill will do its job to help you cook this dish.

2. Place the chicken thighs and linguica sausage on the grill; sear the chicken about 5 minutes per side and cook the sausage, turning, for about 5 minutes. Remove the chicken and sausage to a plate.

3. Place a 15-inch paella pan or cast-iron skillet on the grill. Give it a few minutes to heat up, then add the chorizo. Cook it until browned, crisp, and cooked all the way through, breaking it up with a wooden spoon. Using a slotted spoon, remove the sausage from the pan to the plate. Add the onion and bell pepper to the rendered fat in the pan and cook until softened, about 5 minutes, stirring a few times. Add the sofrito and cook, stirring, for about 2 minutes. Stir in the rice and let toast 2 to 3 minutes. Pour in 2 cups of broth and bring to a boil. Close the dome and cook for 10 minutes.

4. Add the thyme, turmeric, paprika, saffron, and garlic. Stir to work into the rice.

5. Slice the linguica across on an angle into 8 pieces. Add the chicken, sliced sausage, and chorizo to the pan along with another 1 cup of broth and stir, then close the dome.

6. After 20 minutes, stir in the shrimp and peas. If the rice is looking dry, add the remaining cup of broth. Close the dome and cook until the shrimp are done, another 7 to 10 minutes.

7. Remove the pan from the grill and sprinkle with the oregano. Serve immediately.

Boys' Night Out Sweet Potatoes

Serves 6

3 very large sweet potatoes

1 to 2 tablespoons barbecue rub, to taste

½ teaspoon ground cinnamon

6 tablespoons (¾ stick) unsalted butter, cut into 6 pieces

Maple syrup (grade B preferred) for drizzling

I'm part of a group of guys called Boys' Night Out, where we get together, cook, drink, relive the glory days of our past, and argue over current events. With the group being divided between Republicans and Democrats, it can get rowdy. The only rule is no women are allowed. This roasted sweet potato recipe has come out of those dinners and is one of our favorite side dishes. At least it's one thing we agree on. Slide this on the grill alongside a roasting piece of pork or chicken.

1. Slice the sweet potatoes in half lengthwise. With a knife, cut a cross-hatch pattern into the flesh; you want to just barely puncture the flesh, not cut into it deeply. This lets the seasonings get deeper into the sweet potatoes. In a small bowl, combine the barbecue rub and cinnamon, then sprinkle it liberally over the cut sides of the sweet potatoes.

2. Light a fire in the kamado grill using your favorite method. After about 10 minutes, place the grill rack in position and close the dome, then open the upper and lower dampers all the way. When the temperature reaches 500° F, adjust the dampers to maintain the temperature.

3. Place the sweet potatoes on a baking pan. Place the pan on the grill, close the dome, and roast the potatoes for about 45 minutes. Check for doneness by sliding a paring knife into one of the halves; it should go in easily, without resistance. If not, continue roasting for another 15 minutes.

4. Transfer the potatoes to a platter. Cut a slit in each lengthwise and insert a slice of butter. Drizzle lightly with maple syrup and serve.

Brussels Sprouts with Pancetta and Balsamic Vinegar

Serves 4 to 6

1 pound Brussels sprouts, stems trimmed

4 ounces thick-sliced pancetta, diced

2 tablespoons olive oil

3 cloves garlic, minced

2 shallots, chopped

Kosher salt and freshly ground black pepper

2 tablespoons balsamic vinegar

If you had asked me a few years ago what my favorite Brussels sprouts recipe was, I would have laughed and told you there is no such thing as a good Brussels sprouts recipe. This one changed my mind. Now I can't wait for Brussels sprouts to come into season, and I will eat this dish almost every week through late fall and winter and into early spring. This recipe is adapted from a dish initially offered at a local Italian restaurant, Belle Monica, as a special winter appetizer; it has become so popular, they can't take it off the menu.

1. Fill a 3-quart saucepan about half full of water. Place over high heat and bring to a boil. Add the Brussels sprouts and cook 4 to 5 minutes. Drain and run under cold water for a couple of minutes. Arrange a few layers of paper towels on the counter and spread the Brussels sprouts over the paper towels to drain.

2. Light a fire in the kamado grill using your favorite method. After about 10 minutes, place the grill rack in position, close the dome, and open the upper and lower dampers all the way. When the temperature reaches 500° F, adjust the dampers to maintain the temperature.

3. While the grill is coming to temperature, place the pancetta in a cold cast-iron or heavy-bottom sauté pan; I use a carbon-steel skillet for this. Cook over medium-low heat until the pancetta is crisp and has rendered its fat. Remove it from the pan and reserve.

4. To the fat, add the olive oil; place the pan on the grill and close the dome. Wait about 2 minutes, then add the sprouts, garlic, and shallots. Close the dome and roast until the sprouts begin to caramelize, about 15 minutes. Be sure to shake the pan occasionally so that all sides of the sprouts are browning. When the sprouts are tender, add the reserved pancetta. Season with a generous pinch of salt and pepper.

5. Remove the pan from the grill. Add the vinegar to the pan and toss with the sprouts. Transfer to a serving dish and serve hot.

Roasted Carrots, Parsnips, and Shallots with Honey Butter and Sherry Vinegar

Serves 4 to 6

3 large carrots, peeled and cut into 1-inch chunks

3 large parsnips, peeled and cut into 1-inch chunks

8 shallots, peeled and cut in half

2 tablespoons canola oil

Kosher salt and freshly ground black pepper

½ cup honey

6 tablespoons (¾ stick) unsalted butter

3 tablespoons sherry vinegar

1 tablespoon chopped fresh thyme

If you don't try another vegetable dish in this book, try this one. This combination goes with almost anything and changes its character to suit the meal. Add other root vegetables to the mix if you like—sweet potatoes, rutabaga, and winter squash would be good choices.

1. In a medium bowl, combine the carrots, parsnips, and shallots. Drizzle with the oil and sprinkle with salt and pepper.

2. In a small saucepan over medium heat, combine the honey, butter, vinegar, and thyme and bring to a simmer for 1 minute. Pour the mixture over the vegetables and toss to coat the vegetables well.

3. Light a fire in the kamado grill using your favorite method. After about 10 minutes, place the grill rack in position and close the dome, then open the upper and lower dampers all the way. When the temperature reaches 400° F, adjust the dampers to maintain the heat.

4. Pour the vegetables into a rimmed baking pan with the glaze and arrange in a single layer. Place on the kamado grill, close the dome, and roast until the vegetables give easily when pierced with a knife and have some caramelization, about 45 minutes.

5. Transfer the vegetables to a serving bowl and serve immediately.

Roasted Tomatoes

Serves 6

8 large summer-ripe tomatoes or 12 Roma or plum tomatoes

1 cup chopped onion

2 tablespoons olive oil

1 teaspoon dried thyme

1 teaspoon dried oregano

1 teaspoon dried basil

¼ teaspoon kosher salt

¼ teaspoon freshly ground black pepper

Roasting tomatoes concentrates their sweet acidity. This recipe is just a beginning—you can enjoy them as they are right out of the kamado, or use them as the base for homemade marinara sauce, or serve them on bruschetta.

1. Light a fire in the kamado grill using your favorite method. After about 10 minutes, place the grill rack in position, close the dome, and open the upper and lower dampers all the way. When the temperature reaches 375° F, adjust the dampers to maintain the temperature.
2. While the grill comes to temperature, cut the tomatoes in half and arrange, cut side up, on a rack set in a rimmed baking sheet. Sprinkle the onion across the tops of the tomatoes, then drizzle with the olive oil, and sprinkle evenly with the herbs, salt, and pepper.
3. Place the baking sheet on the grill, close the dome, and roast for 1 hour; check to see if they are developing nice charred bits.
4. Close the dome and continue to roast for another 30 minutes, until the tomatoes have taken on a little color.
5. Transfer the tomatoes to a bowl or serving dish and give them a stir. They can be served hot or at room temperature.

Braised Lamb Shanks
(page 198)

5

Steaming & Braising in the Kamado

I expected my kamado to be a great smoker. And it had to be a first-rate grill. Roasting, sure, it should be able to handle that with ease. But my biggest surprise has been what an excellent job of steaming and braising the kamado grill does. The kamado really can do it all with little work or worry on our part.

With steaming, food is cooked, usually in a covered pot on the stovetop, over a small amount of boiling water. Food that is steamed tends to retain more of its nutrients and natural texture and flavor, a boon for more delicate foods.

Braising, on the other hand, requires that the meat or vegetable be browned first and then cooked in liquid at low heat, covered, for a fairly long time. This process breaks down tough fibers, tenderizing the food, and intense flavors develop. Braising is a huge friend to tougher cuts of meat like lamb shanks and lean beef roasts, and to preparations like stew.

So why do I like to use the kamado for steaming and braising? Because it does both so well. Its exacting temperature control creates an environment where you can "set it and forget it"—your own grilling slow cooker, as it were. You also get the added benefit of a layer of smoke flavor, in the case of steamed dishes like Old-Fashioned Oyster Roast that are cooked right on the grill or, in braising, those dishes where the meat is first browned off on the grill directly over the fire, then transferred to its braising liquid and finished off in the kamado.

The grill setup is easy for both steaming and braising—crank up the grill just as you would for direct heat and use the dampers to control the temperatures. Most of the temperatures will be in the midrange, between 300° and 400° F. Don't get panicked if the temperature levels off not exactly where I've indicated. In many of the braising recipes, I'll have you start at a higher temperature to brown the protein and then drop the temperature to braise. The kamado actually helps you with this, the temperature in the grill dropping slightly each time you open the dome to turn the protein while browning it.

While you don't need ceramic plates or other kamado grill gear for steaming and braising, you do need some heavy-duty pots and baking dishes. I like cast iron and porcelain-coated cast iron. You'll also need a roll of heavy-duty aluminum foil as well as disposable aluminum-foil roasting pans and pie plates. Add a steaming rack to your arsenal and you can steam large quantities of shrimp, mollusks, or corn, for instance. With your kamado brought to temperature at 350° F, it should take less than 10 minutes for steam to build in the pot; add your food, cover the pot, close the dome, and steam until done. Five pounds of shrimp will usually take no longer than 15 minutes.

By this point in this cookbook, you might think I've gone past the point of obsession with my kamado. But no, I believe in putting my cooking equipment through its paces, to see what the boundaries of its uses are, even beyond what it is advertised to do. And what I've found is that the kamado steams and braises as well as it smokes. Just call it getting your money's worth from an excellent investment!

Old-Fashioned Oyster Roast

Serves 8: recipe easily doubles or triples

Cocktail sauce

Horseradish sauce

Hot sauce

Melted butter

Lemon wedges

Lots of paper towels
(and I do mean lots!)

8 aluminum-foil pie plates

8 leather garden gloves

8 oyster knives

1 bushel oysters

Damp dish towels

Oysters have been roasted over wood since the first brave soul ventured to open one and partake of it. Thanks to air freight, oysters are available all over the country, and there is no better early-to-late-fall eating than a slew of grill-roasted oysters. The kamado, with its unique moisture-trapping abilities, serves up perfectly roasted oysters, still full of oyster liquor, perfect for slurping. It's simple to do and deliciously messy to eat. Make sure you have plenty of napkins on hand.

1. Light a fire in the kamado grill using your favorite method. After about 10 minutes, place the grill rack in position, close the dome, and open the upper and lower dampers all the way. When the temperature reaches 400° F, adjust the dampers to maintain the temperature.

2. Set all the condiments, melted butter, and lemon wedges on a table close to the grill, along with the paper towels and pie plates. Give each of your guests a pair of gloves and an oyster knife.

3. Place as many of the oysters in a single layer as you can on the grill. Cover with the damp towels and close the dome. As the oysters start to open, usually after about 15 minutes, toss them into the pie plates and encourage everybody to start opening their oysters and topping them off the way they like. Continue cooking the oysters in batches until they're gone. Any oysters that don't open should be discarded.

Steamed Clams with an Asian Twist

Serves 6 or 10 as a first course

CLAMS:

¾ cup dry sake or beer

1½ teaspoons minced, peeled fresh ginger

1½ teaspoons minced garlic

1 teaspoon crushed red pepper

3 green onions, sliced on the bias

3 pounds cherrystone clams, cleaned (see below)

3 tablespoons unsalted butter, cut into small pieces

TOAST:

½ cup olive oil

2 tablespoons hot paprika

1 loaf crusty bread, cut into ½-inch-thick slices

TO SERVE:

3 tablespoons chopped fresh cilantro

1½ limes, quartered

You can serve this sassy take on steamed clams as an entrée, a first course, or an hors d'oeuvre for a cocktail party. The steaming liquid can also be used with shrimp or scallops, as well as with thin white fish fillets like tilapia and flounder. Or use it to steam chicken tenders and then serve them with a sweet chili dipping sauce.

1. In a large measuring cup, combine the sake, ginger, garlic, pepper, and green onions. Pour the mixture into a large disposable aluminum-foil pan. Add the clams. Top evenly with the butter and cover with aluminum foil.

2. Light a fire in the kamado grill using your favorite method. After about 10 minutes, place the grill rack in position, close the dome, and open the upper and lower dampers all the way. When the temperature reaches 400° F, adjust the dampers to maintain the temperature.

3. Place the pan on the grill, close the dome, and steam until all the clams have opened, 10 to 12 minutes. Remove from the grill.

4. Make the toast: Whisk together the oil and paprika and brush the mixture on both sides of the bread. Place on the grill and cook until toasted, 1 or 2 minutes.

5. To serve, remove foil and sprinkle with the cilantro. Divide the clams and their juice between 6 bowls, add the lime wedges and grilled toast, and serve immediately.

Cleaning Mollusks

To purge clams, place in a large bowl, cover with cold water, sprinkle over 1 tablespoon *each* cornmeal and salt, and let stand 1 hour. Drain the clams and rinse.

To clean mussels, all you need to do is take a pair of needle-nose pliers and jerk out the little beards hanging down. You may not even need to do that since most mussels that come to market have already been debearded.

Frogmore Stew for a Party

Serves 8 to 10

4 tablespoons Chesapeake Bay–style seasoning or crab boil seasoning

2 pounds smoked sausage, cut into 2-inch pieces

4 sweet onions, peeled, root ends maintained, then cut into quarters

12 ears corn, shucked, silks removed, and broken in half

4 pounds 3¼-count shrimp

8 stone crab claws (optional)

Cocktail sauce

Melted unsalted butter

Grainy mustard

There are no frogs and no "stew" in Frogmore Stew, but there is a whole lot of ocean-driven flavor in this dish, which is perfect for entertaining at the height of summer. Legend has it that Richard Gay, whose family owns a seafood company near the community of Frogmore on St. Helena Island in South Carolina, invented the stew; it also sometimes goes by the name of Beaufort Stew, the city of Beaufort being just to the west of the island. The reality is that a "stew" like this one can be found in most all Low Country coastal regions of the Southeast.

I like to make this in August when East Coast shrimping really ramps up and the corn is at its sweetest. If I happen to find some, I'll steal an idea from Charleston chef Mike Lata and throw in a few stone crab claws—damn good but not essential. You can easily double or triple the recipe or cut it in half.

1. Take a 6- to 8-quart stockpot and fill two-thirds full of water. Add 3 tablespoons of the seasoning and stir to mix.

2. Light a fire in the kamado grill using your favorite method. After about 10 minutes, place the grill rack in position, close the dome, and open the upper and lower dampers all the way. When the temperature reaches 400° F, adjust the dampers to maintain the temperature.

3. Place the pot on the grill and close the dome. Let the water come to a boil (this will take about 15 minutes). Add the sausage and onions, close the dome, and cook for 5 minutes. Add the corn, close the dome, and cook for 2 to 3 minutes. Add the shrimp and crab claws, if using, close the dome, and cook until the shrimp turn pink and have formed a slight "C" shape, about another 5 minutes.

4. Remove the pot from the grill and drain into a colander. Sprinkle the remaining 1 tablespoon seasoning over the "stew." Dump the stew out over a newspaper-lined table. Call everybody to eat, passing the cocktail sauce, butter, and mustard.

Mussels with Shallots, Tomatoes, and Basil

Serves 4

2 tablespoons olive oil

3 tablespoons finely chopped shallots

1 tablespoon chopped garlic

2 pounds mussels (about 60), debearded (see page 184)

¾ cup Riesling wine

¼ cup fresh lemon juice

¼ cup low-sodium chicken broth

¼ cup diced plum tomatoes or drained canned diced tomatoes (if you're using canned and really like tomatoes, it won't hurt to use a whole 14.5-ounce can, drained)

¼ cup (½ stick) unsalted butter, cut into small pieces

Kosher salt and freshly ground black pepper

3 tablespoons thinly sliced fresh basil

Add some shoestring French fries and you have Belgium in a bowl. Farmed mussels are in the markets year-round and take very little cleaning, making this dish a snap to make even during the week. The flavor that develops, however, says anything but just another weeknight.

1. In a medium skillet over medium heat, heat the oil until it begins to shimmer. Add the shallots and garlic and cook, stirring several times, until soft, about 3 minutes. Pour this mixture into a deep disposable aluminum-foil pan.

2. Light a fire in the kamado grill using your favorite method. After about 10 minutes, place the grill rack in position, close the dome, and open the upper and lower dampers all the way. When the temperature reaches 400° F, adjust the dampers to maintain the temperature.

3. Add the mussels, wine, lemon juice, broth, and tomatoes to the pan. Cover with aluminum foil, place on the grill, and close the dome. Steam until the mussels have opened, about 10 minutes.

4. Remove the pan from the grill and discard any mussels that have not opened. Add the butter to the pan, stirring to blend it with the broth. Season to taste with salt and pepper, sprinkle in the basil, and toss. Divide the mussels and broth among 4 bowls and serve immediately.

New England Shore Dinner Without the Shore

Serves 8

16 small new red potatoes

8 small onions, peeled

3 bunches fresh thyme

5 pounds cherrystone clams, cleaned (see page 184)

8 ears corn, shucked, silks removed, and broken in half

2 pounds mussels, debearded (see page 184)

4 cups bottled clam juice

4 cups water

8 lobster tails (4 to 6 ounces each), thawed if necessary

6 or more lemons cut into wedges for serving

Unsalted butter, melted, for serving

Cocktail sauce for serving

Sliced crusty peasant bread for dipping in the broth

No shore? No problem. Sure, you'll miss the ocean breeze, but not the pit digging or the seagulls trying to steal your food. The fresh thyme takes the place of the seaweed, while also adding a very pleasing flavor note to the broth.

You can use whole lobsters instead of tails if you prefer. When I use whole lobsters, I first put them in a pot of boiling water for a couple of minutes, and then add another 5 minutes to the overall cooking time on the kamado. Try this in July for a change of pace from the standard summer grilling.

1. Place the potatoes and onions in a large, deep roasting pan, like a turkey roaster. Scatter about one-third of the thyme over the vegetables. Arrange the clams evenly over the vegetables, then set the corn on top. Spread the mussels around the corn and scatter the remaining thyme on top.

2. Light a fire in the kamado grill using your favorite method. After about 10 minutes, place the grill rack in position, close the dome, and open the upper and lower dampers all the way. When the temperature reaches 400° F, adjust the dampers to maintain the temperature.

3. Pour the clam juice and water in the pan. Cover with aluminum foil, place on the grill, and close the dome. Let steam for 10 to 15 minutes.

4. Set the lobster tails on top of the other ingredients, recover with the foil, close the dome, and cook until their meat is firm at the exposed end, another 15 minutes.

5. Bring the roasting pan to a table covered with several layers of newspaper. Put out the lemons, butter, cocktail sauce, and bread and let everybody dig in.

Steamed Tilefish with Orange, Ginger, and Green Onions

Serves 6

3 tablespoons orange juice

2 teaspoons grated orange zest

2 tablespoons olive oil

2 tablespoons white wine

2 cloves garlic, minced

1 (2-inch) piece fresh ginger, peeled and cut into matchsticks

¼ cup chopped green onions

2 tablespoons chopped fresh flat-leaf parsley

6 (4- to 6-ounce) tilefish fillets

Kosher salt and freshly ground black pepper

Thin orange slices

Tilefish flesh seems to radiate all the flavors of the ocean that they and we love to eat—lobster, shrimp, crab, and scallops. Because of those delicate flavors, it's a perfect fish to steam, so that every nuance can shine through. If you can't get tilefish, or if the tilefish in your market looks sad, use grouper, snapper, or halibut instead. Please let your guests open their own packets, as the scent of the steam adds to the dining experience.

1. Cut six 10-inch squares of heavy-duty aluminum foil.
2. In a small bowl, whisk the orange juice and zest, oil, wine, and garlic together until blended. Stir in the ginger, green onions, and parsley.
3. Season the fillets with salt and pepper. Place one fillet in each center of the sheet of foil. Pour the orange mixture evenly over the fillets. Top each fillet with orange slices. Fold the foil over the fish and press to seal the edges tightly.
4. Light a fire in the kamado grill using your favorite method. After about 10 minutes, place the grill rack in position, close the dome, and open the upper and lower dampers all the way. When the temperature reaches 400° F, adjust the dampers to maintain the temperature.
5. Place the packets on the grill and close the dome. Grill for 8 minutes.
6. Transfer each packet to a serving plate. Let each diner cut into their own packet to experience the intoxicating smell of the wonderful steam.

Grill-Braised Coq au Vin

Serves 4 to 6

1 large Vidalia onion, cut into 8 wedges

8 cloves garlic, peeled

1 (2-ounce) can oil-packed anchovy fillets, drained

¾ cup fresh flat-leaf parsley leaves

¼ cup fresh rosemary leaves

1 teaspoon kosher salt

½ teaspoon freshly ground black pepper

2 chickens (about 3 pounds each), cut into quarters

1 (750-ml) bottle dry, fruity red wine

Olive oil

8 ounces cremini mushrooms, trimmed and sliced

Here's an American backyard twist on a French classic. Red wine and chicken make for a perfect marriage, in the pot and on the kamado. This isn't as long a braise as for the shanks and other meat cuts in this chapter but the results are just as meltingly tender, with deep, delicious flavors.

1. Place the onion, garlic, anchovy fillets, parsley, rosemary, salt, and pepper in a food processor and pulse until the onion is finely chopped.

2. Take the chicken quarters and place in a 2-gallon zip-top plastic bag. Scrape the onion paste into the bag and add the wine. Squish the marinade around the chicken so that all the pieces are well coated and the wine and solids have blended. Press the air out of the bag and seal. Place in a bowl and refrigerate overnight, turning the bag a few times. Don't panic when the chicken turns red. It's from the wine.

3. Light a fire in the kamado grill using your favorite method. After about 10 minutes, place the grill rack in position, close the dome, and open the upper and lower dampers all the way. When the temperature reaches 375° F, adjust the dampers to maintain the temperature.

4. Remove the chicken from the marinade and pat it dry with paper towels. Pour the marinade into a large cast-iron Dutch oven. Brush the chicken lightly with olive oil and season with salt and pepper. Place on the grill, close the dome, and sear until lightly browned, 3 to 4 minutes per side. Place the chicken and mushrooms in the Dutch oven, cover, place on the grill grate, and close the dome. Braise for about 1½ hours. The breast quarters should have an internal temperature of about 165° F and the thigh quarters about 170° F; the juices should run clear between the thigh and drumstick.

5. Transfer the chicken and mushrooms to a platter and pour the braising liquid over the top. Serve hot or at room temperature.

Italian-Style Braised Rabbit

Serves 4

1 dressed rabbit (about 2½ pounds), thawed if necessary and cut into serving pieces

Kosher salt and freshly ground black pepper

¼ cup olive oil

1 cup chopped onion

2 ribs celery, diced

4 cloves garlic, chopped

½ cup dry white wine

1 tablespoon balsamic vinegar

2 cups unsalted or low-sodium broth

1 cup diced tomatoes (canned is fine)

1 teaspoon dried rosemary

1 teaspoon dried thyme

½ teaspoon dried oregano

½ cup chopped fresh parsley

Rabbit can be found in most large supermarkets today, usually frozen, which is fine for this braise. This is the kind of dish you're likely to find at mom-and-pop eateries throughout Umbria and Tuscany in the fall, more often than not paired with roasted squash or pumpkin. Rabbit is mild and picks up the flavors of the braise, much like chicken. It's a great choice when you feel like you're in a culinary rut, and mighty tasty. Try to keep the dome closed as much as possible at the beginning so you'll have good heat for the braise.

1. Light a fire in the kamado grill using your favorite method. After about 10 minutes, place the grill rack in position, close the dome, and open the upper and lower dampers all the way. When the temperature reaches 400° F, adjust the dampers to maintain the temperature.

2. Season the rabbit pieces generously with salt and pepper. Place the rabbit on the grill, close the dome, and sear until nicely browned, about 3 minutes per side. Transfer to a platter.

3. Place a Dutch oven on the grill, add the olive oil, close the dome, and let the oil heat for about 2 minutes. Throw in the onion and celery, close the dome, and cook for 2 minutes, then stir in the garlic. Place the rabbit back in the pot, add the wine and vinegar, close the dome, bring to a boil (which should take about 5 minutes), and let boil for 2 minutes. Pour in the broth and tomatoes and stir in the dried herbs. Cover the pot, close the dome, adjust the dampers to maintain a temperature of 350° to 375° F, and braise until the rabbit is fork tender, 1 to 1½ hours.

4. Remove the pot from the kamado and stir in the fresh parsley. Taste the broth for salt and pepper, and adjust as needed. Let rest, covered, for at least 20 minutes to let the flavors develop. Serve the rabbit topped with the braising liquid and vegetables.

Pork Osso Buco

Serves 6

1 cup dry white wine

½ cup bourbon

¼ cup molasses

¼ cup cider vinegar

10 cloves garlic, peeled and smashed

8 sprigs fresh thyme

6 bay leaves

4 sprigs fresh rosemary

6 slices pork shank, 1½ to 2 inches thick, skin removed

Kosher salt and freshly ground black pepper

Low-sodium or unsalted chicken broth as needed

Cooked grits, pinto beans, or garlic mashed potatoes for serving

1 cup chowchow

I was going to include a straight-up standard veal osso buco recipe, but pork osso buco has recently become a new standard of Southern cooking. I believe that no matter where you live, you will enjoy this dish. The pork picks up the smoke from the charcoal fire of the kamado quickly and that hint of smoke is reinforced with the addition of molasses and bourbon to the braising liquid. A tip of the hat to chefs Ben Barker, Jason Smith, Frank Stitt, and Jay Pierce for putting the ideas behind this dish into my head.

1. Combine the wine, bourbon, molasses, and vinegar, then stir to combine. Throw in the garlic, thyme, bay leaves, and rosemary. Place the pork in 2-gallon zip-top plastic bag. Add the marinade, seal, and refrigerate for at least 24 hours, turning the bag over several times.

2. Remove the pork from the refrigerator at least 1 hour before cooking. Take the pork from the bag, reserving the marinade, and pat dry. Season liberally with salt and pepper.

3. Light a fire in the kamado grill using your favorite method. After about 10 minutes, place the grill rack in position, close the dome, and open the upper and lower dampers all the way. When the temperature reaches 400° F, adjust the dampers to maintain the temperature.

4. Place the pork on the grill, close the dome, and sear until nicely browned, 3 to 4 minutes per side. Transfer the pork to a large cast-iron Dutch oven, add the reserved marinade, and add enough broth to come even with the top of the pork. Cover. Adjust the dampers to drop the temperature in the kamado to 350° F.

5. Place the pan on the grill, close the dome, and braise the pork until it is super tender, about 2 hours. There should be no resistance when you insert a knife into a thickest section of the pork, and the juices should run clear.

6. Transfer the pork to a plate and tent with aluminum foil. Strain the braising liquid through a fine mesh strainer into a saucepan and bring to a boil. Cook over medium heat until the sauce is reduced by half, usually about 10 minutes. (At this point, you can cover and refrigerate the pork and liquid for up to 2 days. When ready to use, defat both the pork and liquid. Gently rewarm the pork in the broth.)

7. To serve, place a mound of grits, pinto beans, or potatoes in the bottom of a shallow soup bowl. Place one piece of pork on top and divide the chowchow among the servings. Spoon the reduced braising liquid around the pork and serve immediately.

Beef Short Ribs Braised in Red Wine and Balsamic Vinegar

Serves 6

3 pounds short ribs

Kosher salt and freshly ground black pepper

2 medium onions, quartered

2 medium carrots, cut into 1-inch-thick rounds

12 to 16 cloves garlic, peeled

4 bay leaves

1 tablespoon black peppercorns, coarsely crushed

1 teaspoon dried thyme

1 teaspoon dried oregano

3 cups dry red wine (preferably a cabernet sauvignon or other deep, fruity red)

¼ cup balsamic vinegar

3 tablespoons red wine vinegar

2 tablespoons soy sauce (preferably dark, if available)

1 tablespoon cornstarch or potato starch dissolved in 2 tablespoons water

Cooked grits, polenta, or mashed potatoes for serving

1 tablespoon chopped fresh parsley

Short ribs of beef are wonderful grilled (see page 108), but they really come into their own when they're braised, with a rich, dark, earthy flavor perfect for autumn days when the chill is in the air. In a perfect world, you want to make this the day before you intend to serve it. Refrigerate both the ribs and braising liquid and the next day you can simply scrape away the fat, which will have solidified on both. Giving it 24 hours (or even up to three days) in the fridge also allows the flavors time to develop even more. I love serving this over cheese grits made with Gruyère, but just plain old grits, polenta, or mashed potatoes will work fine.

1. Light a fire in the kamado grill using your favorite method. After about 10 minutes, place the grill rack in position, close the dome, and open the upper and lower dampers all the way. When the temperature reaches 500° F, adjust the dampers to maintain the temperature.
2. Season the ribs on both sides with salt and pepper. When the grill is ready, place the ribs on the grill, close the dome, and sear until nicely browned, 3 to 5 minutes per side.
3. Transfer the ribs to a plate. Close the dome and adjust the dampers to drop the temperature to 350° F.
4. Place the onions, carrots, garlic, bay leaves, peppercorns, thyme, oregano, wine, vinegars, soy sauce, and ½ teaspoon salt in a large cast-iron Dutch oven. Set the seared ribs on top and cover. Set the Dutch oven on the grill, close the dome, and braise until the meat is super tender, 2 to 3 hours.
5. Transfer the short ribs to a plate. Strain the braising liquid through a fine mesh strainer into a container. Let both cool, then cover and refrigerate, preferably overnight, which will allow enough time for the fat to rise to the top of the liquid and solidify.
6. Carefully remove all the fat from the braising liquid and scrape any off the ribs. Return the liquid and ribs to the Dutch oven and heat over medium heat until the liquid is simmering, 10 to 15 minutes. Transfer the ribs to a platter and tent with aluminum foil to keep warm. Bring the braising liquid to a boil and whisk in the starch slurry until the liquid thickens.
7. To serve, divide the ribs between 4 dinner plates or large rimmed soup bowls, along with the grits, polenta, or mashed potatoes, and pour some sauce over the top. Sprinkle with the parsley and serve.

Chicago-Style Italian Beef Sandwiches

Serves 8 to 10 or more

1 teaspoon kosher salt

1 teaspoon freshly ground black pepper

1 teaspoon dried oregano

1 teaspoon dried basil

1 teaspoon dried parsley

1 teaspoon onion powder

1 teaspoon garlic powder

1 bay leaf

1 (⅔-ounce) package dry zesty Italian salad seasoning mix

3 cups low-sodium beef broth

1 (5-pound) eye of round roast

Italian or Chicago rolls

Giardiniera

I'm not terribly fond of eye of round roasts, the result of way too many dried-out Sunday roasts in my youth. But I do like to use eye of round for this recipe. It's lean, so it throws off much less fat, but it still takes well to braising and the vibrant flavors of this Chicago classic. This makes a lot, so it's great for a block party or other large gathering, but it also freezes nicely and can be reheated in minutes with the help of a microwave. These sandwiches are a messy, delightful treat.

If you're not familiar with giardiniera, it's a pickled mixture of cauliflower, carrots, celery, and usually a hot pepper. It gives the sandwiches a welcome kick of heat and sour, as well as crunch.

1. Place all the seasonings and the broth in a large cast-iron Dutch oven. Stir to blend, then put in the roast. It's okay if you need to cut it in half. Cover.

2. Light a fire in the kamado grill using your favorite method. After about 10 minutes, place the grill rack in position, close the dome, and open the upper and lower dampers all the way. When the temperature reaches 350° F, adjust the dampers to maintain the temperature.

3. Place the Dutch oven on the grill, close the dome, and braise until the meat is fork tender, 3 to 4 hours.

4. Remove the Dutch oven from the kamado and discard the bay leaf. Shred the meat with a fork right in the pot with the juices. The meat juices are a big part of the sandwich. Serve on toasted Chicago or Italian rolls with giardiniera on the side and plenty of napkins.

Braised Lamb Shanks

Serves 6

4 tablespoons olive oil

1 cup diced onion

5 cloves garlic, peeled and crushed

4 ribs celery, cut into ½-inch-thick slices

2 medium carrots, cut into ½-inch-thick rounds

2 cups dry red wine

2 bay leaves

6 oil-packed anchovy fillets

2 cups low-sodium beef broth

1 (32-ounce) can plum tomatoes, drained

10 black peppercorns

6 (1- to 1¼-pound) lamb shanks

Kosher salt and freshly ground black pepper

I didn't grow up eating lamb, because my father, who served with the Army Air Force in England during World War II, had more than his fill of mutton and refused to have anything similar to it in our house. If he were alive today, I believe I could get him to change his mind with this recipe. I first had lamb shank at the Tavern at the Beekman Arms in Rhinebeck, New York. I never was able to get them to part with the recipe, but this version satisfies my taste memory of it. Lamb shanks are perfect candidates for braising, developing layer upon layer of flavor, each deeper and more complex than the last, all of them melding into perfection. (See photo on page 180).

1. In a large skillet over medium heat, heat 2 tablespoons of the oil, then add the onion, garlic, celery, and carrots and cook, stirring a few times, until the vegetables have slightly softened, 3 to 5 minutes. Add 1 cup of the wine and stir, scraping up any browned bits from the bottom of the skillet. Pour the contents of the skillet into a large disposable aluminum-foil pan. Add the remaining 1 cup wine, the bay leaves, anchovies, broth, tomatoes, and peppercorns.

2. Light a fire in the kamado grill using your favorite method. After about 10 minutes, place the grill rack in position, close the dome, and open the upper and lower dampers all the way. When the temperature reaches 325° F, adjust the dampers to maintain the temperature.

3. Brush the lamb shanks with the remaining 2 tablespoons oil and season with salt and pepper. Place the shanks on the grill, close the dome, and sear until nicely browned on all sides, turning the shanks every 2 to 3 minutes.

4. Transfer the lamb shanks to the foil pan, cover with foil, and set the pan on the grill. Close the dome and adjust the dampers to drop the temperature in the kamado down to about 325° F. Braise until the meat is exceedingly tender, about 2½ hours.

5. Transfer the shanks to a platter and cover with foil. Strain the braising liquid through a fine-mesh strainer into a medium saucepan. Bring to a boil and reduce until nicely thickened. Pour the sauce over the lamb shanks and serve.

Kamado Brunswick Stew

Serves 15 to 18

1 cup (2 sticks) unsalted butter

3 cups finely diced onions (about 2 large)

2 tablespoons finely chopped garlic

1 tablespoon freshly ground black pepper

1 cup Lexington-Style "Dip" (page 246)

¼ cup Worcestershire sauce

¼ cup yellow mustard

¼ cup honey

1 pound leftover boneless smoked pork

1 pound leftover boneless smoked beef

1 pound leftover smoked poultry

2 (28-ounce) cans crushed tomatoes

3 cups fresh corn kernels (from 4 to 6 ears)

4 cups baby butter beans (lima beans)

2 quarts unsalted or low-sodium chicken broth

Kosher salt

2 cups mashed potatoes

Proper Cornbread (page 217)

Your favorite hot sauce

An award-winning chronicler of Southern foods and someone I'm proud to call a friend, Jim Villas, calls Brunswick stew "the aristocrat of American stews." I couldn't agree more and it's time this stew made its way north of the Mason-Dixon Line. The kamado offers a way to cook the stew the way it should be done—over a wood fire in a cast-iron pot. Historically, the stew was made in a cast-iron wash-pot nestled in a wood fire, and required almost constant stirring. The kamado mimics that method, capturing that time-honored flavor of smoke but with a whole lot less stirring.

Of course, all things Southern seem to come with a basket full of controversy, and this stew is no different. Is it from Brunswick County, Georgia, or Brunswick County, Virginia, or Brunswick County, North Carolina? Should it include smoked meats? Stewed meats? But good stew is like good barbecue: It really doesn't matter what its origins are, as long as the flavor and traditions are in the pot. This recipe is more Georgia, with its inclusion of smoked meats. If you like, swap out the smoked chicken for fresh as a counterpoint to all that smoked flavor. When I'm smoking pork butts, brisket, or chickens, I always hold some back and freeze it so I have the beginnings of a good Brunswick stew on hand. The stew is perfect for putting up in your freezer, so don't worry about the big yield.

1. Light a fire in the kamado grill using your favorite method. After about 10 minutes, place the grill rack in position, close the dome, and open the upper and lower dampers all the way. When the temperature reaches 300° F, adjust the dampers to maintain the temperature.

2. Set the largest cast-iron Dutch oven pot you have on the stove over medium heat and melt the butter. Add the onions and garlic and cook, stirring a few times, until softened, 5 to 10 minutes. Stir in the pepper, dip, Worcestershire, mustard, and honey and heat through. Stir in the meat, poultry, tomatoes, corn, beans, and broth and heat through.

3. Place the pot on the grill, close the dome, and let simmer for 2 to 3 hours, stirring occasionally. Taste the stew after 2 hours and see if it's to your liking. You might want to add some salt at this point and then taste again. You want a deep flavor with sweet, smoky notes. If the flavor's right, stir in the mashed potatoes, close the dome, and cook for another 30 minutes. I highly encourage you to wait at least 3 hours and, if you have the patience, up to 4 hours, before considering the stew done.

4. Remove the pot from the grill, ladle the stew into bowls, and serve with cornbread and hot sauce, if desired.

German Pancake with Strawberries (page 203)

6
Baking in the Kamado

My grandmother had two ways to cook in her rural North Carolina home—one of those newfangled (to her) electric stoves and her trusty wood stove. It took her a while to completely trust the electric stove, and most mornings, her biscuits came from the wood-fired oven—and they were absolutely the best biscuits I have ever eaten. That wood oven added something unique to her biscuits that electric or gas just couldn't deliver—an essence of smoke and an outer crispness that belied their soft, flaky insides. I thought that was lost forever until I purchased a kamado grill and realized what an exceptional baking apparatus it is.

Wood-fired ovens are all the rage in the restaurant and bakery world, and with good reason—the tasty results yielded from cooking with wood speak for themselves. And the kamado's superior heat retention and precise temperature control, along with its ability to trap moisture and circulate heat perfectly, mimics and improves upon the wood- or charcoal-fired brick oven.

I used to be what is known in the culinary world as a "bone roaster." Give me meat to cook, and I was happy. That changed when I got my kamado. Now I love to bake breads, pies, and cakes in the kamado, and I've had a blast with breakfast items as well as baked entrees. The kamado has made it simple and fun to bake great crusty bread, enjoy naan right off the grill, give an extra layer of flavor to baked fish, bake a pie that gets a double dose of apple flavor because I can cook it over an applewood fire, or savor a pizza that will rival any you can buy at a wood-fired oven pizzeria.

So how does it happen? On the temperature scale, baking happens from a low of 300° F to a high of 450° to 500° F, but mostly in the lower range. This is what differentiates it from roasting, where you use higher temperatures to help create a tasty crust on your food.

Baking is an indirect method of cooking, meaning the food will not come directly in contact with the flame. In the recipes that follow, you will see that this is achieved in several ways. In the first and simplest method, the dish is placed on the grill grate in a cooking vessel. Cast-iron is a great choice for this, but anything that is flame-proof will work.

Second, the ceramic plate is inserted in the kamado and allowed to thoroughly heat up, then the food is either placed directly on that plate or in a cooking vessel on the plate. In this case, you don't have to use flameproof cookware; oven-proof—like Pyrex—will work fine.

In the final method, the ceramic plate is inserted and then a baking stone or pizza stone is placed on top of that and allowed to heat up before the food is placed directly on the stone. I think of this "stone on stone" cooking. It's important to cook pizza using this method, as the stone draws moisture from the crust as it bakes, giving you that authentic, crispy crust that you cannot achieve in an indoor oven or, for that matter, any other grill I've ever tried. Once you've made pizza in your kamado, I doubt you'll ever pick up the phone again to call for delivery.

In the end, you should choose the method that's the least trouble for you. There's really no right or wrong way.

If you'd like to give your food an extra shot of smoke while it's cooking, you can add wood chunks (not chips). Don't bother soaking them in advance. Just be sure to pick a wood that will play nice with your food, like cherry wood for a berry crisp. Hickory is a little strong for most baking, but can be tasty when firing up a pizza.

Temperature control is critical when baking on your Kamado, and you must resist the temptation to open the dome. That said, don't panic over slight temperature variations while your dish is baking. That happens in your indoor oven as well, it's just not made obvious to you as it is with the temperature gauge on the front of your kamado. It takes a little practice to bake in a kamado, but I doubt that you'll ruin any foods along the way.

There are wonderful recipes in this chapter and I hope you try them all. When it comes to baking, the kamado once again proves its worth as a multitasking cooking marvel.

German Pancake with Strawberries

Serves 4

3 tablespoons confectioners' sugar, plus more for serving

1 cup chopped ripe strawberries

3 tablespoons unsalted butter, divided

3 tablespoons firmly packed light brown sugar

8 large eggs

1 (3-ounce) package cream cheese, softened

1 cup whole milk

3 tablespoons honey

1 cup all-purpose flour

½ teaspoon kosher salt

½ teaspoon baking powder

¼ teaspoon ground cinnamon

This pancake puffs up so pretty, a perfect choice for Mother's Day or a weekend without the kids. I like it with strawberries, but apples, pears, and other berries are nice as well. (See photo on page 200.)

1. In a medium bowl, combine the confectioners' sugar and strawberries and toss to coat. Set aside.

2. Light a fire in the kamado grill using your favorite method. After about 10 minutes, place the grill rack in position, close the dome, and open the upper and lower dampers all the way. When the temperature reaches 425° F, adjust the dampers to maintain the temperature.

3. Take 1 tablespoon of the butter and smear it over the bottom and sides of a 12-inch cast-iron skillet. Dust the butter with the brown sugar, shaking out any excess. Place the remaining 2 tablespoons butter in the skillet and set aside.

4. Place the eggs, cream cheese, milk, honey, flour, salt, baking powder, and cinnamon in a blender or food processor and puree until smooth and batter-like.

5. Place the skillet on the grill, close the dome, and let the skillet preheat for about 5 minutes. Open the dome and pour in the batter. Close the dome and bake until puffed up and golden brown, 20 to 25 minutes.

6. Remove the skillet from the kamado and dust the pancake with confectioners' sugar. Cut into servings and spoon the strawberries over each serving.

Biscuit Breakfast Pudding

Serves 6 to 8

20 to 24 baked tea biscuits
or 8 baked regular biscuits
(baked frozen biscuits are okay)

1 pound mild or hot country
breakfast sausage

3 tablespoons all-purpose flour

2 cups whole milk

Freshly ground black pepper

6 large eggs, beaten

1 cup shredded cheese (I like a
mixture of cheddar and Gruyère)

Maple syrup for serving

This is Southern to the core and unbelievably good. Each component is great on its own, but put them together, add some smoke, and you have a world-class breakfast or brunch. Great when you have company.

1. Line the bottom of a 15-inch cast-iron baking pan or skillet with the biscuits. You should have some left to crumble on top.

2. In a large skillet over medium heat, brown the sausage, using a spatula to break apart large chunks. This will take 8 to 10 minutes. Once all the pink is gone, sprinkle in the flour and stir to coat the sausage. Continue to cook for another 1 to 2 minutes. Slowly start stirring in the milk. You may not need the entire 2 cups. You want the gravy to build and thicken but not be too thick; this usually takes about 5 minutes. Season to taste with pepper. Spoon the gravy evenly over the biscuits. Use all the gravy. Pour the beaten eggs over the top. Crumble the remaining biscuits over the eggs. Scatter the cheese evenly over everything.

3. Light a fire in the kamado grill using your favorite method. After about 10 minutes, place the grill rack in position, close the dome, and open the upper and lower dampers all the way. When the temperature reaches 350° F, adjust the dampers to maintain the temperature.

4. Place the baking pan on the grill, close the dome, and bake until the cheese has browned a bit and the center of the pudding feels a little firm to the touch, but is still slightly liquid, 20 to 25 minutes.

5. Remove the pan from the grill and let sit 10 minutes. Cut into serving pieces and drizzle with maple syrup if desired. Serve immediately.

Pancetta Frittata

Serves 4 to 6

8 large eggs

2 tablespoons milk

1 cup shredded fontina cheese

Kosher salt and freshly ground black pepper

1 tablespoon unsalted butter

½ cup diced onion

4 ounces pancetta, diced

¼ cup sour cream for serving (optional)

I love omelets and they are perfect for just two folks, but how about for four or more? Enter the frittata, the Italian open-faced omelet. This one stays on the Italian theme using pancetta, which is bacon that is cured but not smoked. I've also added some caramelized onions for good measure. Feel free to customize the ingredients as you like—diced cooked potatoes, tomatoes, and squash are some other nice choices.

1. Light a fire in the kamado grill using your favorite method. After about 10 minutes, place the grill rack in position, close the dome, and open the upper and lower dampers all the way. When the temperature reaches 400° F, adjust the dampers to maintain the temperature.

2. In a large bowl, whisk the eggs, milk, cheese, and salt and pepper to taste together.

3. In a 12-inch cast-iron skillet over medium heat, melt the butter; when it foams, add the onion and cook until it is soft and some color develops, about 10 minutes, stirring occasionally. Add the pancetta and cook, stirring a few times, until it takes on a little color, about 5 minutes. Pour the egg mixture into the pan and stir it around with a spatula so that the eggs make full contact with the bottom of the pan.

4. Immediately, take the pan and place it on the grill. Close the dome and bake until the frittata is puffed up and golden brown, 20 to 25 minutes.

5. Remove the skillet from the grill and let cool for about 10 minutes. Slice the frittata into wedges and serve with sour cream, if desired.

Country Sausage-Laced Baked Beans

Serves 8 to 10 or more

3 (32-ounce) cans pork and beans, drained

2 pounds country breakfast sausage, browned and crumbled

2 medium onions, thinly sliced into half moons

1 cup firmly packed light brown sugar

1 cup dark corn syrup

¼ cup prepared yellow mustard

1 tablespoon dry mustard

2 teaspoons Worcestershire sauce

My neighbors had been after me for this recipe for years, and when I finally gave it up, it took on a life of its own. It has since been passed on to friends and relatives in North Carolina, South Carolina, Maryland, Tennessee, Indiana, and even as far west as Texas. Since I published a version of it in my newspaper column, it has become my second most-requested recipe, after my ribs (page 47).

1. Light a fire in the kamado grill using your favorite method. After about 10 minutes, place the grill rack in position, close the dome, and open the upper and lower dampers all the way. When the temperature reaches 350° F, adjust the dampers to maintain the temperature.

2. Pour the drained pork and beans in a 9- x 13-inch disposable aluminum-foil baking pan or a cast-iron Dutch oven. Add the sausage and onions and stir to mix. Add the remaining ingredients and stir to blend well.

3. Set the baking pan on the grill, close the dome, and bake for at least 1 hour; 1½ hours is better. Cooking the beans the day before and reheating them for about 30 minutes in a preheated 350° F oven will get you the very best flavor.

Cowboy Beans

Serves 8 to 10

1 pound dried pinto beans, soaked overnight in enough water to cover them

½ pound thick-cut bacon, diced

1 cup chopped onion

Freshly ground black pepper

¼ cup firmly packed light brown sugar

¼ cup molasses

1 tablespoon red wine vinegar

1 tablespoon dry mustard

1 tablespoon granulated garlic powder

2 cups brewed black coffee

1 cup tomato-based barbecue sauce

½ cup ketchup

Pinto beans and coffee are two of the main components in this rambunctious pot of flavors worthy of a Clint Eastwood or John Wayne Western. While these beans go with most any grilled food, they are at their best when paired with a piece of smoked beef. Do not salt the beans until the end, and don't be tempted to add the tomato-based products until the beans have cooked for an hour. Doing either will make the beans tough. The cooking time will also depend on the age of the beans.

1. Drain and rinse the beans; set aside. In a cast-iron Dutch oven over medium heat, cook the bacon until it is crisp and the fat is rendered, about 10 minutes. Spoon off all but 3 to 4 tablespoons of the bacon fat. Add the onion to the pot and season with pepper. Cook until softened, 5 to 8 minutes, stirring a few times. Stir in the beans, brown sugar, molasses, vinegar, dry mustard, and garlic. Pour in the coffee and enough water to just cover the beans. Stir to combine and remove from the heat until your fire is ready.

2. Light a fire in the kamado grill using your favorite method. After about 10 minutes, place the grill rack in position, close the dome, and open the upper and lower dampers all the way. When the temperature reaches 300° F, adjust the dampers to maintain the temperature.

3. Place the Dutch oven on the grill and partially cover the pot. Close the dome and cook for about 1 hour.

4. Stir in the barbecue sauce and ketchup and partially cover the pot again. Close the dome, cook another hour, and then taste. If the beans are still firm, cook for another hour. Give the beans a stir about every half hour. When done, the beans should be tender and flavorful and the sauce deep brown and thick. Serve at once or at room temperature.

Twice-Baked Potatoes

Serves 6

3 large russet potatoes

¼ cup extra-virgin olive oil

Kosher salt

¾ cup heavy cream

½ cup chopped green onions

3 tablespoons unsalted butter

1½ cups grated Gruyère
or smoked Gouda cheese
(about 6 ounces)

Freshly ground black pepper

Who doesn't like twice-baked potatoes? These are really rich and really cheesy. Feel free to add your choice of herbs and spices and change up the cheese to your liking. Cooking a steak? Start the potatoes early, then add some charcoal to bring the temperature up to grilling speed; as you grill the steaks, slide the stuffed potatoes back onto the grill to finish.

1. Light a fire in the kamado grill using your favorite method. After about 10 minutes, place the grill rack in position, close the dome, and open the upper and lower dampers all the way. When the temperature reaches 450° F, adjust the dampers to maintain the temperature.

2. Brush the potatoes all over with the oil. Pierce them with the tines of a fork and sprinkle with salt. Wrap each potato in aluminum foil and place on the grill. Close the dome and cook until the potatoes are soft and easily pierced with a knife, about 1 hour.

3. Remove the potatoes from the grill and let rest for about 15 minutes. Heat the cream in a small saucepan until hot (but not boiling) and throw in the green onions. Remove from the heat.

4. Unwrap the potatoes, cut each one in half lengthwise, and scoop out the flesh. Be careful not to tear the skin. Place the potato flesh in a large bowl and add the butter and 1 cup of the cheese. Pour in the hot cream; using a sturdy fork, mix together until the mixture is smooth and the cheese is melted. Season with salt and pepper, then spoon the mixture into each of the potato-skin shells. Sprinkle the tops evenly with the remaining ½ cup cheese.

4. Put the potatoes in a flameproof baking pan and place on the grill. Close the dome and heat until the cheese is melted, about 5 minutes. Serve immediately.

Grilled Pizza

Makes 4 pizzas

1 cup warm water (105° to 110° F)

1 teaspoon sugar

1 teaspoon active dry yeast

3 cups unbleached all-purpose flour, plus more as needed

1 teaspoon kosher salt

1 teaspoon olive oil

Your choice of toppings

Cornmeal for dusting

Some Thoughts on Pizza Toppings

Pizza is really a flatbread with toppings, and the crust should always be part of the taste experience, so don't put the kitchen sink on your pizza. Beside the traditional Margherita of fresh mozzarella, tomato slices, and basil, or pepperoni and marinara sauce, think beyond the norm. Smear some Bacon-Onion Jam (page 256) on the dough, then top with mozzarella, baby spinach, and thinly sliced red onion. Or make your pizza bianco, sprinkling chopped garlic over the crust, followed by mozzarella, ricotta, Asiago, and goat cheese, topped with torn basil. Use grilled vegetables or sliced artisanal sausage. Drizzle a little extra virgin olive oil over the finished pizza for an extra flourish. Leftover barbecued chicken, barbecue sauce, and pepper jack cheese is another winning combination. If you like something, you can probably make a pizza out of it. Have fun!

There's no doubt about it—the best pizzas come out of wood- or coal-fired ovens, and your kamado makes a great pizza oven. Please use this pizza dough—it's designed to give you a thin crust. Here are a couple of tricks I've learned: Put the cheese down first, then the sauce, and don't put more than four ingredients on your pizza, so it will slide off the peel easily. Also, the cornmeal is critical for success; it acts as a "ball bearing" to help the pizza off the peel.

1. Pour the water into a measuring cup, add the sugar, and sprinkle the yeast over the water. Let it sit until frothy, 5 to 10 minutes.
2. In the bowl of a stand mixer fitted with the dough hook, combine the flour and salt. Add the yeast mixture and mix on low speed until well combined. Pour in the oil and continue to mix on low. When all the ingredients are blended, knead the dough on medium speed until it becomes smooth and elastic, about 5 minutes.
3. Dust the surface of the dough lightly with flour and form into a ball. Spray a bowl with cooking spray and place the dough in the bowl. Cover with plastic wrap and let sit in a warm place until doubled in size, about 1½ hours.
4. Turn the dough out onto a floured work surface and knead 4 or 5 times. Form the dough into a ball and cut into 4 equal parts. Shape each into a disc and dust with flour.
5. Light a fire in the kamado grill using your favorite method. After about 10 minutes, place the ceramic plate in position, close the dome, and open the upper and lower dampers all the way. When the temperature reaches 500° F, set a baking stone on the ceramic plate, close the dome, and let it heat up for about 10 minutes. Adjust the dampers to maintain the temperature.
6. Using a rolling pin, roll each disc into a 10- to 12-inch circle. Lightly dust a pizza peel or a large rimless cookie sheet with cornmeal, lay out the dough on the peel, then arrange your desired toppings over the dough.
7. Dust the baking stone with cornmeal. Carefully slide the pizza off the peel onto the preheated baking stone. Close the dome and cook until the crust is crisp and the cheese is melted, about 10 minutes.
8. Remove to a cutting board and cut into serving slices. Repeat with the additional discs and toppings.

Savory Baked Apples

½ cup finely chopped onion

1 tablespoon unsalted butter

½ pound country breakfast sausage

½ teaspoon ground cinnamon

¼ teaspoon ground allspice

¼ teaspoon ground ginger

¼ teaspoon kosher salt

9 medium Granny Smith apples

1 cup chopped pecans

2 cups apple cider, warmed

Baked apples are a natural for the fall, especially when stuffed with country sausage. Serve them as a side dish or make a meal of them, serving up two per person. Of course, they're delicious with pork, but they also partner beautifully with smoked or roasted beef as well as turkey and chicken.

1. Place a medium skillet over medium heat and add the onion and butter. Cook until the onion is soft, about 5 minutes, stirring a few times. Add the sausage, using a spatula to break it apart into chunks. Sprinkle the spices and salt over the sausage and cook until the sausage is no longer pink, about 12 minutes.

2. Peel and core one of the apples and cut into small chunks. Add to the sausage and cook for a couple of minutes. Stir in the pecans. Remove from the heat and let cool.

3. Core the remaining apples and stuff with the sausage mixture. Place the stuffed apples in a shallow flameproof baking pan and pour the warm cider around them.

4. Light a fire in the kamado grill using your favorite method. After about 10 minutes, place the grill rack in position, close the dome, and open the upper and lower dampers all the way. When the temperature reaches 350° F, adjust the dampers to maintain the temperature.

5. Place the baking pan on the grill and close the dome. Bake until the apples still hold their shape but can be easily pierced with a knife, about 40 minutes. Serve warm or at room temperature.

Chicken Tagine with Tomato and Honey Jam

Serves 6 to 8

6 pounds ripe heirloom tomatoes, seeded and coarsely chopped

½ cup sugar

¼ cup honey

6 pounds chicken parts, a mixture of breasts and thighs

2 cups finely chopped onions

¼ cup extra-virgin olive oil

1 tablespoon finely chopped garlic

1 teaspoon ground cumin

1 teaspoon ground cinnamon

½ teaspoon ground coriander

¼ teaspoon ground ginger

¼ teaspoon crumbled saffron threads placed in ¼ cup warm water

1 cup low-sodium chicken broth

½ cup unsalted roasted shelled pistachios

3 cups cooked basmati rice

You can take a trip to Morocco without leaving your backyard by preparing this dish. The deep flavors of this tagine, which takes its name from the vessel it is traditionally cooked in, will drive your taste buds crazy. If you have a tagine, all the better, but a Dutch oven works just fine. My former neighbor in New York City, a native of Morocco, gave me this recipe. Be sure to make the jam at least one day in advance.

1. The day before you plan to make this dish, make the jam. In a large skillet, combine the tomatoes, sugar, and honey and bring to a boil. Reduce the heat to low and cook, uncovered, stirring occasionally, until the mixture is thickened and jamlike, about 1 hour. Let cool completely, then refrigerate in an airtight container until ready to serve; it will keep for up to a week.

2. Light a fire in the kamado grill using your favorite method. After about 10 minutes, place the grill rack in position, close the dome, and open the upper and lower dampers all the way. When the temperature reaches 375° F, adjust the dampers to maintain the temperature.

3. While the grill comes to temperature, toss the chicken, onions, oil, and garlic together in a large bowl. Sprinkle with the spices and toss to coat. Add the saffron mixture and toss one more time. Arrange the chicken mixture in the bottom of a tagine or cast-iron Dutch oven. Pour in the broth, cover, and place on the grill. Close the dome and cook until the internal temperature of the thighs is 165° F, about 1 hour.

4. Remove the tagine from the grill and place on a trivet at your table. Remove the lid (be careful of the steam that will come out) and spoon some of the tomato jam over each piece of chicken. Sprinkle with the pistachios and serve immediately with basmati rice.

Mediterranean Baked Fish

Serves 4

6 plum tomatoes, roughly chopped

1 cup pitted Kalamata olives

½ cup thinly sliced fennel bulb

4 cloves garlic, run through a press

1 shallot, finely chopped

1 teaspoon Creole seasoning

1 teaspoon dried herbes de Provence

4 (6-ounce) tilapia or other sturdy white fish fillets

This is a very simple recipe that belies just how good it is. If you have folks in your house who are not big fish eaters, give this a try and I bet they will change their tune. You can substitute shrimp for the fish; just reduce the cooking time by 5 minutes.

1. Place the tomatoes, olives, fennel, garlic, and shallot in a 9- x 13-inch baking pan or disposable aluminum-foil pan or cast-iron skillet.
2. In a small bowl, combine the Creole seasoning and herbes de Provence. Sprinkle this mixture over the fish fillets, coating them well on both sides. Nestle the fish fillets in among the vegetables in the pan.
3. Light a fire in the kamado grill using your favorite method. After about 10 minutes, place the grill rack in position, close the dome, and open the upper and lower dampers all the way. When the temperature reaches 350° F, adjust the dampers to maintain the temperature.
4. Place the baking dish on the grill, close the dome, and bake until the tip of a cake tester inserted into the center of one of the fillets is just warm to your lip, about 20 minutes.
5. Transfer the fish to a platter and cover with the tomato mixture and all the juices that have accumulated in the pan. Serve immediately.

Sweet Potato Biscuits with Orange-Honey Butter

Makes 10 to 12

1 cup self-rising soft wheat flour

1 tablespoon firmly packed light brown sugar

½ teaspoon baking powder

⅛ teaspoon ground cinnamon

¼ cup (½ stick) cold unsalted butter

1 large sweet potato, baked until tender and flesh removed from skin, or 1 (15.5-ounce) can sweet potatoes, drained and mashed

½ cup (1 stick) unsalted butter, softened

1 tablespoons honey

Grated zest of 1 orange

This is a nice change of pace from regular biscuits, and the earthiness of the sweet potato partners well with the smoke. These are very tasty sliced and served with a slice of ham.

1. Light a fire in the kamado grill using your favorite method. After about 10 minutes, place the grill rack in position, close the dome, and open the upper and lower dampers all the way. When the temperature reaches 500° F, adjust the dampers to maintain the temperature.

2. While the grill comes to temperature, in a large bowl, combine the flour, brown sugar, baking powder, and cinnamon. Cut the cold butter into pieces and scatter on top of the flour. Work the butter into the flour with a pastry cutter, two knives, or your fingertips if you have cold hands until the mixture resemble large peas. Stir at least ¾ cup of the sweet potato into the flour until a dough forms. Lightly flour a work surface and knead the dough 2 or 3 times.

3. Put a silicone baking mat or sheet of parchment paper on a flameproof baking sheet. Pat the dough until it is ½ inch thick. Flour a 2-inch biscuit cutter and cut out as many biscuits as possible, placing them on the baking sheet with their sides touching. Pat the scraps together and cut out more biscuits.

4. Place the baking sheet on the grill, close the dome, and bake until the tops are brown, 10 to 12 minutes.

5. While the biscuits are baking, cream the softened butter, honey, and orange zest together.

6. Transfer the biscuits to a plate and serve hot or at room temperature with the orange-honey butter.

Proper Cornbread

Serves 8

2 cups self-rising cornmeal mix

1⅓ cups buttermilk

¼ cup corn oil

1 large egg, slightly beaten

1 to 2 tablespoons sugar if you were born north of the Mason-Dixon line

In my opinion, all cornbread is to die for, if it's done right. Here's the proper way to make cornbread to accompany a plate of ribs.

1. Spray an 8- or 10-inch cast-iron skillet or an 8-inch square flameproof baking pan with 2-inch sides with cooking spray.
2. Light a fire in the kamado grill using your favorite method. After about 10 minutes, place the grill rack in position, close the dome, and open the upper and lower dampers all the way. When the temperature reaches 375° F, adjust the dampers to maintain the temperature. Place the prepared pan on the grill and close the dome
3. In a large bowl, whisk the cornmeal mix, buttermilk, oil, egg, and sugar, if using, together.
4. Pour the batter into the heated skillet. Close the dome and bake until the cornbread pulls away from the side of the pan and a toothpick inserted in the center comes out clean, 20 to 25 minutes for a 10-inch skillet or 25 to 30 minutes for an 8-inch skillet or pan.
6. Remove the skillet from the oven, cut the cornbread into 8 wedges or squares, and serve hot.

Kamado Naan

Makes 14 naan

1 (¼-ounce) package
active dry yeast

1 cup warm water (105° to 110° F)

¼ cup sugar

3 tablespoons whole milk

1 large egg, beaten

2 teaspoons regular table salt,
not kosher

2 cups whole wheat flour

2½ cups bread flour

¼ cup (½ stick) unsalted butter,
melted

Kosher salt

Middle Eastern Za'tar Seasoning
(page 235; optional)

There are a lot of similarities between a tandoori oven and a kamado grill. Both are charcoal fired and well insulated. Use your kamado to cook up some great-tasting naan. Try them with Braised Lamb Shanks (page 198) or Chicken Tagine with Tomato and Honey Jam (page 213).

1. In the bowl of a stand mixer fitted with a dough hook, dissolve the yeast in the warm water and let stand until frothy, about 10 minutes. On low speed, mix in the sugar, milk, egg, regular salt, and whole wheat flour. As that mixes, slowly add in the bread flour. Turn the mixer speed up one notch and let the machine knead the dough for 6 to 8 minutes, until you have a smooth dough that attaches itself to the dough hook.

2. Transfer the dough to a greased bowl. Cover with a damp cloth and let rise until doubled in volume, about 1 hour.

3. Punch down the dough and pinch off golf ball–size portions. Roll these into balls and place on a baking sheet. Cover with a clean kitchen towel and let rise until doubled in size, about 30 minutes.

4. Light a fire in the kamado grill using your favorite method. After about 10 minutes, place the ceramic plate in position, close the dome, and open the upper and lower dampers all the way. When the temperature reaches 500° F, set a baking stone on the ceramic plate, close the dome, and let it heat up for about 10 minutes. Adjust the dampers to maintain the temperature.

5. On a floured work surface with a floured rolling pin, roll each ball of dough into a circle about ¼ inch thick. Place as many pieces of dough as will fit on your stone, close the dome, and cook for 2 to 3 minutes. Turn the pieces, close the dome, and cook for another 2 to 4 minutes, until nicely browned.

6. As you remove the naan from the grill, brush with the butter and sprinkle with kosher salt and za'tar if using. Continue until all the naan has been baked. You can freeze the dough for later use if desired. Just let the balls thaw and rise before cooking. Naan is best eaten hot but you can store leftovers in a zip-top bag for a couple of days; just reheat in your oven before serving.

Pita Bread

Makes 8 to 12 pitas

1½ cups unbleached all-purpose flour

½ cup whole wheat flour

2 teaspoons regular table salt, not kosher

2 teaspoons instant yeast

2 tablespoons olive oil

1¼ cups warm water (105° to 110° F)

Homemade pita bread beats the heck out of store-bought any day. Pita is easy to make and bakes perfectly in a kamado. I think the charcoal fire really enhances the flavor, yielding a more authentic taste. To improve the flavor, a rest in the refrigerator is best, but taking the dough right to the grill will still give you a result you can't buy in a store. This is a fun bread to get the kids to help with.

1. Make the dough at least 1½ hours before baking. This will yield better flavor. In the bowl of a stand mixer fitted with a paddle attachment, combine all of the ingredients and mix on low speed until the flour is fully moistened. This will take less than a minute. Change to the dough hook and let the machine run on medium speed for about 10 minutes. The dough will clean the bowl and be smooth, soft, and a little sticky.

2. Spray the inside of a large bowl with cooking spray. Place the dough in the bowl and lightly spray the top. Cover with plastic wrap and let rise at room temperature until the dough doubles in size. This will take about 1½ hours, but you can let the dough continue to rise for up to 8 hours. You can refrigerate the risen dough for up to 3 days.

3. Transfer the dough to a lightly floured work surface and cut it into 8 to 12 equal pieces. Work with one piece at a time, keeping the rest covered with a damp cloth. Shape each piece into a ball and then flatten it into a disc. Cover the dough with plastic wrap sprayed with cooking spray and let rest for 20 minutes at room temperature.

4. Light a fire in the kamado grill using your favorite method. After about 10 minutes, place the ceramic plate in position, close the dome, and open the upper and lower dampers all the way. When the temperature reaches 475° F, set a baking stone on the ceramic plate, close the dome, and let it heat up for about 10 minutes. Adjust the dampers to maintain the temperature.

5. Roll each disc into a circle about ¼ inch thick. Allow them to rest for 10 minutes, uncovered, before baking.

6. Quickly place as many pieces of dough as will fit on your stone, about an inch apart. If they don't drop into perfect circles, don't worry, they will still taste good. Close the dome and bake for about 3 minutes. Turn the pitas, close the dome, and bake for another 2 to 3 minutes. They may puff up; if they do, flatten them with a spatula. They're ready to come off the grill when they just turn from a raw flour look to a light brown with probably a few darker spots in places.

7. Transfer the baked pitas to a clean kitchen towel and wrap them up. Continue until all the pitas are baked. Serve hot or, when completely cool, store in a zip-top plastic bag for up to 3 days or in the freezer for up to 2 months. The pitas can be reheated for about 30 seconds in a hot oven before serving.

No-Knead Artisanal Bread

Makes 1 loaf

3 cups unbleached all-purpose flour

2 teaspoons regular table salt, not kosher

1 teaspoon active dry yeast

1⅔ cups warm water (105° to 110° F)

Bread baked in a wood-fired oven is exceptional in every way—you get a great crust, a soft, flavorful inside, and a hint of wood smoke that is just not possible in a conventional oven. Your kamado is the perfect wood-fired oven. It delivers superb heat, steam, and flavor, all of which you want when baking bread. Feel free to add 2 to 3 tablespoons of chopped fresh herbs to the dough or, for a special treat, a handful of white chocolate chips. You will need a large metal mixing bowl, sometimes referred to as a "dough bowl," for this recipe. Also, be sure to use regular table salt, not kosher; it mixes into the flour more evenly than kosher would, giving you better flavor throughout the bread.

Do you really need to let the dough sit in the fridge overnight? Yes. The slow fermentation develops layers of flavor in the bread.

My method has you bake the bread on the baking stone. If you prefer, you can forgo the ceramic plate and stone and bake the bread in a cast-iron Dutch oven set directly on the grill grate. You will need to preheat the Dutch oven (with its lid on) for a good 10 minutes. Then place the dough in it, put the lid back on, close the dome, and bake as directed below, removing the lid after 30 minutes.

1. In a large bowl, combine the flour, salt, and yeast and mix well. Stir in the water until you have a very sticky, shaggy-looking dough. Cover with plastic wrap and let rise in the refrigerator for 18 to 24 hours.

2. Flour the work surface. Remove the plastic wrap from the bowl. The dough will have risen and be covered with bubbles. Transfer the dough to the work surface and dust the top with flour. Fold the dough in half, form it into a ball by stretching and tucking the edges of the dough underneath it. Flour a kitchen towel and place the dough on it. Top with another floured towel; let rise until doubled in size, about 2 hours.

3. Light a fire in the kamado grill using your favorite method. After about 10 minutes, place the ceramic plate in position, close the dome, and open the upper and lower dampers all the way. When the temperature reaches 450° F, set a baking stone on the ceramic plate, close the dome, and let it heat up for about 10 minutes. Adjust the dampers to maintain the temperature.

4. Gently turn the dough ball onto the baking stone, seam side down. Cover the dough with a large metal mixing bowl. Close the dome and bake for 30 minutes. Remove the bowl and continue to bake until the crust is golden brown, 15 to 20 minutes. You can also judge doneness by taking the internal temperature of the bread, which should be 110° F.

5. Transfer the bread to a wire rack and let cool before slicing—if you can wait that long.

Measuring Flour

When making bread, the first key to success is to measure the flour properly. For all of the bread, biscuit, pastry, and cake recipes in this chapter, the method I used was to spoon flour into a dry measuring cup to overflowing, then level it off with a knife. If you use your measuring cup to scoop up flour and level it, the flour becomes compacted and the measurements will not be the same.

Coconut-Coffee-Chocolate Pie

*Makes one 9-inch pie;
serves 8*

**4 ounces Baker's German's Sweet
Chocolate**

¼ cup (½ stick) unsalted butter

**2 tablespoons coffee-flavored
liqueur**

1 (12-ounce) can evaporated milk

1½ cups sugar

3 tablespoons cornstarch

⅛ teaspoon kosher salt

2 large eggs, lightly beaten

1 teaspoon vanilla extract

**1 (9-inch) unbaked deep-dish
pie shell**

1½ cups shaved coconut

1 cup pecan halves

Whipped cream (optional)

This is a killer pie made even more delicious by cooking it in the kamado. Its time in the grill imbues it with just a slight undercurrent of smoke, which accentuates the coffee flavor.

Any pie plate that you can put in your regular oven will work here, although ceramic and glass work the best. With a metal pie plate, lower the temperature by 25 degrees; the cook time will be the same.

1. Light a fire in the kamado grill using your favorite method. After about 10 minutes, place the grill rack in position, close the dome, and open the upper and lower dampers all the way. When the temperature reaches 375° F, adjust the dampers to maintain the temperature.

2. While the grill comes to temperature, heat the chocolate and butter together in a medium saucepan over low heat, stirring until they are melted and the mixture is smooth. Remove from the heat and whisk in the liqueur and evaporated milk.

3. In a medium bowl, combine the sugar, cornstarch, and salt. Beat in the eggs and vanilla. Fold in the chocolate mixture. Pour the filling into the pie shell. Combine the coconut and pecans and sprinkle evenly over the filling.

4. Place the pie on the grill, close the dome, and bake until the coconut is toasted and the edge of the filling is set but the center is still a bit jiggly, about 45 minutes. Let cool before serving. Serve with whipped cream, if desired.

Rustic Apple Pie with Bacon-Cheddar Crust and Salted Caramel-Cider Syrup

PIE CRUST:

½ teaspoon kosher salt

⅓ cup ice water

2 slices thick-cut bacon, finely chopped and frozen

2 cups unbleached all-purpose flour, plus more for rolling

½ cup grated extra-sharp cheddar cheese

½ cup (1 stick) unsalted butter, cut into ¼-inch-thick slices and frozen

FILLING:

¼ cup water

2 teaspoons cornstarch

1 teaspoon vanilla extract

1 tablespoon unsalted butter

1 teaspoon canola oil

6 Granny Smith apples, cut into quarters, cored, and thinly sliced

⅓ cup firmly packed dark brown sugar

1 teaspoon fresh lemon juice

½ teaspoon kosher salt

1 large egg, beaten

1 or 2 tablespoons water

2 tablespoons granulated sugar

2 tablespoons cornmeal

SYRUP:

20 caramels, unwrapped

1 tablespoon water

1 teaspoon cider vinegar

½ teaspoon coarse sea salt

Ice cream for serving

. . . .

Recommended wood: Apple

Everything that's good when paired with an apple is in this free-form pie: cheddar cheese, bacon, and caramel. You can also make it with pears or a combination of apples and pears. Around the holidays, I'll stir dried cranberries into the filling. Baking it on a stone adds a nice texture to the pie. And for some extra apple flavor, I usually throw a few chunks of apple wood on the charcoal.

Why make two pies? You'll be glad you did when you see how fast they go. If your baking stone is too small to fit them both, bake one at a time, but let the stone heat up for a few minutes before baking the second one. My baking guru, Belinda Ellis, is responsible for this recipe.

1. Make the crust: Dissolve the salt in the water. Take the frozen bacon and toss it with the flour to coat it. Put the flour and bacon in a food processor and pulse until coarse crumbs form. Add the cheese and butter and pulse a few times. Pour in the salted water and pulse until a dough develops.

2. Flour a work surface and remove the dough from the food processor. Divide the dough into two equal pieces and shape into disks; the dough will be slightly sticky. Wrap each disk tightly with plastic wrap and refrigerate for at least 1 hour and up to 3 days.

3. Make the filling: In a small bowl, stir the water, cornstarch, and vanilla together until smooth. Set aside.

4. In a large skillet over medium-high heat, melt the butter with the oil. Add the apples and cook, stirring occasionally, until they are lightly caramelized, about 5 minutes. Add the brown sugar, lemon juice, and salt and cook for another 2 minutes, stirring a few times. Stir in the cornstarch mixture and cook another minute or two, until the liquid thickens. Remove from the heat and let cool completely.

5. Light a fire in the kamado grill using your favorite method. After about 10 minutes, add the wood chunks, if using, then place the ceramic plate in position, close the dome, and open the upper and lower dampers all the way. When the temperature reaches 375° F, set a baking stone on the ceramic plate, close the dome, and let it heat up for about 10 minutes. Adjust the dampers to maintain the temperature.

6. Line a rimless cookie sheet with parchment paper.

7. Lightly flour a work surface and rolling pin. Remove the dough from the refrigerator and roll into two ¼-inch-thick rounds. Transfer the rounds to the cookie sheet. Divide the filling between the two rounds, leaving a 2-inch border all around. Fold the dough at the edge of that border up and around the apples. The center will be open.

8. In a small bowl, beat the egg and water together to form an egg wash. Brush this over the dough, then sprinkle with the granulated sugar.

9. Slide the pies and parchment paper onto the baking stone and close the dome. Bake until the crust is golden brown, about 45 minutes. Transfer the pies to a wire rack and let cool completely.

10. Meanwhile, place the caramels and water in a microwave-safe bowl. Microwave on high for 1 minute, then stir until smooth. Stir in the vinegar and sea salt. Drizzle over the pies. Serve with ice cream, if desired.

Kamado S'Mores

Serves 6 to 8

12 ounces semisweet baking chocolate, coarsely chopped

4 cups miniature marshmallows

Graham crackers

This is a recipe my daughter and I used to make on YMCA camping trips. I know it will become a favorite of your kids (and grown-up friends) as well.

1. Light a fire in the kamado grill using your favorite method. After about 10 minutes, place the grill rack in position, close the dome, and open the upper and lower dampers all the way. When the temperature reaches 450° F, adjust the dampers to maintain the temperature.

2. Sprinkle the chocolate evenly in the bottom of a 10-inch cast-iron skillet. Cover the chocolate with the marshmallows. Place the skillet on the grill, close the dome, and bake until the marshmallows are browned, about 5 minutes.

3. Remove the skillet from the kamado and let stand for 5 minutes. Serve with the graham crackers, using them to dip into the skillet.

Pig-Picking Fudge Cake

Makes on 12-inch cake: serves 12

8 ounces semisweet chocolate, chopped

½ cup heavy cream

½ cup hot water

3 ounces bittersweet chocolate, roughly chopped

1 tablespoon espresso powder

½ cup (1 stick) unsalted butter, softened

2 cups sugar

2 large eggs

1 teaspoon vanilla extract

2 cups sifted cake flour

1 teaspoon baking soda

1 cup sour cream

1 cup sweetened whipped cream (optional; it wouldn't be my first choice, but you could use Cool Whip if you like)

Chocolate cake with its own fudge topping baked right in—goodness, what a treat! At many of the pig-pickings I've been to in North Carolina, someone has snuck this cake onto the pit to bake as the pig roasted. The kamado does the cake just as much justice as a barbecue pit. I added some espresso for a modern twist.

1. Light a fire in the kamado grill using your favorite method. After about 10 minutes, place the ceramic plate in position, close the dome, and open the upper and lower dampers all the way. When the temperature reaches 350° F, set a baking stone on the ceramic plate, close the dome, and let it heat for about 10 minutes. Adjust the dampers to maintain the temperature.

2. While the grill comes to temperature, mix up the cake. Combine the semisweet chocolate and cream in a microwave-safe bowl. Microwave on high for 1 minute, then let the mixture sit for 4 to 5 minutes.

3. In a medium bowl, combine the hot water, bittersweet chocolate, and espresso powder. Stir until the chocolate melts, the espresso powder has dissolved, and the mixture is smooth. Set aside.

4. In a large bowl with an electric mixer, beat the butter and sugar together on high speed until airy. Add the eggs and vanilla and beat on medium speed until combined; the mixture should be pale yellow. Stir in the melted chocolate-espresso mixture. Add the flour, baking soda, and sour cream and stir in just until combined. Pour the batter into a 12-inch cast-iron skillet.

5. Whisk the cream and chocolate mixture together until smooth, then pour over the batter in the skillet. Place the skillet on the baking stone and close the dome. Bake until the cake pulls away from the pan slightly and a cake tester inserted in the center comes out clean, 25 to 30 minutes. Serve warm directly from the skillet with whipped cream, if desired.

Oatmeal-Berry Crisp

Serves 6 to 8

1½ cups hulled and quartered fresh strawberries

1½ cups fresh blueberries

1½ cups fresh raspberries

⅓ cup granulated sugar

2 cups all-purpose flour

2 cups rolled (old-fashioned) oats

1½ cups firmly packed light brown sugar

1 teaspoon ground cinnamon

½ teaspoon ground nutmeg

¾ cup (1½ sticks) cold unsalted butter

Ice cream (optional)

As a Southerner, I'm supposed to be crazy for fruit cobblers, but I'd much rather have a crisp. The addition of oats provides a wonderful textural foil to the fruit. The oats also seem to take on a faint hint of the charcoal smoke—just enough to be interesting, without killing the overall sweetness of the dish. This is one you can cook right on the grill grate if you want, or you can add the ceramic plate; if you do, increase your cooking time by about 10 minutes. This is one of my favorite recipes.

1. At least 2 hours before you plan to bake the crisp, toss the fruit and granulated sugar together in a large bowl. Set aside at room temperature, tossing the mixture together occasionally.

2. Light a fire in the kamado grill using your favorite method. After about 10 minutes, place the grill rack in position, close the dome, and open the upper and lower dampers all the way. When the temperature reaches 350° F, adjust the dampers to maintain the temperature.

3. While the grill comes to temperature, combine the flour, oats, brown sugar, cinnamon, and nutmeg in another large bowl. Work the butter into the mixture, using a pastry cutter, two knives, or your fingertips, until it has the texture of small peas. Press half the mixture into the bottom of a 9- x 13-inch cast-iron or other flameproof baking pan. Pour in the berries with their juice. Sprinkle the remaining crumble mixture over the top of the berries.

4. Place the baking pan on the grill, close the dome, and bake until the fruit is bubbly and the topping is golden brown, 30 to 40 minutes. Serve warm with ice cream, if desired.

7

Rubs, Marinades, and Injections:
The Building Blocks of Flavor

hefs talk about building layers of flavor all the time. That layering can be achieved in many different ways, and how you do it is how you can make the food you cook on your kamado uniquely your own. Salt and pepper are your starting point. Then add spices and herbs to create seasoning rubs and blends. Add moisture (oil, vinegar, citrus juice, soy sauce, etc.) and fresh herbs and you've got a marinade. Add more liquid (broth, fruit juice) and an injection or brine develops.

Just by using your kamado you will create two very distinct layers: that of the fire and the smoke. Don't do anything at all but season your food with salt and pepper and chances are you're going to end up with something damn tasty. But the fact that you have bought a kamado tells me that you are serious about food and that you are an adventurer. This chapter will give you what you need to make your own culinary adventure.

Rubs, or seasoning blends, are combinations of spices and herbs whose goal is to bring out and enhance the natural flavors of what you are cooking. They can also take you to another world, whether it be Texas or North Africa. What you'll find here are the blends I use most frequently in my own cooking.

Sometimes you want to take the flavor a little deeper; that's where marinades, injections, and brines come in. I am careful with these recipes. Fish never needs much more than an hour or a two in a marinade, but other proteins can go for up to a few days. Be careful, though, because the acids (like lemon juice and vinegar) that are typically found in marinades can start to break down proteins after a time and change the texture of the food. I like it when that happens to a leg of lamb but not so much on chicken, so adjust your timing accordingly.

Injections are shot right into the meat to provide flavor as well as moisture and work well with large pieces of meat, especially lean pork cuts or a pork butt you intend to smoke. Brines have become the rage over the last decade, which I personally find kind of odd. We are just putting back in the very brine solutions that we want removed from the meat and poultry we buy at the supermarket. I much prefer dry brines to wet brines (see Dry-Brined Roast Turkey on page 170); I think they better preserve the integrity of the meat. There's another good reason why you don't need to wet brine—you own a kamado, which has a superior moisture lock. The grill itself does a great job of making sure you end up with a moist result. The choice is yours as to whether or not to brine (and I've included a couple of brine recipes here if you decide you do want to), but I would recommend you first give your kamado the chance to prove how unnecessary a wet brine is.

This chapter and the next, on sauces, can really impact your cooking world. As I said earlier: You're an adventurer—go blaze your trail.

Best Ever Barbecue Rub

This is my "go to" barbecue rub. Whether you are smoking, roasting, or grilling, this rub will amplify the flavor of the fire and smoke. You may think there is an error in the amount of sugar but it's correct. White sugar doesn't burn as fast as brown sugar, but I like the depth of flavor that brown sugar brings to a rub. The mix below provides that depth without burning too quickly. At times, I'll also add a pinch of cinnamon or some onion powder.

Makes almost 2 cups

½ cup sweet paprika

¼ cup granulated sugar

2 tablespoons light brown sugar

2 tablespoons kosher salt

2 tablespoons freshly ground black pepper

2 tablespoons chili powder

2 tablespoons ground cumin

2 tablespoons granulated garlic

1 tablespoon dry mustard

2 teaspoons cayenne pepper

Combine all the ingredients and store in an airtight container in a cool, dry place. Will keep indefinitely.

Texas Brisket Rub

Makes about 1½ cups

½ cup kosher salt

½ cup granulated garlic

⅓ cup freshly ground black pepper

¼ cup sweet paprika (optional)

Most all store-bought rubs that say "Texas" have too many ingredients. My Texas friends just start cussing like crazy when they talk about what a brisket rub should and shouldn't be; here's what the true flavor of Texas is all about.

Combine all the ingredients and store in an airtight container in a cool, dry place.

Cajun Rub

Makes about 1½ cups

3 tablespoons sweet paprika

3 tablespoons kosher salt

3 tablespoons freshly ground black pepper

3 tablespoons granulated garlic

3 tablespoons granulated onion

4 teaspoons dried oregano

4 teaspoons dried thyme

1 tablespoon smoked paprika

1 tablespoon cayenne pepper

"Rustic" best describes this rub, with its earthy notes and sassy flavors. There's not much this seasoning is not good on—and be sure to try it with grilled or roasted vegetables.

Combine all the ingredients and store in an airtight container in a cool, dry place. It will keep for several months.

Canadian-Style Steak Seasoning

This blend is very close to what is sold in stores as Montreal seasoning. It's a wonderful spice and herb combination that will enhance the flavor of any red meat.

Makes about 6 tablespoons

1 tablespoon crushed black peppercorns

1 tablespoon sweet paprika

1½ teaspoons kosher salt

1½ teaspoons granulated garlic

1½ teaspoons granulated onion

1½ teaspoons ground coriander

1½ teaspoons dill seeds, lightly crushed

1½ teaspoons crushed red pepper

Combine all the ingredients and store in an airtight container in a cool, dry place.

Middle Eastern Za'tar Seasoning

Za'tar is as ubiquitous in North Africa and the Middle East as salt is in this country. Its primary flavor component is powdered red sumac, which has a fruity sourness. Look for it online or in specialty spice shops or Middle Eastern food markets. Use this to season lamb, pork, and especially fish.

Makes about ¼ cup

3 tablespoons dried thyme

2 teaspoons ground sumac

½ teaspoon kosher salt or to taste

1 tablespoon toasted sesame seeds

Using a mortar and pestle, grind together the thyme, sumac, and salt until pulverized. Add the sesame seeds and taste for seasoning. Store in an airtight container in a cool, dry place.

Japanese Shichimi

Makes about 3 tablespoons

1 tablespoon Szechuan peppercorns

1½ teaspoons dried orange peel

1 teaspoon black sesame seeds

1 teaspoon white sesame seeds

1½ teaspoons ground red chile

1 teaspoon crushed nori

1 teaspoon granulated garlic

A blend of pepper and citrus flavors, this seasoning is particularly good with fish and steak. The toasting causes the natural oils in the ingredients to be more pronounced, giving them a deeper flavor profile. You can use any type of ground red chile except chipotle; its smokiness would interfere with the flavor you're trying to create. Hotter chiles will overshadow the citrus notes in the blend, so consider that as well. I like to use cayenne for this.

1. Toast the peppercorns in a small skillet over medium heat for 1 minute, then grind into a powder using a mortar and pestle or a coffee or spice grinder. Transfer to a small bowl.
2. Toast the orange peel and sesame seeds in the skillet over medium heat for 1 minute. Add to the peppercorns. Toast the chile for 30 seconds. Add to the peppercorns, along with the nori and garlic. Stir to blend. Store in an airtight container in a cool, dry place.

Asian-Style Rub

Makes about 1 1/2 cups

½ cup kosher salt

⅓ cup Chinese five-spice spice powder

¼ cup granulated sugar

¼ cup firmly packed light brown sugar

¼ cup freshly ground black pepper

½ teaspoon cayenne pepper

Trying to duplicate the deep, sweet spice notes you find in true Chinese barbecue is difficult, but this rub comes close. Use it on ribs, chicken, pork loin and shoulders, and especially duck.

Combine all the ingredients and store in an airtight container in a cool, dry place. It will keep for about a month.

North African Spice Rub

Makes about 1/2 cup

2 tablespoons smoked paprika

2 tablespoons light brown sugar

1 tablespoon sesame seeds

1 tablespoon ground cinnamon

2 teaspoons ground cumin

2 teaspoons ground coriander

2 teaspoons kosher salt

1 teaspoon freshly ground black pepper

1 teaspoon ground ginger

1 teaspoon ground turmeric

½ teaspoon ground fenugreek

In the mood for exotic? Try this rub on seafood, pork, chicken, and especially lamb. Couple it with Tangy Pomegranate Glaze (page 252) for a kicking result.

Combine all the ingredients and store in an airtight container in a cool, dry place. It will keep for a couple of months.

Tandoori Seasoning

Makes about ¼ cup

3 tablespoons curry powder

1 teaspoon hot paprika

1 teaspoon sweet paprika

1 teaspoon ground cumin

1 teaspoon ground turmeric

1 teaspoon ground coriander

½ teaspoon freshly grated nutmeg

½ teaspoon ground ginger

½ teaspoon ground cardamom

This blend is built on a curry powder blend but goes much further than that in the flavor department. It will give your food the beautiful red-orange color of a tandoori oven–cooked meal.

Combine all the ingredients and store in an airtight container in a cool, dry place.

Nikki's Lamb Marinade

Makes 1 ¾ cups

¾ cup vegetable oil

½ cup red wine vinegar

½ cup chopped onion

2 teaspoons Dijon mustard

2 teaspoons kosher salt

½ teaspoon dried oregano

½ teaspoon dried basil

⅛ teaspoon freshly ground black pepper

2 cloves garlic, bruised

1 bay leaf

My friend Nikki Parrish shared this recipe. She serves a grill-roasted leg of lamb for her annual Derby Day party that marinates a good long time in this marinade. It's perfect for any cut of lamb, but it also works with wild game or pork. It's one of my most-requested recipes.

In a medium bowl, whisk all the ingredients together. Use it to marinate your choice of protein at least 24 hours and up to 48 hours.

Lemon-Herb Marinade

Lemon-Herb Marinade

Makes about 1 cup

½ cup extra-virgin olive oil

¼ cup chopped fresh rosemary

¼ cup chopped fresh thyme

¼ cup chopped fresh basil

1¼ teaspoons kosher salt

1 teaspoon freshly ground black pepper

4 cloves garlic, minced

Grated zest and juice of 2 lemons

This marinade is so versatile—it marries well with pork, most all poultry, lamb, and fish. Use it as your default marinade—you pretty much can't go wrong with it!

In a small bowl, whisk all the ingredients together. For poultry or meat, use it to marinate for up to 2 days; for fish, no more than 2 hours.

Limeade Pacific Seafood Marinade

Makes about 2 cups

¾ cup extra-virgin olive oil

¾ cup tamari

6 ounces frozen limeade concentrate, thawed

2 tablespoons minced garlic

2 tablespoons chopped fresh rosemary

I got this recipe from Chris Smiley, a culinary intern who was helping out at a Knights of Columbus crab feed in Mendocino, California. Not only is it good tossed in with steamed crabs, it is a righteous marinade to use with salmon—especially king and coho—swordfish, and halibut. Shrimp are superb after a bath in this stuff. But don't let anything sit in it for more than an hour or two.

In a medium bowl, whisk all the ingredients together.

Gene's Fort Bragg Special Marinade

Makes enough to coat 4 to 6 salmon fillets

½ cup chopped fresh dill

½ cup chopped shallots

2 tablespoons freshly ground black pepper

2 tablespoons olive oil

1 tablespoon maple syrup

Juice of 1 lemon

2 garlic cloves, minced

1 green onion, chopped

All my cookbooks include a recipe from Gene Mattiuzzo, the "Mayor" of Noyo Harbor, near Fort Bragg, California. More of a crust for fish than a marinade, this is really sumptuous with rich, fatty salmon. Just pack it on the fish right before cooking.

In a small bowl, combine all the ingredients together. Cover and refrigerate for an hour to let the flavors meld, then use to coat your fillets.

Herb Poultry Marinade

Makes about 1 quart

1 cup canola oil

½ cup tamari

⅓ cup red wine vinegar

¼ cup fresh lemon juice

3 tablespoons Worcestershire sauce

1½ tablespoons dry mustard

1 tablespoon dried parsley flakes

1 tablespoon dried rosemary

2 teaspoons freshly ground black pepper

1½ teaspoons salt

1 teaspoon dried oregano

½ teaspoon dried thyme

4 cloves garlic, finely chopped

This is particularly nice with whole chicken and turkey breast but also works with pork tenderloin, roast, and ribs, as well as with lamb ribs.

In a large bowl, whisk all the ingredients together. This marinade will keep in an airtight container in the refrigerator for several weeks. Whisk well before using.

Low and Slow Pork Injection or Brine

Using a Flavor Injector

When buying a flavor injector, get a good one made from metal, with at least two needle sizes. When injecting, insert the injector into the meat as far as it will go. Then start to pull the needle back out, slowly depressing the plunger at the same time; be sure to stop pressing on the plunger before the needle comes out of the meat. When you inject this way, the flavor injection won't pool in one place. Now move the injector a few inches over and do it again. Keep repeating this all around the meat or until more injection liquid is coming out of the holes than going in.

This is a down-and-dirty injection solution that will add both moisture and flavor to a smoked pork shoulder. If you want to use it as a brine rather than an injection, double the salt.

Makes about 8 cups

2 quarts low-sodium chicken broth

2 cups apple juice

½ cup olive oil

1 cup of your favorite barbecue spice rub, divided

½ cup sugar

¼ cup kosher salt

¼ cup Worcestershire sauce

2 cups (4 sticks) unsalted butter, melted

In a large bowl, whisk all the ingredients together until the sugar and salt dissolve. If using as an injection, load up your injector and give the pork all it will take. If brining, let the pork sit in it overnight and up to 2 days.

Apple-Infused Poultry or Pork Brine

Makes about 8 ½ cups

4 cups water

4 cups cider or apple juice

5 tablespoons kosher salt

2 tablespoons dried basil

2 tablespoons coriander seeds

1 tablespoon black peppercorns

1 tablespoon yellow mustard seeds

1 teaspoon granulated garlic

2 bay leaves

This is great for chicken, turkey, duck, and pork.

In a large bowl, whisk all the ingredients together until the salt dissolves. Brine chicken for no more than 8 hours in this; 4 to 6 hours will usually do the trick—same for duck. For a whole turkey or a pork shoulder, let it sit in the brine for 24 to 48 hours.

8

Sauces:
The Final Flavor

In your culinary toolbox, sauces are the closers, meant to gild, not hide, the wonderful flavors you have developed by cooking your food in the kamado. The right sauce will highlight the natural flavor of the food itself as well as knit together the added nuances of the fire, the smoke, and any rub or other seasoning you may have initially applied. Sauces can be basted onto your food, allowing for a nice final touch of caramelization over the flames, or simply served on the side, for your guests to help themselves.

Think about a pork chop or a piece of chicken. It's just a canvas waiting for you to make it special. A sauce turns the everyday into something special, even truly awesome.

The recipes in this chapter will take you on an adventure through the different barbecue regions of this country—Memphis, Texas, Kansas City, South and North Carolina—as well as around the world. Every time you light up your kamado, you can transport yourself somewhere new!

Use these recipes to exercise your culinary brain and continue your training as a kamado grill master—remember, the secret is in the sauce!

Eastern North Carolina Vinegar BBQ Sauce

Makes about 3 cups

1½ cups cider vinegar

1½ cups distilled white vinegar

1 tablespoon sugar

1 tablespoon crushed red pepper

1 tablespoon freshly ground black pepper

1 tablespoon salt

1 tablespoon hot pepper sauce

This sauce is going to pucker your taste buds. You can use it as a "mop" or basting sauce while smoking pork, or you can toss it with pulled pork before serving it up on buns, with some extra sauce offered on the side.

In a medium bowl, whisk all the ingredients together. Store in an airtight container at room temperature; it will keep up to 2 months.

North Carolina's Feuding BBQ Sauces

North Carolinians argue about barbecue probably more than the citizens of any other state. The two primary points of contention are the sauce and what cut of pork is used. Down East, when you say "barbecue," you're talking about smoking a whole hog and serving the resulting pulled pork with a mostly vinegar sauce that contains no ketchup. In the Piedmont, it's pork shoulders that get smoked and the sauce gets a little more sugar and contains a shot of ketchup. Both are damn good when done right, and either of these sauces will enhance your barbecue experience.

Lexington-Style "Dip"

Makes about 3 cups

2 cups cider vinegar

½ cup water

½ cup ketchup

2 tablespoons light brown sugar

1 tablespoon hot pepper sauce

2 teaspoons crushed red pepper

2 teaspoons kosher salt

1 teaspoon freshly ground black pepper

In the Piedmont, which includes the city of Lexington, pork shoulders are smoked and the sauce includes some ketchup. "Dip" is the age-old word for sauce that this part of North Carolina has used. Like the Eastern style, it is not meant to cover the taste of the pork. North Carolinians also love to dip their fried pork skins in the stuff. You can toss this with pulled pork, chicken, or turkey, and it makes an excellent table sauce as well. People who prefer "dry" ribs often use this sauce as a mop during the last few minutes of cooking.

In a medium bowl, whisk all the ingredients together until the sugar and salt dissolve. Use immediately or store in an airtight container in the refrigerator for up to 1 month. Shake before using.

East Tennessee–Style Sauce

Makes about 3 1/2 cups

1 cup ketchup

1 (8-ounce) can tomato sauce

1 cup firmly packed light brown sugar

1 cup cider vinegar

1 tablespoon Worcestershire sauce

1 tablespoon paprika

1½ teaspoons onion salt

1 teaspoon dry mustard

1 to 2 teaspoons hot pepper sauce or to taste

East Tennessean Belinda Ellis shared this recipe with me. It's a hybrid of the Memphis and Lexington styles and, quite frankly, is darn good stuff. Thicker than Eastern North Carolina vinegar sauce, it still has that characteristic bite. Use this on smoked pork shoulder and other pork cuts, as well as on chicken. If using this to baste with, brush it on near the end of the cooking so its sugars don't burn.

In a small saucepan, combine all the ingredients. Cook, stirring, over low heat until the sugar dissolves and the ingredients are blended. Reduce the heat as low as it can go and let simmer about 10 minutes. Can be used warm or cool as a basting or table sauce. Store in an airtight container in the refrigerator for up to 2 weeks.

Clockwise from the center: Low Country Mustard Sauce, East Tennessee–Style Sauce, Lexington-Style "Dip," Texas Barbecue Joint–Style Sauce, North Alabama White Sauce, Eastern North Carolina Vinegar BBQ Sauce

Righteous Memphis-Style Sauce

Makes about 4 cups

2½ cups ketchup

1¼ cups water

⅓ cup cider vinegar

⅓ cup firmly packed light brown sugar

⅓ cup granulated sugar

2 teaspoons freshly ground black pepper

2 teaspoons granulated onion powder

2 teaspoons dry mustard

1 tablespoon fresh lemon juice

1 tablespoon Worcestershire sauce (homemade preferred, see page 252)

Memphis is located in the sweet spot of barbecue. Its masters pull from three different directions—the vinegar of the Carolinas, the sweet of Kansas City, and the spice of Texas. This sauce incorporates all those flavors into a truly authentic Memphis barbecue sauce. While you can cook this sauce on a stovetop, I've found that throwing all the ingredients in a slow cooker set on low makes for easy work. Use it with just about any kind of pork cut; it's equally at home with chicken. Keep some of this in your refrigerator at all times.

1. In a 3-quart saucepan, combine all the ingredients except the lemon juice and Worcestershire. Bring to a boil over medium heat, stirring to dissolve the sugar. Reduce the heat to low and simmer, uncovered, until the sauce thickens a bit, about 1½ hours, stirring occasionally.

2. Stir in the lemon juice and Worcestershire and simmer for another 30 minutes. Remove from the heat and let cool. Use or store in an airtight container in the refrigerator. It will keep for up to 3 weeks but I doubt it will last that long. Use it as a finishing baste or a table sauce.

Slow-Cooker Variation: Combine all the ingredients in a small slow cooker, cover, set on low, and let cook 4 hours. Remove the lid and let cook for another 2 hours.

Kansas City Perfection

Makes about 2 cups

2 cups ketchup

¼ cup cider vinegar

¼ cup red wine vinegar

¼ cup firmly packed dark brown sugar

¼ cup fresh lemon juice

2 tablespoons Worcestershire sauce

2 tablespoons molasses

½ cup (1 stick) unsalted butter

2 cloves garlic, smashed

1 tablespoon paprika

1 tablespoon chili powder

1 teaspoon onion powder

1 teaspoon ground ginger

1 teaspoon kosher salt or to taste

Several dashes hot pepper sauce or to taste

Kansas City–style barbecue sauce is thick and sweet, with a little heat at the back end. Primarily used as a rib and brisket sauce, it also does chicken and pork chops proud.

In a 2-quart saucepan, combine all the ingredients. Cook, stirring, over low heat until the sugar and butter have melted and the sauce is well blended. Continue to simmer 20 to 30 minutes, stirring frequently. Use warm or let cool and store in an airtight container in the refrigerator; it will keep for up to 3 weeks. Warm before serving.

Texas Barbecue Joint-Style Sauce

Makes about 4 cups

1 tablespoon olive oil

2 cups finely diced onions

5 cloves garlic, finely minced

1 cup ketchup

½ cup Worcestershire sauce

¼ cup firmly packed light brown sugar

¼ cup cider vinegar

¼ cup fresh lemon juice

1 tablespoon ancho chile powder (if you'd like a smokier and much hotter flavor, use chipotle chile powder instead)

2 tablespoons yellow mustard

1 teaspoon kosher salt or to taste

Okay, this is a two-part sauce. What makes a great Texas brisket sauce is the secret ingredient—drippings from the brisket. When smoking a brisket, place it on a rack over a drip pan to catch all its juices. Texas barbecue expert and cookbook author Robb Walsh suggests making a base sauce such as this, then adding 1 cup of drippings for every 2 cups of sauce. Or you can use this sauce as is; both are good table sauces to serve with barbecued beef ribs, chicken, and goat.

1. In a 3-quart saucepan, heat the oil over medium heat; when it shimmers, add the onions and cook, stirring, until wilted, about 3 minutes. Throw in the garlic and cook for another minute. Stir in the remaining ingredients, reduce the heat to low, and simmer until it thickens, about 45 minutes, stirring frequently. If you like a chunky sauce, leave as is; otherwise, place it in a blender or food processor and puree.

2. If you want to go true Texas style, add 1 cup of brisket drippings for every 2 cups of sauce. You can serve immediately or let cool and store in an airtight container in the refrigerator; it will keep for 3 to 4 weeks. Reheat before serving.

North Alabama White Sauce

Makes about 2 cups

1 cup mayonnaise

1 cup cider vinegar

1 tablespoon fresh lemon juice

1 tablespoon prepared horseradish

1½ tablespoons freshly cracked black peppercorns

½ teaspoon kosher salt

¼ teaspoon cayenne pepper

Only in northern Alabama will you see anything like this. Most all of the BBQ joints in that part of the state have a take on this recipe, which is one of the few truly regional specialties left in barbecue land. It's unbelievably good with smoked chicken, particularly wings (see my recipe on page 69). In North Alabama, this is used both as a marinade and a table sauce.

In a small bowl, whisk all the ingredients together. Store in an airtight container in the refrigerator for up to 4 days.

Low Country Mustard Sauce

Makes about 2 cups

1 cup prepared yellow mustard

¼ cup balsamic vinegar

¼ cup cider vinegar

¼ cup firmly packed light brown sugar

2 tablespoons honey

2 tablespoons unsalted butter

1 tablespoon Worcestershire sauce

1 tablespoon fresh lemon juice

1 teaspoon cayenne pepper (optional)

This sauce is found almost exclusively along the coasts of South Carolina and Georgia. It's delicious with pulled pork and not bad with ribs either. Next time you smoke a pork shoulder, make a batch of this sauce—you'll be pleasantly surprised. Mainly used as a table sauce, it can also be brushed over ribs and chicken during the last 10 minutes of cooking.

In a 2-quart saucepan, whisk all the ingredients together. Bring to a simmer over medium heat, stirring until the sugar is dissolved. Reduce the heat to low and simmer for 30 minutes, stirring occasionally. Use warm or at room temperature or let cool and store in an airtight container in the refrigerator; it will keep for a couple of weeks.

Korean Spicy and Sweet Barbecue Sauce

Makes about 2 ½ cups

½ cup ketchup

½ cup rice wine vinegar

½ cup tamari

¼ cup firmly packed dark brown sugar

½ cup peeled, cored, and finely grated Asian pear

½ cup pear juice

2 tablespoons sesame seeds

1 tablespoon hot pepper paste (optional)

½ teaspoon freshly ground black pepper

3 green onions, chopped

1 tablespoon garlic paste (in a tube)

1 tablespoon ginger paste (in a tube)

1 tablespoon toasted sesame oil

You can use this sauce as a marinade, basting sauce, or table sauce. Look beyond Korean beef short ribs and brush it on grilled halibut. Marinate chicken pieces in it for a subtle Asian note. Pork chops, especially boneless, gain character with a little help from Korea.

1. In a 2-quart saucepan, whisk all the ingredients except the sesame oil together. Bring to a simmer over medium heat, then reduce the heat to low and cook at a gentle simmer until thickened, about 20 minutes.

2. Remove the sauce from the heat and stir in the sesame oil. Use immediately or let cool and store in an airtight container in the refrigerator; it will keep for 5 days.

Spicy and Smoky Southwestern Sauce

Makes about 2 cups

1 cup ketchup

¼ cup fresh lime juice

¼ cup distilled white vinegar

½ cup firmly packed light brown sugar

1 jalapeño chile, seeded and finely chopped

2 chipotle chiles packed in adobo sauce

1 tablespoon adobo sauce

1 tablespoon ancho chile powder

2 teaspoons ground cumin

1 teaspoon chipotle chile powder

½ teaspoon kosher salt, or to taste

This is sort of Texas style with an added kick, courtesy of the addition of chipotle. Try it on brisket or ribs. It's also crazy awesome ladled onto a burger that's been topped with jack cheese and avocado, and killer used as a baste for swordfish.

In a 2-quart saucepan, whisk all the ingredients together. Bring to a simmer over medium-low heat, stirring until the sugar dissolves. Continue to simmer, stirring occasionally, until the sauce reaches your desired thickness, about another 5 minutes. Taste and adjust the seasonings as needed. Use warm. It will keep in an airtight container in the refrigerator for 2 to 3 weeks.

Cheerwine Madness

Makes about 4 cups

1 (18-ounce) bottle hickory-smoked barbecue sauce

1 (12-ounce) can or bottle Cheerwine or Dr. Pepper

¾ cup firmly packed light brown sugar

½ cup molasses

¼ cup distilled white vinegar

½ teaspoon freshly ground black pepper

½ teaspoon cayenne pepper

¼ teaspoon crushed red pepper

2 or 3 shakes liquid smoke, or more to taste (optional)

Cheerwine is a cherry-flavored cola that's been a special part of North Carolinians' lives for decades. Besides drinking the stuff, we use Cheerwine as an ingredient in all sorts of things—cakes, pies, ice cream, and this zesty barbecue sauce. It's a thin sauce, as are most hailing from North Carolina, and it is excellent tossed with chopped smoked pork or beef brisket, or brushed on chicken and ribs. Cheerwine is available nationally these days and there are plenty of Southern food websites that will be glad to ship you a six-pack, but a Dr. Pepper works here as well.

In a 3-quart saucepan, combine all the ingredients. Bring to a boil over medium-high heat, stirring until the sugar dissolves. Reduce the heat to medium and simmer for 5 minutes, stirring occasionally. Remove from the heat and use immediately or let cool and store in an airtight container in the refrigerator; it will keep for about 2 weeks. Reheat the sauce slightly before using.

Tangy Pomegranate Glaze

Makes about 1 1/4 cups

1 cup pomegranate molasses

1/4 cup prepared horseradish, very well drained

1 tablespoon Dijon mustard

1/2 teaspoon kosher salt

1/2 teaspoon coarsely ground black pepper

This glaze has a nice balanced kick and is perfect for brushing on duck, chicken, lamb chops, shrimp, or tuna just before it comes off the grill. Look for pomegranate molasses in specialty or Middle Eastern food stores.

In a small bowl, whisk all the ingredients together. Store in an airtight container in the refrigerator; it will keep for up to 2 days. Bring the glaze to room temperature before using.

18 Seaboard Worcestershire Sauce

Makes about 4 cups

2 tablespoons olive oil

4 large yellow onions, coarsely chopped

5 jalapeño chiles, seeded and chopped

4 cups light corn syrup

2 cups dark corn syrup

2 cups water

1 cup distilled white vinegar

6 (2-ounce) cans flat anchovies, drained

6 cloves garlic, minced

1 tablespoon molasses

1 teaspoon whole cloves

1/2 teaspoon freshly ground black pepper

1 cup drained prepared horseradish

2 cups low-sodium beef broth

Juice of 4 lemons, plus more to taste, rinds reserved

Kosher salt

Jason Smith is the chef-owner of 18 Seaboard, a casual upscale restaurant in Raleigh, North Carolina. I've tried making my own Worcestershire following a lot of different recipes but I like Jason's best because he gets that big Worcestershire flavor with fewer ingredients. Make this once and you will be hooked on having your own house-made Worcestershire on hand to liven up any dish you cook.

1. In a 5-quart cast-iron Dutch oven, heat the oil over medium heat until it shimmers. Add the onions and jalapeños and cook, stirring occasionally, until the onions take on some color and are soft, 5 to 10 minutes. Stir in the two corn syrups, water, vinegar, anchovies, garlic, cloves, pepper, and horseradish. Adjust the heat to a simmer and cook, uncovered, until the mixture has reduced by about one half; this could take as long as 2 hours. Keep a close eye on the pot and stir occasionally to prevent anything from sticking to the bottom.
2. Stir in the broth, lemon juice, and reserved rinds and keep the sauce at a simmer until it reduces so that it is a bit syrupy and will coat the back of a spoon, about another hour.
3. Strain the sauce through a fine-mesh strainer, discarding the solids. Let cool slightly, then taste and add salt or more lemon juice as you see fit. Cool completely and store in an airtight container in the refrigerator, where it will keep indefinitely.

Variation: To use this as a marinade, thin it, adding one part hot water to 3 parts sauce. You'll end up with a consistency close that of commercial Worcestershire sauce.

Kamado 157 Steak Sauce

Makes about 2 cups

1 large orange

½ cup cold water

¼ cup golden raisins

½ cup balsamic vinegar

¼ cup Worcestershire sauce

¼ cup ketchup

¼ cup Dijon mustard

1 tablespoon anchovy paste

1 tablespoon drained prepared horseradish

½ teaspoon celery seeds

¼ teaspoon kosher salt

¼ teaspoon freshly ground black pepper

1 clove garlic, cut in half

This is a good all-purpose steak and chop sauce with a taste somewhere between A1 and Heinz 57—but, of course, much better than either one.

1. Cut the orange in half and cut one of the halves into quarters. Reserve the half.
2. Combine the remaining ingredients in a 3-quart saucepan. Squeeze the orange quarters into the pan; discard the rinds. Stir to combine. Bring to a simmer over medium heat and let simmer until thickened, about 15 minutes. Strain through a fine-mesh strainer, then squeeze in the juice of the reserved orange half and stir to combine. Refrigerate until cool before using; it'll keep, refrigerated, up to 2 weeks.

Heaven's Ketchup

Makes about 2 cups

¾ cup ketchup

¼ cup canola oil

½ cup chopped onion

3 tablespoons sugar

2 tablespoons Worcestershire sauce

2 tablespoons cider vinegar

2 tablespoons molasses

2 teaspoons spicy brown mustard

1 teaspoon hot pepper sauce

1 clove garlic, peeled

Kosher salt and freshly ground black pepper to taste

When barbecue scholar John Shelton Reed says he hopes this is what ketchup is like in heaven, you should sit up and take notice. It's a copycat version of the ketchup served at The Ridgewood, a barbecue joint in Piney Flats, Tennessee. The actual recipe is a closely guarded secret (aren't they all?), but this recipe comes close. Fries dip pretty good in it, but it works best as a barbecue sauce with smoked fresh ham, which is what The Ridgewood uses for its barbecue, as well as chicken and beef. Just a really good sauce.

Pour all the ingredients in a blender or food processor and process until smooth. Pour into a 1-quart saucepan and place over medium heat. Simmer, stirring often, until slightly thickened, about 20 minutes. Use immediately or let cool and then store in an airtight container in the refrigerator; it will keep for 2 to 3 weeks. Best served slightly warm.

Honey Mustard

Makes about 1 cup

⅔ cup ground yellow or brown mustard seeds

¼ cup cider vinegar

¼ cup white balsamic vinegar

⅓ cup honey

½ teaspoon kosher salt

This quick homemade version is so superior to store-bought that you will wonder why you ever used to buy it. Use it as you would use honey mustard, even to make a salad dressing. It's great on left-over pork roast sandwiches or painted on pork ribs to hold a coating of rub.

In a small saucepan, combine all the ingredients. Cook over medium heat, stirring, until the mustard dissolves and the sauce has thickened, about 5 minutes. Serve warm or store in an airtight container in the refrigerator; it will keep for a week.

Tzatziki Sauce

Makes about 2 cups

1 (16-ounce) container plain Greek yogurt

2 cucumbers, peeled, seeded, and finely diced

2 tablespoons olive oil

2 tablespoons fresh lemon juice

3 cloves garlic, peeled

2 tablespoons chopped fresh dill

Kosher salt and freshly ground black pepper to taste

We think of tzatziki as going with gyros, but it's so much more. Use it to dip homemade pita (page 220) and naan (page 218) into. Serve it alongside grilled fish or shellfish, or use it as snappy base for potato salad. Any lamb dish will benefit from being served with some tzatziki by its side.

1. Place all the ingredients in a food processor or blender. Pulse 4 or 5 times, then run the machine to combine. Don't fully puree it; you want this sauce slightly chunky.
2. Pour into an airtight container and refrigerate for at least 2 hours so the flavors can marry. The sauce will last for about 4 days in the refrigerator.

Jezebel Sauce

Makes about 1 cup

¼ cup pineapple preserves

½ cup apple jelly

⅓ cup stone-ground mustard

1 tablespoon drained prepared horseradish

This is an old Southern sauce that is most often remembered as being served with crackers and a block of cream cheese. It also happens to be one of the best sauces ever to serve with grilled sausages or to pour over a grilled pork chop or tenderloin. The sweetness of the pineapple and apple paired with the heat of the mustard and horseradish creates something remarkable.

1. In a 1-quart saucepan, whisk all the ingredients together. Cook, stirring, over low heat until the sauce begins to bubble around the edges and the preserves and jelly melt. This should take about 3 minutes.
2. Remove from the heat and let cool slightly. Serve immediately or let cool completely and store in an airtight container in the refrigerator; it will keep for up to 1 month. This sauce is better if slightly warm.

Easy Lemon Mayonnaise

Makes about 1 cup

1 cup good-quality mayonnaise

Juice of 2 lemons

1 teaspoon chopped fresh chives

Freshly ground black pepper to taste

For absolutely foolproof nonstick grilled fish, rub this mayonnaise over the fillets before putting them on the grill. It will add flavor and help the fish release from the grill magically. It's a tasty dipping sauce alongside any kind of seafood—grilled, baked, or fried.

In a small bowl, whisk all the ingredients together. Cover and refrigerate for an hour before using; it will keep for about week before the lemon gets too strong.

Bacon-Onion Jam

Makes almost 3 cups

1½ pounds center-cut sliced bacon, chopped

2 cups chopped sweet onions

4 cloves garlic, chopped

⅓ cup firmly packed light brown sugar

¼ cup pure maple syrup (grade B preferred)

¼ cup molasses

⅓ cup sherry vinegar

¼ cup strong brewed coffee

2 bay leaves

What can I say about this stuff? Damn good? Holy righteous? Awesome? How did I ever live without it? No, all those words of praise can't do this stuff justice. I use it as a filling in the pork loin recipe on page 158 and instead of tomato sauce on pizza. Spread this marvelous goo on a burger after you flip it for an extravagance of flavor you will want to repeat time and again.

1. Cook the bacon slowly in a large skillet over medium heat until it is nicely browned and the majority of the fat has rendered. Drain the fat off.
2. Place the bacon and the remaining ingredients in a small slow cooker. Cook, uncovered, on high until the mixture has a nice syrupy consistency, 3 to 4 hours.
3. Remove the bay leaves and transfer the mixture to a food processor or blender. Pulse the mixture several times until it forms a spreadable jam but is still a bit chunky. Let cool completely, then store in an airtight container in the refrigerator; it will keep for up to 4 weeks. Heat for 10 to 15 seconds in the microwave before serving.

Metric Equivalents

WEIGHTS

1 ounce = 28 grams

4 ounces (¼ pound) = 113 grams

8 ounces (½ pound) = 227 grams

16 ounces (1 pound) = 454 grams

VOLUME MEASURES

¼ teaspoon = 1.25 ml

½ teaspoon = 2.5 ml

1 teaspoon = 5 ml

1 tablespoon = ½ fluid ounce = 15 ml

2 tablespoons = 1 fluid ounce = 30 ml

¼ cup = 2 fluid ounces = 60ml

⅓ cup = 3 fluid ounces = 80 ml

½ cup = 4 fluid ounces = 120ml

⅔ cup = 6 fluid ounces = 160ml

¾ cup = 6 fluid ounces = 180ml

1 cup = 8 fluid ounces = 235 ml

1 pint = 16 fluid ounces = 475 ml

1 quart = 32 fluid ounces = 945 ml

1 gallon = 128 fluid ounces = 3,755 ml
(3¾ liters)

TEMPERATURE EQUIVALENTS

(rounded to the nearest 5)

°F	°C	Gas Mark
90	30	
100	40	
110	45	
125	50	
135	55	
250	120	½
275	135	1
300	150	2
325	165	3
350	175	4
375	190	5
400	205	6
425	220	7
450	230	8
475	245	9
500	260	10

LENGTH MEASURES

1 inch = 2.5 cm

1 foot = 30.5 cm

Index

Page numbers in italics indicates illustrations and sidebars.